City of Chelsea, Mass.

Roll of Honor of the City of Chelsea

A list of the soldiers and sailors who served on the quota of Chelsea, in the great

Civil War for preservation of the Union from 1861 to 1865

City of Chelsea, Mass.

Roll of Honor of the City of Chelsea
A list of the soldiers and sailors who served on the quota of Chelsea, in the great Civil War for preservation of the Union from 1861 to 1865

ISBN/EAN: 9783337221096

Printed in Europe, USA, Canada, Australia, Japan

Cover: Foto ©Andreas Hilbeck / pixelio.de

More available books at **www.hansebooks.com**

ROLL OF HONOR

OF THE

CITY OF CHELSEA,

A LIST OF THE

SOLDIERS AND SAILORS

WHO SERVED ON THE

QUOTA OF CHELSEA,

IN THE GREAT CIVIL WAR FOR THE PRESERVATION OF THE
UNION FROM 1861 TO 1865, WITH A PARTIAL RECORD
OF EACH MAN ALPHABETICALLY ARRANGED.

ALSO AN

APPENDIX

INCLUDING THE NAMES OF CHELSEA MEN WHO SERVED TO THE
CREDIT OF OTHER STATES, CITIES AND TOWNS.

CHELSEA:

H. MASON & SON, PRINTERS, NO. 132 WINNISIMMET STREET.

1880.

Published by authority of the City Council, under direction of the Joint Standing Committee on Military Affairs.

JOHN H. CRANDON, Chairman.
DENNIS A. O'BRIEN,
CHARLES C. RIVERS,
JOHN J. CONNELLY,
SEYMOUR A. BOSTWICK.
      Committee on Military Affairs.

CHELSEA, 1880.

NOTE.

The Joint Standing Committee on Military Affairs, to whom was delegated the authority to compile, in suitable form for reference and preservation, the names and record of the soldiers and sailors who served to the credit of Chelsea in the great conflict for supremacy of law and the maintenance of the Union, present this record, in book form, as the result of their labors. That the work is as full, complete, and accurate as is possible to make it, the Committee feel assured. Every known authority h: **CHELSEA**, Mass. Roll of Honor of the City nly to and List of Soldiers and Sailors who served in the Civil cause War. 8° wrappers. Chelsea, 1880 ge of this work. Her sons were upon nearly every battle field from the commencement to the close of the war, and many of them filled positions of high trust and honor; and while their deeds will be imperishable to the end of time, indelibly inscribed on the tablet of every loyal heart, this little book, filled with such a record of patriotism, including privations, sufferings, and even death, for the perpetuation of republican institutions and the blessings of civil and religious liberty, will be fondly cherished and preserved by a grateful people, who are now in the full enjoyment of all that was bequeathed us by their patriotism and valor.

JOHN H. CRANDON,
for the Committee.

ROLL OF HONOR.

ADAMS, CHARLES T. Corporal Company H, 43d Regiment Infantry, mustered September 20, 1862, for nine months, discharged July 30th, 1863, expiration of service.

ADAMS, GEORGE Q. Private Company G, 40th Regiment Infantry, mustered Sept. 5th, 1862, for three years, died January 27th, 1864, at Boston, Mass., from chronic diarrhœa.

ADAMS, JOHN. Third United States Artillery, mustered March 15th, 1864.

ADAMS, JOHN Q. First Lieutenant 4th company unattached Infantry, commissioned May 3, 1864, for ninety days, resigned June 6, 1864.

ADAMS, JONATHAN S. Private Company H, 43d Regiment Infantry, mustered September 20, 1862, for nine months, discharged July 30, 1863, expiration of service.

ADAMS, SAMUEL M. Private Company I, New Battalion 1st Cavalry, mustered December 5, 1863, for three years, discharged June 25, 1865, expiration of service, absent sick.

ADAMS, SYLVESTER R. Private Co. H, 43d Regiment Infantry, mustered Sept. 20, 1862, for nine months, discharged July 30, 1863, expiration of service.

ADAMS, WILLIAM L. Corp. Co. C. 13th Regiment Infantry mustered July 16, 1861 for three years. Appointed Sergt. Nov. 1, 1862 ; discharged Feb. 14, 1863 for promotion, and commissioned 1st Lieut. Ullman's 2d Brigade Corps D'Afrique, Feb. 7, 1863.

AHERN, STEPHEN. Private Co. H, 48th Regiment Infantry, mustered Sept. 25, 1862, for nine months. Deserted Oct. 2, 1862.

ALCOTT, CHARLES H. Private Co. H, 24th Regiment Infantry, mustered Oct. 15, 1861, for three years ; appointed Corporal Aug. 1862. Deserted Aug. 6, 1863.

ALDEN, GEORGE W. Private Co. C, 35th Regiment Infantry, mustered Aug. 19, 1862, for three years. Killed at Antietam, Md., Sept. 17, 1862.

ALGER, CHARLES H. Private Co. H, 1st Regiment Infantry, mustered May 23, 1861, for three years ; discharged May 25, 1864, expiration of service.

ALLEN, ANDREW. Artificer Co. K, 3d Regiment Heavy Artillery, mustered May 12, 1864, for three years ; discharged Sept. 18, 1865, expiration of service.

ALLEN, HIRAM W. Private Co. H, 1st Regiment Infantry, mustered May 23, 1861, for three years ; discharged for promotion Aug. 13, 1863. Commissioned 2d Lieutenant 36 Regiment U. S. C. T., Aug. 13, 1863 ; commissioned Capt. Sept. 3, 1865 ; mustered out Nov. 29, 1866, at Hampton, Va.

9

ALLEN HOSEA. Wagoner Co. K, 4th Regiment Heavy Artillery, mustered Aug. 18, 1864, for 1 year, discharged June 17, 1865.

ALLEN NATHANIEL. Private Co. H, 1st Regiment Infantry, mustered May 23, 1861, for three years; wounded at White Oak Swamp, Va., June 30, 1862, discharged May 25, 1864, expiration of service.

ALLEN, NEWELL B. Private 1st Light Battery, mustered May 18, 1861, for three months, discharged Aug. 2, 1861, expiration of service. Re-enlisted as private, 8th Light Battery, mustered May 30, 1862, for six months, discharged Nov. 29, 1862, expiration of service. Commissioned 2d Lieut. 1st Regiment Cavalry, Dec. 16, 1863; promoted and mustered 1st Lieut. Oct. 7, 1864, discharged June 5, 1865, expiration of service.

ALLEN, WILLIAM H. Private Co. F, 61st Regiment Infantry, mustered Oct. 10, 1864, for one year, discharged July 16, 1865, expiration of service.

ALLISON, DANIEL. Private Co. L, 3d Regiment Heavy Artillery, mustered May 30, 1864, for three years, discharged Sept. 18, 1865, expiration of service.

ALLSTON, ISAAC. Private Co. H, 1st Regiment Infantry, mustered May 23, 1861, for three years. Wounded near Manassas, Va., Aug. 29, 1862, appointed Corporal, Nov. 1, 1862, appointed Sergeant, June 20, 1863, discharged May 25, 1864, expiration of service.

AMES, GEORGE F. Private, Veteran Reserve Corps, mustered Aug. 16, 1864, discharged Nov. 17, 1865, by order of War Department.

ANDERSON, JAMES A. Private 4th Co. Unattached Infantry, mustered May 3, 1864, for ninety days, discharged
Aug. 6, 1864, expiration of service.

ANDERSON, JOHN. Unassigned recruit 2d Regiment Cavalry, mustered March 17, 1864, for three years ; transferred April 2, 1864, to Navy.

ANDERSON, JOHN H. Private Co. C, 54th Regiment Infantry, mustered May 13, 1863, for three years, discharged
April 26, 1864, for disability.

ANDERSON, JOHN J. Private Co. L, 2d Regiment Cavalry,
mustered March 29, 1864, for three years. Deserted
April 16, 1864.

ANDREWS, ELWYN. Private Co. K, New Battalion 1st
Cavalry, mustered Dec. 23, 1863, for three years, died
July 5, 1864, at Chester, Va.

ANDREWS, GEORGE H. Private 8th Light Battery, mustered June 3, 1862, for six months, discharged Nov. 29,
1862, expiration of service.

ANDREWS, STEPHEN H. Capt. Co. A, 35th Regiment
Infantry, mustered Aug. 1, 1862, resigned April 24, 1863.

ANDREWS, WALTER B. Private Co. H, 1st Regiment Infantry, mustered Oct. 17, 1861, for three years. Killed
at Yorktown, Va., April 26, 1862.

APPLETON, CHARLES A. J. Private Co. H, 1st Regiment
Infantry, mustered May 23, 1861, for three years, discharged July 30, 1861, disability. Private 1st Light Battery, mustered Aug. 31, 1861, for three years, discharged
Jan'y 3, 1864, to re-enlist, mustered Jan'y 4, 1864, for
three years. Killed Oct. 19, 1864, in Battery M, 5th U.
S. Artillery at Cedar Creek, Va.

ARROWSMITH, ABRAHAM. Unassigned recruit, 28th Regiment Infantry, mustered March 30, 1864, for three years, transferred Jan'y 5, 1865, to V. R. C.

ARCHIBALD, WILLIAM D. Private Co. I, 59th Regiment Infantry, mustered April 2, 1864, for three years ; transferred June 1, 1865, to 57th Regiment, discharged July 30, 1865, expiration of service.

ASHMAN, SAMUEL. Private Co. G, 1st Regiment Infantry, mustered Aug. 13, 1862, for three years, discharged May 25, 1864, expiration of service.

ATKINSON, RICHARD P. Band, 12th Regiment Infantry, mustered July 10, 1861, for three years, discharged May 8, 1862, order of War Department.

ATWOOD, DANIEL A. Private Co. I, 24th Regiment Infantry, mustered Jan'y 2, 1864, for three years, discharged Jan'y 20, 1866, expiration of service. Served three years on quota of Boston prior to this enlistment.

ATWOOD, SOLOMON R. Private 4th Co. Unattached Infantry, mustered May 3, 1864, for ninety days, discharged Aug. 6, 1864, expiration of service. Mustered, Jan'y 2, 1865, Q. M. Sergeant, Co. D, 1st Battalion Frontier Cavalry on quota of Lee, Mass., discharged June 30, 1865.

ATWOOD, WILLIAM S. Private Co. G, 44th Regiment Infantry, mustered Sept. 12, 1862, for nine months, discharged June 18, 1863, expiration of service.

AUSTIN, ALBERT S. 1st Lieutenant, Co. H, 1st Regiment Infantry, mustered May 25, 1861, for three years, discharged Aug. 7, 1862, for promotion. Commissioned Capt. and C. S. U. S. V. Appointed Q. M., Aug. 1, 1861, acting chief of subsistence Hooker's Division, appointed on Gen. Hooker's Staff (Grand Central Division), rank of Lt. Col. on Gen. Stoneman's Staff (Cavalry Corps) in 1863. Dismissed April, 1864.

AUSTIN, EDWARD J. Private 1st Light Battery, mustered Jan'y 15, 1864, for three years, transferred March 12, 1865, to 9th Light Battery, discharged May 22, 1865, expiration of service.

AVERILL, CHARLES S. Private Co. H, 50th Regiment Infantry, mustered Sept. 29, 1862, for 9 months, discharged Aug. 24, 1863, expiration of service.

AVERILL, GEARY C. Private Co. G, 4th Cavalry, mustered Jan'y 27, 1864, for three years, discharged Nov. 14, 1865, expiration of service.

AYER, CHARLES C. Corporal Co. I, 32d Regiment Infantry, mustered Aug. 11, 1862, for three years, discharged March 22, 1863, for disability.

AYERS, CHARLES. Private Co. G, 2d Regiment Heavy Artillery, mustered Dec. 7, 1863, for three years. Taken prisoner at Plymouth, N. C., April 20, 1864, paroled Dec. 8, 1864. Drowned April 23, 1865.

AYERS, CHARLES. Private Co. C, 35th Regiment Infantry, mustered Aug. 19, 1862, for three years, discharged Jan'y 11, 1863, for disability. Re-enlisted and mustered Oct. 19, 1863, private Co. C, 1st Battery Heavy Artillery, discharged Oct. 20, 1865, expiration of service.

AYLWARD, JOHN. Private Co. H, 50th Regiment Infantry, mustered Sept. 29, 1862. for nine months, discharged Aug. 24, 1863, expiration of service.

B

BACON, ANDREW J. Corporal Co. G, 40th Regiment Infantry, mustered Sept. 5, 1862, for three years ; appointed Sergeant January, 1864, appointed 1st Sergeant June 18, 1864, discharged Nov. 14, 1864, for promotion. Commissioned as 1st Lieutenant 29th Co. Unattached Heavy Artillery, Nov. 14, 1864, for one year, discharged June 16, 1865, expiration of service.

BACON, GEORGE. Private Co. H, 1st, Regiment Infantry, mustered May 23, 1861, for three years. Killed at Blackburn's Ford, Va., July 18, 1861.

BACON, LEWIS. Private Co. G, 40th Regiment Infantry, mustered Sept. 5, 1862, for three years, transferred to V. R. C., discharged 1864.

BADETT, ELI. Private Co. B, 28th Regiment Infantry, mustered March 18, 1864, for three years ; absent since May 5, 1864.

BADGER, WILLARD, JR. Private Co. F, 44th Regiment Infantry, mustered Sept. 12, 1862, for nine months, discharged June 18, 1863, expiration of service.

BAIER, HEINRICH. Private Co. B, 20th Regiment Infantry, mustered July 26, 1861, for three years. Wounded at Antietam, Md., Sept. 17, 1862, transferred to V. R. C., Nov. 1, 1863, discharged July 26, 1864.

BAIRD, WILLIAM. Private Co. I, 2d Regiment Infantry, mustered May 25, 1861, for three years, appointed Corporal, Feb'y 16, 1863, discharged to re-enlist Dec. 30, 1863, mustered same date for three years, and discharged July 14, 1865, expiration of service.

BAILEY, AUGUSTUS S. Corporal Co. E, 1st Regiment
Heavy Artillery, mustered March 31. 1864, for three
years, discharged Aug. 16, 1865, expiration of service.

BAILEY, CHARLES A. Private Co. G, 42d Regiment Infantry, mustered Sept. 23, 1862, for nine months, discharged Aug. 20, 1863, expiration of service. Re-enlisted
and mustered March 29, 1864, for three years, private
14th Light Battery, discharged June 15, 1865, expiration
of service.

BAILEY, DAVIS W. Capt. Co. H, 42d Regiment Infantry,
mustered Sept. 24. 1862, for nine months, discharged
August 30, 1863, expiration of service.

BAILEY, HENRY S. P. Private Co. G, 40th Regiment Infantry, mustered Sept. 5. 1862, for three years, transferred
Aug. 9, 1864. to V. R. C., discharged July 6, 1865, expiration of service.

BAILEY, JOHN D. Private Co. H, 50th Regiment Infantry,
mustered Sept. 29, 1862, for nine months, discharged
Aug. 24, 1863, expiration of service. Died in Chelsea,
April 7, 1864.

BAILEY, JOSHUA M. Private Co. G, 40th Regiment Infantry, mustered Sept. 5, 1862, for three years. Died at
Folly Island, S. C., Oct. 22, 1863, of chronic diarrhœa.

BAILEY, WILLIAM. Private Co. E, 26th Regiment Infantry,
mustered Dec. 20, 1864, for three years. Deserted Feb.
10, 1865.

BAKER, ALEXANDER B. Private Co. H, 19th Regiment
Infantry, mustered Aug. 28, 1861, for three years, dis-
charged Oct. 28, 1861, for disability. Mustered a private
Co. H, 1st Regiment Infantry, Jan. 31, 1862, discharged
August, 1862, for disability. Insane.

BAKER, JOSEPH. Private Co. G, 40th Regiment Infantry,
mustered Sept. 5, 1862, for three years; transferred Nov.
13, 1863, to V. R. C., discharged June 10, 1864.
Drowned Nov. 6, 1871, Boston Harbor.

BALLSDON, GEORGE. Private Co. H, 43d Regiment Infantry, mustered Sept. 20, 1862, for nine months, discharged July 30, 1863, expiration of service.

BALLIE, ROBERT. Private 13th Light Battery, mustered
Oct. 20. 1862, for three years. Died August 8, 1863, at
Port Hudson, La.

BALLMAN, CHARLES. General Service U. S. A., mustered
March 17, 1864.

BANGS, JAMES F. F. Private Co. C, 11th Regiment Infantry, mustered June 13, 1861, for three years, discharged
June 24, 1864, expiration of service.

BARAIN, PATRICK. Private Co. H, 48th Regiment Infantry, mustered Sept. 25, 1862, for nine months. Deserted Oct. 27, 1862.

BARKER, GEORGE. Unassigned recruit 28th Regiment Infantry, mustered April 15, 1864, for three years; transferred May 17, 1864, to Navy.

BARNABY, WILLIAM H. Wagoner Co. C, 26th Regiment Infantry, mustered Oct. 17, 1861, for three years, discharged Dec. 31, 1863, to re-enlist. Mustered January 1, 1864, for three years, discharged April 3, 1865, for disability.

BARNES, FRANKLIN O. Corp. Co. H, 43d Regiment Infantry, mustered Sept. 20, 1862, for nine months, discharged July 30, 1863, expiration of service.

BARRETT, JOHN. Private Co. H, 42d Regiment Infantry, mustered Sept. 24, 1862, for nine months, discharged Aug. 20, 1863, expiration of service.

BARRINGTON, JOHN C. Hospital Steward 28th Regiment Infantry, mustered Jan. 1, 1862, for three years, discharged for promotion, Dec. 5, 1862. Commissioned as Assistant Surgeon Dec. 5, 1862, resigned June 17, 1864. Commissioned as Assistant Surgeon 2d Regiment Heavy Artillery, Jan. 11, 1865, discharged Sept. 3, 1865, expiration of service. Died Jan. 15, 1867.

BARRINGTON, JOHN F. Private Co. G, 40th Regiment Infantry, mustered Sept. 5, 1862, for three years. Killed at Cold Harbor, Va., June 1, 1864.

BARRINGTON, RICHARD. Sergt. 4th Co., unattached Infantry, mustered May 3, 1864, for ninety days, discharged Aug. 6, 1864, expiration of service.

BARRY, CHARLES W. Corp. Co. K, 4th Regiment Cavalry, mustered March 1, 1864, for three years, discharged May 25, 1865; promoted Lieut. U. S. C. T.

BARTLETT, BENJAMIN F.   1st Lieut. 28th Regt. Infantry, mustered October 8, 1861 ; resigned Dec. 16, 1862.

BASSETT, CHARLES Z.   Private Co. H, 43d Regt. Infantry, mustered September 20, 1862, for 9 months, discharged July 30, 1863, expiration of service.

BASSETT, SAMUEL B.   Private Co. H, 1st Regt. Infantry, mustered May 23, 1861, for three years ; appointed corporal May 25, 1861 ; appointed Sergeant Jan'y 15, 1863, wounded at Gettysburg, Pa., July 2, 1863, discharged May 25, 1864, expiration of service.

BASSETT, WILLIAM H.   Private Co. G, 2d Regiment Cavalry, mustered April 14, 1864, for three years.   Died at Baltimore, Md., Aug. 3, 1864.

BATCHELDER, EZRA A.   Private Co. H, 1st Regiment Infantry, mustered May 23, 1861, for three years, discharged at Georgetown, D. C., July 22, 1861, for disability.

BATCHELDER, JOSIAH H.   Private Co. C, 35th Regiment Infantry, mustered Aug. 19, 1862, for 3 years.   Wounded at Antietam, Md., Sept. 17. 1862 ; discharged March 4, 1864.   Died in Chelsea, May 25, 1864.

BATCHELDER, SAMUEL, JR.   Private Co. G, 40th Regiment Infantry, mustered Sept. 5, 1862.   Killed at Drury's Bluff, May 16, 1864.

BATES CHARLES G.   Private Co. C, 35th Regiment Infantry, mustered Aug. 19, 1862, for three years ; wounded July 4, 1864, near Petersburg, Va.   Died July 5, 1864.

BATSON, WILLIAM.   Artificer 13th Light Battery, mustered March 29, 1864 for three years ; discharged July 28, 1865, expiration of service.

BAUER, HENRY. Private Co. B, 3d Regiment Cavalry, mustered July 22, 1864, for three years ; discharged Sept. 28, 1865, expiration of service.

BAYLEY, GRANVILLE B. Musician Co. G, 40th Regiment Infantry ; mustered Sept. 5, 1862, for three years ; discharged June 16, 1865, expiration of service.

BAYLEY, GEORGE F. H. Private Co. G, 40th Regiment Infantry, mustered Sept. 5, 1862, for three years ; discharged June 20, 1865, by order of War Department.

BEAN, GEORGE. Private 4th Co. Unattached Infantry, mustered May 3, 1864, for 90 days ; discharged Aug. 6, 1864, expiration of service.

BEAN, JOHN E. Private 4th Co. Unattached Infantry, mustered May 3, 1864, for 90 days ; discharged Aug. 6, 1864, expiration of service.

BEARCE, WILLIAM A. Private Co. G, 59th Regiment Infantry, mustered March 4, 1864, for three years ; discharged for promotion and mustered 1st Lieut., March 25, 1865. Transferred 1865 to 57th Regiment ; discharged July 30, 1865, expiration of service.

BEARD, WILLIAM. Private Co. I, 16th Regiment, mustered Aug. 28, 1861, for three years ; discharged Feb. 12, 1863, for disability. Re-enlisted in V. R. C. Sept. 16, 1864, on quota of Dedham.

BEARNS, DANIEL. Private Co. H, 48th Regiment Infantry, mustered Sept. 25, 1862, for nine months. Deserted Oct. 6, 1862.

BEATLEY, CHARLES S. Private Co. H, 43d Regiment Infantry, mustered Sept. 20, 1862, for nine months ; discharged July 30, 1863, expiration of service.

BEARY, THOMAS F. Private Co. H, 48th Regiment Infantry, mustered Sept. 25, 1862 for nine months. Deserted Oct. 8, 1862.

BEECHER, JOHN G. Private Co. E, 45th Regiment Infantry, mustered Sept. 26, 1862, for nine months. Deserted Oct. 7, 1862.

BELCHER, CHARLES B. Private Co. I, New Battalion 1st Regiment Cavalry, mustered Jan. 14, 1864, for three years. Appointed Corporal, June 30, 1864 ; discharged June 29, 1865, expiration of service.

BENDER, DANIEL. Private Co. G, 40th Regiment Infantry, mustered Sept. 5, 1862, for three years. Wounded at Olustee, Fla., Feb. 20, 1864 ; appointed Corporal, Oct. 1, 1864 ; discharged June 15, 1865, expiration of service.

BENNETT, CHESTER. Private Co. I, 2d Regiment Infantry, mustered July 7, 1864, for three years ; discharged July 10, 1865, expiration of service.

BENNETT, OCTAVE. Private Co. H, 19th Regiment Infantry, mustered March 26, 1864, for three years ; discharged June, 30, 1865, expiration of service.

BENNER, EDWIN. Private Co. H, 43d Regiment Infantry, mustered Sept. 20, 1862, for nine months ; discharged July 30, 1863, expiration of service.

BENTLEY, GEORGE F. Hospital Steward U.S A., mustered March 30, 1864.

BETTS, ELLIOTT B. Private Co. F. 30th Regiment Infantry, mustered Nov. 5, 1861, for three years. Died at Baton Rouge, La., Aug. 21, 1862.

BETTIS, JONAS A. Private Co. H, 43d Regiment Infantry, mustered Sept. 20, 1862, for nine months; discharged July 30, 1863, expiration of service.

BETZLER, ANDREW. Private V. R. C., mustered May 28, 1864.

BICKERS, JAMES E. Private Co. D, 3d Regiment Cavalry, mustered Dec. 8, 1863, for three years ; discharged Sept. 28, 1865, expiration of service.

BICKERS, JOSEPH P. Private Co. H, 50th Regiment Infantry, mustered Sept. 29, 1862, for nine months ; discharged Aug. 24, 1863, expiration of service.

BICKERS, WILLIAM H. Private Co. G, 42d Regiment Infantry, mustered Sept. 16, 1862, for nine months. Died at Algiers, La., July 26, 1863.

BICKFORD, GEORGE F. Private Co. H, 50th Regiment Infantry, mustered Sept. 29, 1862, for nine months. Died at Baton Rouge, La., April 25, 1863.

BICKFORD, HENRY P. Private Co. H, 50th Regiment Infantry, mustered Sept. 29, 1862, for nine months ; discharged Aug. 24, 1863, expiration of service.

BICKNELL, EMERSON. Private Co. A, 8th Regiment M. V. M., mustered April 20, 1861, for three months ; discharged Aug. 1, 1861, expiration of service. Mustered on quota of Boston, Aug. 19, 1861, for three years as private; promoted to 2d Lieut., Sept. 19, 1862 ; discharged July 18, 1863, disability.

BIERMAN, LUDWIG. Private Co. A, 2d Regiment Infantry, mustered July 6, 1864, for three years. Deserted at Atlanta, Ga., Aug. 13, 1864.

BIGELOW, JOSEPH H. Private Co. H, 1st Regiment Infantry, mustered May 25, 1861, for three years ; wounded near Manassas, Va., Aug. 29, 1862. Died from wounds in hospital at Alexandria, Va., Sept. 22, 1862.

BIGELOW, THOMAS H. Private Co. H, 1st Regiment Infantry, mustered May 23, 1861, for three years, appointed Corporal Nov. 1, 1861 ; wounded near Manassas Junction, Va., Aug. 29, 1862 ; appointed Sergeant, Nov. 1, 1862 ; wounded at Chancellorsville, Va., May 3, 1863. Died at Corps Hospital, June 2, 1863.

BILLINGS, JAMES M. Private Co. E, 26th Regiment Infantry, mustered Oct. 7, 1861, for three years. Died at New Orleans, La., Feb. 5, 1863.

BIRD, JAMES H. Private Co. H, 42d, Regiment Infantry, mustered Sept. 24, 1862, for nine months ; discharged Aug. 20, 1863, expiration of service.

BIRD, PATRICK H. Private Co. H, 28th Regiment Infantry, mustered Jan. 10, 1862, for three years ; wounded Aug. 29, 1862, near Manassa, Va. ; appointed Sergeant, Sept. 1, 1862 ; wounded Dec. 13, 1862, at Fredericksburg, Va. ; appointed 1st Sergeant, Sept. 1, 1863 ; discharged Jan. 1, 1864, to re-enlist ; mustered 1st Sergeant Jan. 2, 1864, for three years ; discharged May 22, 1864, for promotion. Commissioned 1st Lieut., May 22, 1864 ; wounded June 3, 1864, at Cold Harbor, Va. ; Commissioned Capt. Aug. 16, 1864 ; wounded April 2, 1865, near Five Forks, Va. ; discharged June 30, 1865, expiration of service.

BISBEE, ORVILLE. Private Co. H, 1st Regiment Infantry, mustered May 23, 1861, for three years; wounded at Bull Run, Va., July 18, 1861; appointed Corporal Nov. 1, 1862; taken prisoner at Chancellorsville, Va., May 3, 1863; exchanged Sept. 1, 1863; wounded at Wilderness May 12, 1864, discharged May 25, 1864, expiration of service.

BISHOP, CHARLES. Private Co. H, 2d Regiment Heavy Artillery, mustered Aug. 6, 1864, for three years; transferred January 17, 1865, to 17th Regiment Infantry, and discharged July 27, 1865, expiration of service.

BLAISDELL, BENJAMIN F. Private Co. G, 19th Regiment Infantry, mustered March 28, 1864, for three years, discharged Oct. 8, 1864, for disability.

BLAISDELL, SARGENT. Private Co. H, 1st Regiment Infantry, mustered Sept. 28, 1861, for three years, discharged May 25, 1864, expiration of service. Died at Canaan, N. H.

BLAKE, GEORGE B. 1st Sergeant 4th Co. Unattached Infantry, mustered May 3, 1864, for ninety days, discharged Aug. 6, 1864, expiration of service.

BLAKE, HENRY N. Musician, Band 24th Regiment Infantry, mustered Oct. 3, 1861, discharged Aug. 30, 1862, order War Dep't.

BLAKELY, FREDERICK F. Private Co. C, 35th Regiment Infantry, mustered Aug. 19, 1862, for three years, discharged Dec. 1, 1862, disability.

BLAKERNEY, ALONZO. Private V. R. C., mustered May 28, 1864.

BLANCHARD, ALFRED, JR. Corporal Co. C, 35th Regiment Infantry, mustered Aug. 19, 1862, for three years; appointed Sergeant April 19, 1863; 1st Sergeant Sept. 6, 1864; commissioned 2d Lieutenant Sept. 8, 1864; taken prisoner near Petersburg, Va., Sept. 20, 1864; commissioned 1st Lieut., Nov. 29, 1864; paroled February, 1865; discharged June 9, 1865, expiration of service.

BLANCHARD, CLIFTON A. 1st Lieut. Co. C, 35th Regiment Infantry, mustered Aug. 13, 1862; commissioned Captain January 1, 1863; resigned and discharged for disability June 16, 1863; re-commissioned Captain Co. C, June 30, 1863; wounded near Petersburg, Va., July 30, 1864; resigned and discharged Nov. 28, 1864, disability from wound. Died Sept. 23, 1879.

BLANCHARD, EDWARD B. Private Co. H, 43d Regiment Infantry, mustered Sept. 20, 1862, for nine months, discharged July 30, 1863, expiration of service.

BLANCHARD, GEORGE E. Private 2d Light Battery, mustered March 16, 1864, for three years, discharged Aug. 11, 1865, expiration of service.

BLOOD, CHARLES. Corporal 6th Light Battery, mustered Dec. 20, 1864, for three years, discharged Aug. 7, 1865, expiration of service.

BLOOD, THOMPSON B. Private Co. A, 18th Regiment Infantry, mustered Sept. 3, 1861, for three years; appointed corporal March 8, 1862; taken prisoner near Beverly Ford, Va., Oct., 1863. Died at Andersonville, Ga., May 23, 1864.

BOANS, PATRICK. Private Co. B, 26th Regiment Infantry, mustered Jan. 6, 1864, for three years, discharged Aug. 26, 1865, expiration of service.

BOHEMER, FREDERICK. Private Co. A, 2d Regiment Infantry, mustered May 16, 1864, for three years ; prisoner of war, no record.

BOHAN, DANIEL. Private Co. H, 50th Regiment Infantry, mustered Oct. 31, 1862, for three years, deserted Nov. 30, 1862, at New York.

BOHAN, John. Private Co. B, 28th Regiment Infantry, mustered Jan. 6, 1862, for three years ; wounded at Gettysburg, Pa., July 2, 1863, discharged Jan. 10, 1864, disability from wound.

BORCHARDT, JOHN. Private Co. H, 31st Regiment Infantry, mustered April 15, 1864, for three years, discharged June 15, 1865, expiration of service.

BOSS, BERNHARD. Private Co. D, 2d Regiment Infantry, mustered July 6, 1864, for three years, discharged July 14, 1865, expiration of service.

BOSS, WILLIAM. Private Co. I, 1st Regiment Infantry, mustered Dec. 31, 1861, for three years, discharged May 25, 1864, expiration of service.

BOWEN, DANIEL E. Sergeant Co. G, 40th Regiment Infantry, mustered Sept. 5, 1862, for three years ; promoted Sergeant Major, Jan. 1, 1863 ; promoted 2d Lieut. ; mustered Jan. 16, 1863 ; promoted 1st Lieut. ; mustered Nov. 7, 1863, June 1, 1864, resigned. Died in Boston, April 8, 1867, small pox.

BOWEN, WILLIAM. Private Co. C, 35th Regiment Infantry, mustered Aug. 19, 1862, for three years ; discharged May 3, 1863, disability.

BOWZER, HENRY W. Private Co. D, 5th Regiment Cavalry, mustered Jan. 29, 1864, for three years. Deserted March 17, 1864.

BOYD, CHARLES O. Private 6th Light Battery, mustered May 10, 1864, for three years ; discharged May 6, 1865, expiration of service.

BRABROOK, WILLIAM F. Private Co. E, 18th Regiment Infantry, mustered Aug. 24, 1861, for three years ; discharged June 16, 1862, for disability.

BRACKETT, EDWIN F. A. Corporal Co. H, 50th Regiment Infantry, mustered Sept. 29, 1862, for nine months ; discharged Aug. 24, 1863, expiration of service.

BRACKETT, SAMUEL P. Private Co. G, 40th Regiment Infantry, mustered Sept. 5, 1862, for three years ; discharged June 16, 1865, expiration of service.

BRACKETT, THOMAS D. Corporal 6th Light Battery, mustered Dec. 23, 1864, for three years ; discharged Aug. 7, 1865, expiration of service.

BRADBURY, WILLIAM. 1st Lieutenant Co. H, 43d Regiment Infantry, mustered Sept. 20, 1862, for nine months ; discharged July 30, 1863, expiration of service.

BRAHN, CHARLES. Private V. R. C., mustered July 20, 1864.

BRANNON, PETER. Private Co. A, 1st Regiment Cavalry, mustered Dec. 4, 1864, for three years ; discharged June 26, 1865, expiration of service.

BRAUER, BERNARD. Private Co. K, 4th Regiment Cavalry, mustered July 23, 1864, for three years ; discharged Nov. 14, 1865, expiration of service.

BRENER, HENRY. Private Co. G, 19th Regiment Infantry, mustered Dec. 3, 1864, for three years ; discharged June 30, 1865, expiration of service.

BRIGHAM, JOHN L. Commissary Sergeant 1st Regiment Cavalry, mustered Dec. 17, 1861, for three years ; promoted 1st Lieut., March 7, 1862 ; discharged Oct. 24, 1864, expiration of service ; Brevet Major.

BRIGGS, EDWARD P. Private Co. H, 50th Regiment Infantry, mustered Sept. 29, 1862, for nine months ; discharged Aug, 24, 1863, expiration of service.

BRIGGS, ELIJAH E. Private Co. C, 35th Regiment Infantry, mustered Aug. 19, 1862, for three years ; discharged June 27, 1863, for disability.

BROOKS, DAVID P. Private Co. F, 29th Regiment Infantry, mustered Dec. 14, 1861, for three years ; discharged Jan. 1, 1864, to re-enlist ; mustered Jan. 2, 1864, for three years ; discharged July 29, 1865, expiration of service.

BROOKS, KENDALL. Private Co. F, 29th Regiment Infantry, mustered Nov. 28, 1861, for three years ; discharged Oct. 22, 1862, to enlist in U. S. A.

BROWN, CHARLES. Private Co. G, 2d Regiment Cavalry, mustered April 9, 1863, for three years ; deserted March 14, 1864.

BROWN, CHARLES E. Private Co. A, 1st Battalion Heavy Artillery, mustered March 1, 1862, for three years ; discharged March 4, 1864, to re-enlist ; mustered March 4, 1864, on quota of Cambridgeport.

BROWN, CHARLES E. Private 4th Co. Unattached Infantry, mustered May 3, 1864, for ninety days ; discharged Aug. 6, 1864, expiration of service.

BROWN, CHARLES H. Private Co. B, 1st Regiment Infantry, mustered May 23, 1861, for three years ; wounded near Manassas, Va., Aug. 29, 1862. Transferred to V. R. C., Dec. 1, 1863 ; discharged May 30, 1864.

BROWN, CHARLES S. Unassigned recruit 1st Regiment Cavalry, mustered March 15, 1864, for three years. Died April 21, 1864, near Washington, D. C.

BROWN, FRANK A. Private Co. G, 40th Regiment Infantry, mustered Sept. 5, 1862, for three years ; appointed Corporal, June, 1863 ; Sergeant, May 1, 1864 ; 1st Sergeant, Jan. 1, 1865 ; discharged, June 16, 1865, expiration of service.

BROWN, GEORGE. Corporal Co. K, 3d Regiment Heavy Artillery, mustered May 12, 1864, for three years ; discharged Sept. 18, 1865, expiration of service.

BROWN GEORGE F. Private Co. H, 50th Regiment Infantry, mustered Sept. 29, 1862, for nine months ; discharged May 11, 1863, to re-enlist ; transferred to 7th Regiment Illinois Cavalry.

BROWN, HENRY. Sergeant Co. G, 2d Regiment Cavalry, mustered May 10, 1864, for three years ; discharged July 20, 1865, expiration of service.

BROWN, JAMES. Private Co. E, 28th Regiment Infantry, mustered March 26, 1864, for three years ; transferred Feb. 10, 1865, to V. R. C.

BROWN, JOHN. Private Co. L, 3d Regiment Heavy Artillery, mustered May 30, 1864, for three years. Deserted Nov. 1, 1864.

BROWN, PHILIP. Private Co. H, 48th Regiment Infantry, mustered Sept. 25, 1862, for nine months. Deserted Dec. 21, 1862.

BROWN, ROBERT. Private Co. L, 3d Regiment Heavy Artillery, mustered May 30, 1864, for three years ; discharged Sept. 18, 1865, expiration of service.

BROWN, RUDOLPH. Corporal Co. D, 28th Regiment Infantry, mustered March 30, 1864, for three years ; discharged June 30, 1865, expiration of service.

BROWN, RUFUS F. Private Co. H, 48th Regiment Infantry, mustered Sept. 25, 1862, for nine months ; discharged Sept. 3, 1863, expiration of service.

BROWN, THOMAS. Unassigned recruit 28th Regiment Infantry, mustered May 11, 1864, for three years.

BRUNSON, CHARLES F. Unassigned recruit 2d Regiment Cavalry, mustered May 17, 1864, for three years.

BRUTT, AUGUST. Private Co. C, 35th Regiment Infantry, mustered July 23, 1863, for three years ; transferred June 9. 1865, to 29th Regiment Infantry ; discharged July 29, 1865. expiration of service.

BRYANT, ANDREW A. Private Co. F, 2d Regiment Infantry, mustered Feb. 15, 1864, for three years; discharged July 14, 1865, expiration of service.

BRYANT, GEORGE. Private Co. H, 48th Regiment Infantry, mustered Sept. 25, 1862, for nine months; discharged Sept. 3, 1863, expiration of service.

BRYANT, MARSHALL. Private 4th Co. Unattached Infantry, mustered May 3, 1864, for ninety days; discharged Aug. 6, 1864, expiration service.

BRYANT, MARSHALL P. Private Co. I, 28th Regiment Infantry, mustered Dec. 13, 1861, for three years; discharged Aug. 12, 1863, for disability. Mustered on quota of Woburn, private Co. A, 4th Regiment Cavalry, Dec. 31, 1864, for three years; discharged Nov. 14, 1865, expiration of service.

BRYANT, RICHARD R. 1st Sergeant Co. I, 28th Regiment Infantry, mustered Dec. 13, 1861, for three years. Died June 1, 1862, at Hilton Head, S. C., of typhoid fever.

BRYANT, SOUTHWORTH. Corporal Co. H, 43d Regiment Infantry, mustered Sept. 20, 1862, for nine months; discharged July 30, 1863, expiration of service.

BRYANT, WILLIAM B. Private Co. H. 43d Regiment Infantry, mustered Sept. 20, 1862, for three years; discharged July 30, 1863, expiration of service.

BUCHANAN, ALBERT L. Private Co. D, 2d Regiment Heavy Artillery, mustered June 14, 1864, for three years. Died Sept. 23, 1864.

BUCHANAN, WILLIAM E. Private Co. D, 2d Regiment
Heavy Artillery, mustered June 11, 1864, for three years.
Deserted June 28, 1865.

BUCK, GEORGE H. Private Co. G, 40th Regiment Infantry, mustered Sept. 5, 1862, for three years; discharged
June 16, 1865, expiration of service.

BUCK, THEODORE H. Private Co. G, 40th Regiment Infantry, mustered Sept. 5, 1862, for three years. Wounded
at Olustee, Fla., Feb. 20, 1864; discharged May 13, 1864,
disability from wound.

BUNTEN, GILBERT. Private Co. H, 43d Regiment Infantry, mustered Sept. 20, 1862, for nine months ; discharged
July 30, 1863, expiration of service.

BUOCK, LEWIS. Private Co. L, 3d Regiment Heavy Artillery, mustered May 30, 1864, for three years. Deserted
Feb. 20, 1865

BURKETT, HENRY A. Private Co. H, 50th Regiment Infantry, mustered Sept. 29, 1862, for nine months ; discharged Aug. 24, 1863, expiration of service.

BURNHAM, EDWARD W. Private Co. H, 50th Regiment
Infantry, mustered Sept. 29, 1862, for nine months ; discharged Aug. 24, 1863, expiration of service.

BURKE, GEORGE W. Private Read's Co., 3d Regiment
Cavalry, mustered Sept. 30, 1861, for three years ; appointed saddler, Nov. 15, 1861 ; discharged June 28,
1862, disability.

BURKE, JOSEPH J. Private Co. A, 43d Regiment Infantry, mustered Oct. 11, 1862, for nine months ; discharged July 30, 1863, expiration of service.

BURKE, MICHAEL. Private 12th Light Battery, mustered Nov. 28, 1862, for three years ; discharged July 25, 1865, expiration of service.

BURRILL, HADLEY P. 2d Lieutenant 4th Co. Unattached Infantry, mustered May 3, 1864, for ninety days ; discharged Aug. 6, 1864, expiration of service.

BURWELL, AUGUSTUS B. 1st Sergeant 2d Light Battery, mustered July 1, 1861, for three years, discharged Aug. 16, 1864, expiration of service.

BUSH, BENJAMIN. Private Co. K, 3d Regiment Heavy Artillery, mustered May 12. 1864, for three years ; deserted July 6, 1864.

BUTTS, CHARLES G. Sergeant Co. H, 43d Regiment Infantry, mustered Sept. 20, 1862, for nine months, discharged July 30, 1863, expiration of service. Mustered May 3d, 1864, Sergeant 4th Co. Unattached Infantry, for ninety days, discharged Aug. 6, 1864, expiration of service.

BUTTS, EDWIN H. Private Co. H, 43d Regiment Infantry, mustered Sept. 20, 1862, for nine months, discharged July 30, 1863, expiration of service. Mustered May 3, 1864, Sergeant 4th Co. Unattached Infantry, for ninety days, discharged Aug. 6, 1864, expiration of service.

BUTLER, ALFRED C. Private Co. C, 35th Regiment Infantry, mustered Aug. 19, 1862, for three years ; appointed Corporal Dec. 1, 1864, discharged June 9, 1865, expiration of service.

BUTLER, ALFRED M. S. Corporal Co. H, 43d Regiment Infantry, mustered Sept. 20, 1862, for nine months, discharged July 30, 1863, expiration of service.

BUTLER, BENJAMIN H. Private Co. G, 40th Regiment Infantry, mustered Sept. 5, 1862, for three years; discharged May 19, 1865, order War Department.

BUTLER, GEORGE W. Private 8th Light Battery, mustered May 30, 1862, for six months, discharged Nov. 29, 1862, expiration of service. Mustered July 28, 1863, for three years, Private Co. A, 2d Regiment Heavy Artillery, discharged Sept. 3, 1865, expiration of service.

BUTLER, ORVILLE W. Private Co. H, 50th Regiment Infantry, mustered Sept. 29, 1862, for nine months; discharged Aug. 24, 1863, expiration of service.

BUTLER, THOMAS W. Private Co. G, 1st Regiment Infantry, mustered Aug. 8, 1862, for three years. Deserted Dec. 17, 1862.

BUZZELL, HIRAM H. Private Co. G, 40th Regiment Infantry, mustered Sept. 5, 1862, for three years. Wounded near Petersburg, Va., June 30, 1864; discharged June 16, 1865, expiration of service. Died April 22, 1867, at National Soldiers' Home, Togus Springs, Me.

C

CABELLO, MAURICE. Private Co. C, 5th Regiment Cavalry, mustered Jan. 29, 1864, for three years ; discharged Oct. 31, 1865, expiration of service.

CADIAN, AMBROSE. Private Co. L, 3d Regiment Heavy Artillery, mustered May 30, 1864, for three years. Deserted Feb. 17, 1865.

CADY, CHARLES. Private Co. I, 30th Regiment Infantry, mustered Dec. 8, 1861, for three years. Died Jan. 14, 1863, at New Orleans, La.

CAFFREY, EDWARD. Private Co. E, 2d Regiment Infantry, mustered June 10, 1864, for three years ; discharged July 14, 1865, expiration of service.

CALEF, HORATIO S. Private Co. H, 50th Regiment Infantry, mustered Oct. 15, 1862, for nine months. Deserted Oct. 25, 1862 ; Boxford, Mass.

CALEF, ISAAC W. Private Co. H, 50th Regiment Infantry, mustered Sept. 29, 1862, for nine months ; discharged Aug. 24, 1863, expiration of service.

CAMPBELL, CHARLES A. Sergeant Co. G, 40th Regiment Infantry, mustered Sept. 5, 1862, for three years, appointed Q. M. Sergeant ; promoted 2d Lieut. Aug 30, 1863 ; resigned Feb. 6, 1864, for disability contracted in the service.

34

CAMPBELL, GEORGE W. Private Co. H, 1st Regiment Infantry, mustered Sept. 10, 1861, for three years ; wounded at Yorktown, Va., April 26, 1862 ; discharged Sept. 25, 1862, disability from wound. Mustered Dec. 28, 1863, for three years, private Co. M, 2d Regiment Heavy Artillery ; discharged Sept. 3, 1865, expiration of service.

CAMPBELL, JOHN. Private Co. G, 50th Regiment Infantry, mustered Sept. 19, 1862, for nine months ; discharged Aug. 24, 1863, expiration of service.

CAMPBELL, JOHN. Private V. R. C., mustered July 23, 1864.

CAMPBELL, WILLIAM H. Private Co. H, 1st Regiment Infantry, mustered May 23, 1861, for three years ; discharged July 30, 1861, at Fort Albany, Va., for disability. Mustered Jan. 31, 1862, private Co. D, 17th Regiment Infantry, for three years ; discharged Jan. 31, 1865, expiration of service.

CANNELIN, HERMAN. Private Co. H, 2d Regiment Infantry, mustered June 14, 1864, for three years ; discharged July 14, 1865, expiration of service.

CANNON, OWEN. Unassigned recruit 35th Regiment Infantry, mustered Dec. 31, 1863, for three years ; discharged March 5, 1864, rejected recruit.

CAPEN, EDMUND A. Private Co. C, 35th Regiment Infantry, mustered Aug. 19, 1862, for three years ; appointed Corporal, April 14, 1864 ; wounded near Petersburg, Va., July 30, 1864 ; appointed Sergeant, Sept. 1, 1864 ; discharged June 9, 1865, expiration of service.

CARLETON, WILLIAM F. Private, Read's Co. 3d Regiment Cavalry, mustered Nov. 8, 1861, for three years; discharged Aug. 26, 1862, for promotion; commissioned 2d Lieut. 2d Regiment, La. Cavalry, 1863; commissioned Captain.

CARLTON, WILLARD F. Sergeant Co. H, 50th Regiment Infantry, mustered Sept. 29, 1862, for nine months; discharged Aug. 24, 1863, expiration of service.

CARLINE, WILLIAM. Private Co. C, 11th Regiment Infantry, mustered July 10, 1861, for three years; discharged Oct. 18, 1862, disability.

CARR, CHARLES. Private Co. F, 24th Regiment Infantry, mustered Nov. 23, 1861, for three years; discharged April 19, 1862, disability; mustered private Co. A, 56th Regiment Infantry, March 19, 1864, for three years. Deserted at Annapolis, Md.

CARR, JOSEPH. Private Co. G, 2d Regiment Cavalry, mustered May 11, 1864, for three years. Deserted July 13, 1864.

CARR, WILLIAM. Private Co. H, 43d Regiment Infantry, mustered Sept. 20, 1862, for nine months. Deserted Sept. 25, 1862, Readville, Mass.

CARR, WILLIAM M. Private Co. I, 5th Regiment Infantry, , mustered May 1, 1861, for three months; discharged July 31, 1861, expiration of service.

CARROLL, JOHN. Private Co. B, 2d Regiment Heavy Artillery, mustered Aug, 16, 1864, for three years; discharged Sept. 3, 1865, expiration of service.

36

CARROLL, MICHAEL. Private Co. D, 2d Regiment Infantry, mustered July 7, 1864, for three years. Deserted
Aug. 8, 1864.

CARRUTH, SUMNER. Capt. Co. H, 1st Regiment Infantry, mustered May 22, 1861, for three years; wounded
near Richmond, Va., June 25, 1862 ; commissioned Major
35th Regiment Infantry, Aug. 20, 1862 ; commissioned
Lieut. Col. Aug. 27, 1862 ; wounded at Antietam, Md.,
Sept. 17, 1862 ; taken prisoner at Sulphur Springs, Va.,
Nov. 13, 1862 ; exchanged Jan. 1863 ; commissioned Colonel, April 25, 1863 ; discharged June 9, 1865, Brevet
Brig. General.

CARRUTHERS, JAMES O. Sergeant Co. I, 28th Regiment
Infantry, mustered Dec. 31, 1861, for three years ; appointed 1st Sergeant, April 1, 1862 ; discharged July 22,
1862, for promotion; commissioned 2d Lieut., July 27,
1862 ; commissioned 1st Lieut. Dec. 7, 1862 ; August 24,
1863, resigned; mustered Dec. 31, 1863, 1st Lieut. 56th
Regiment Infantry; resigned Jan. 7, 1864.

CARTER, HORACE. Private Co. H, 50th Regiment Infantry, mustered Sept. 29, 1862, for nine months. Died
July 31, 1863, at Vicksburg, Miss.

CASEY, MICHAEL F. Private Co. D, 28th Regiment Infantry, mustered May 4, 1864, for three years; transferred to V. R. C. ; discharged June 22, 1865.

CASS, FREDERICK P. Private Co. D, 3d Regiment Heavy
Artillery, mustered Dec. 23, 1863, for three years ; discharged Sept. 18, 1865, expiration of service.

CASWELL, GEORGE A. Private Co. E, 30th Regiment Infantry, mustered March 26, 1864, for three years. Deserted Dec. 14, 1865.

CASWELL, GEORGE W. Private 4th Co. Unattached Infantry, mustered May 3, 1864, for ninety days ; discharged Aug. 6, 1864, expiration of service.

CATE, WILLIAM W. Private Co. D, 28th Regiment Infantry, mustered March 22, 1864, for three years ; transferred to V. R. C. ; discharged July 29, 1865.

CHADWICK, JOHN O. Unassigned recruit 3d Regiment Heavy Artillery, mustered May 7, 1864, for three years ; May 13, 1864, rejected and discharged.

CHANCE, CHARLES. Private Co. I, 2d Regiment Cavalry, mustered June 14. 1864, for three years ; discharged July 20, 1865, expiration of service.

CHAMBERS, WILLIAM. Private Co. B, 17th Regiment Infantry, mustered Aug. 22, 1861, for three years ; discharged Dec. 4, 1863, to re-enlist ; mustered Dec. 5, 1863, for three years ; discharged July 11, 1865, expiration of service.

CHANDLER, HORACE W. Musician Co. G, 61st Regiment Infantry, mustered Nov. 12, 1864, for one year ; discharged July 16, 1865, expiration of service.

CHANDLEY, CHARLES F. Private Co. G, 61st Regiment Infantry, mustered Nov. 16, 1864, for one year ; discharged Feb. 1, 1865, order of War Department.

CHANNEL, JOHN F. Private Co. C, 35th Regiment Infantry, mustered Aug. 19, 1862, for three years; appointed
Corporal, Sept. 1, 1863; discharged June 9, 1865, expiration of service.

CHANNELL, HERBERT. Private 4th Co. Unattached Infantry, mustered May 3, 1864, for ninety days; discharged
Aug. 6, 1864, expiration of service.

CHAPMAN, ENOCH W. Private Co. A, 30th Regiment Infantry, mustered Sept. 27, 1861, for three years. Died
Jan. 4, 1863, at New Orleans, La.

CHAPMAN, WILLIAM. Private 13th Light Battery, mustered Nov. 28, 1862, for three years. Deserted Jan. 17,
1863.

CHASE, IRA C. Hospital Steward U. S. A., mustered March
30, 1864.

CHEEVER, HENRY A. 1st Lieutenant Co. D, 17th Regiment Infantry, mustered Feb. 20, 1862, for three years;
appointed Adjutant, Nov. 1862. Wounded and taken
prisoner near Newbern, N. C., Feb. 1, 1864; discharged
Aug. 4, 1865, expiration of service.

CHEEVER, JOSEPH C. F. Private Co. G, 40th Regiment
Infantry, mustered Sept. 5, 1862, for three years; ap-
pointed Corporal Sept. 16, 1862; appointed Sergeant
Jan. 1, 1863; discharged June 20, 1865, order of War
Department.

CHEEVER, TRACY P. Capt. Co. C, 35th Regiment Infantry, mustered Aug. 13, 1862, for three years. Wounded
by concussion of shell at Antietam, Md.; discharged June
23, 1863, for disability.

CHENEY, GILBERT. Musician Co. L, 3d Regiment Heavy Artillery, mustered May 30, 1864, for three years ; discharged July 10, 1865, disability.

CHITTENDEN, ALBERT A. 2d Lieutenant Co. H, 6th Regiment Infantry, mustered July 16, 1864, for 100 days ; discharged Oct. 27, 1864, expiration of service.

CHURCH, JOSEPH. Captain 59th Regiment Infantry, mustered July 31, 1864, for three years ; discharged July 1, 1865.

CHURCH, SAMUEL. Unassigned recruit 15th Regiment Infantry, mustered March 18, 1864, for three years.

CHUTE, RICHARD H. Private Co. C, 35th Regiment Infantry, mustered Aug. 19, 1862, for three years ; discharged Nov. 11, 1863, for promotion ; mustered Dec. 4, 1863, 2d Lieut. 59th Regiment Infantry; commissioned 1st Lieut. Feb. 18, 1864. Wounded at North Anna River, May 24, 1864 ; commissioned Capt. June 23, 1864 ; taken prisoner, June, 1864 ; exchanged, 1864 ; resigned and discharged, Feb. 27, 1865, disability from wounds.

CLAPP, GEORGE I. Private Co. A, 17th Regiment Infantry, mustered Jan. 4, 1864, for three years ; discharged July 20, 1865, expiration of service.

CLAPP, GEORGE W. Sergeant Co. G, 40th Regiment Infantry, mustered Sept. 5, 1862, for three years. Wounded at Cold Harbor, Va., June 1, 1864 ; discharged June 16, 1865, expiration of service.

CLARK, EDWIN R. Private 7th Co. Unattached Infantry, mustered May 4, 1864, ninety days ; discharged Aug. 5, 1864, expiration of service.

CLARK, FRANK. Unassigned recruit 2d Regiment Cavalry, mustered Aug. 11, 1864, for three years.

CLARK, GEORGE L. Private Co. G, 40th Regiment Infantry, mustered Sept. 5, 1862, for three years; discharged June 16, 1865, expiration of service.

CLARK, HENRY. Private Co. C, 35th Regiment Infantry, mustered Aug. 19, 1862, for three years. Wounded at Antietam, Sept. 17, 1862; discharged March 16, 1863, disability from wound.

CLARK, JAMES. Unassigned recruit 28th Regiment Infantry, mustered April 15, 1864, for three years.

CLARK, JAMES. Private Co. M, new Battery, 1st Regiment Cavalry, mustered Jan. 14, 1864, for three years; discharged June 26, 1865, expiration of service.

CLARK, JOSEPH H. Private 7th Co. Unattached Infantry, mustered May 4, 1864, for ninety days; discharged Aug. 5, 1864, expiration of service.

CLARK, LEWIS. Private Co. H. 50th Regiment Infantry; mustered Sept. 29, 1862, for nine months; discharged Aug. 24, 1863, expiration of service.

CLARK, THOMAS B. Private Co. L, 2d Regiment Cavalry, mustered April 15, 1864, for three years; transferred Jan. 1, 1865, V. R. C.

CLARK, WILLIAM E. Corporal Co. K, 6th Regiment Infantry, mustered Aug. 31, 1862, for nine months; discharged, June 3, 1863, expiration of service.

CLEMENT, ANDREW J. 1st Sergeant Co. M, 1st Regiment Cavalry, mustered Oct. 5, 1861, for three years; transferred to Co. M, 4th Regiment Cavalry; discharged Oct. 5, 1864, expiration of service.

CLEMENT, FRANK. Private 4th Co. Unattached Infantry, mustered May 3, 1864, for ninety days; discharged Aug. 6, 1864, expiration of service.

CLEMENT, WILLIAM B. Private Co. H, 1st Regiment Infantry, mustered May 23, 1861, for three years; discharged Jan. 24, 1863, disability..

CLIFFORD, GEORGE W. Private 12th Light Battery, mustered Dec. 1, 1862, for three years. Deserted Feb. 12, 1863.

CLIFFORD, WELLS W. Private 2d Co. Sharpshooters, mustered Aug. 13, 1862, for three years; discharged Nov. 4, 1862, disability.

CLOSEY, DAVID. Unassigned recruit 31st Regiment Infantry, mustered June 10, 1864.

CLOUGH, HENRY A. Private Co. C, 35th Regiment Infantry, mustered Aug. 19, 1862, for three years. Wounded at South Mountain, Md., Sept. 14, 1862; transferred Sept. 1, 1863, to V. R. C.; discharged Aug. 18, 1865. Died March 19, 1866, at Chelsea.

COBB, GEORGE H. Private Co. H, 50th Regiment Infantry, mustered Oct. 13, 1862, for nine months; discharged Aug. 24, 1863, expiration of service.

COBURN, CHARLES M. Corporal Co. H, 43d Regiment Infantry, mustered Sept. 20, 1863, for nine months; discharged July 30, 1863, expiration of service.

COBURN, JOSEPH N.   Private Co. E, 3d Regiment Cavalry,
mustered Jan. 4, 1864, for three years.   Died 1864, Boston, Mass.

COETHEN, ARTHUR.   Corporal Co. A, 2d Regiment Infantry, mustered May 6, 1864, for three years ; discharged
June 26, 1865, expiration of service.

COFFIN, EPHRAIM A.   Private Co. C, 11th Regiment Infantry, mustered June 11, 1861, for three years.   Deserted
Aug. 9, 1861.

COFFRAIN, HENRY P.   Private Co. I, 1st Regiment Cavalry, mustered Dec. 5, 1863, for three years, discharged
June 29, 1865, expiration of service.

COHEN, LEOPOLD.   General service U. S. A., mustered
March 17, 1864.

COITEUX, JOSEPH.   Private Co. K, 43d Regiment Infantry,
mustered Sept. 16, 1862, for nine months ; discharged
July 30, 1863, expiration of service.

COLBURN, GEORGE.   Unassigned recruit 28th Regiment Infantry, mustered March 21, 1864, for three years ; discharged April 15, 1864, disability.

COLBY, EUGENE D.   Private Co. C, 35th Regiment Infantry, mustered Aug. 19, 1862, for three years ; appointed
Corporal Sept. 1, 1864 ; discharged June 9, 1865, expiration of service.

COLBY, OSCAR F.   Private Co. G, 40th Regiment Infantry,
mustered Sept. 5, 1862, for three years ; discharged June
16, 1865, expiration of service.

COLE, CHARLES A. Private Co. C, 45th Regiment Infantry, mustered Sept. 26, 1862, for nine months; discharged July 7, 1863, expiration of service; mustered Corporal 4th Co. Unattached Infantry, May 3, 1864, for ninety days; discharged Aug. 6, 1864, expiration of service; mustered Jan. 5, 1865, on quota of Lee, Mass., for one year, Sergeant Co. D, 1st Battalion Frontier Cavalry; discharged June 30, 1865, expiration of service.

COLE, DAVID. Private Co. A, 17th Regiment Infantry, mustered Jan. 5, 1864, for three years; discharged June 26, 1865, expiration of service.

COLE, GEORGE W., JR. Private Co. C, 45th Regiment Infantry, mustered Sept. 26, 1862, for nine months; discharged July 7, 1863, expiration of service.

COLE, HERBERT S. Private Co. G, 40th Regiment Infantry, mustered Sept. 5, 1862, for three years. Wounded at Olustee, Fla., Feb. 20, 1864; appointed Corporal Jan. 1, 1865; discharged June 16, 1865, expiration of service.

COLE, SOLOMON A. Private Co. H, 50th Regiment Infantry, mustered Sept. 29, 1862, for nine months; discharged Aug. 24, 1863, expiration of service.

COLEMAN, JOHN. Private Co. K, 2d Regiment Cavalry, mustered May 25, 1864, for three years; discharged July 12, 1865, expiration of service.

COLEMAN, JOSEPH. Corporal Co. C, 3d Regiment Cavalry, mustered Dec. 7, 1863, for three years; discharged Sept. 28, 1865, expiration of service.

COLEMAN, WILLIAM. Private Co. G, 4th Regiment Cav alry, mustered June 10, 1864, for three years; discharged Nov. 14, 1865, expiration of service.

COLESWORTHY, CHARLES J. Private Co. H, 43d Regiment Infantry, mustered Sept. 20, 1862, for nine months; discharged July 30, 1863, expiration of service.

COLESWORTHY, D. C. JR. 2d Lieutenant Co. H, 43d Regiment Infantry, mustered Sept. 20, 1862, for nine months; discharged July 30, 1863, expiration of service.

COLESWORTHY, GEORGE E. Corporal Co. H, 43d Regiment Infantry, mustered Sept. 20, 1862, for nine months; discharged July 30, 1863, expiration of service. Mustered Corporal 4th Co. Unattached Infantry, May 3, 1864, for ninety days; discharged Aug. 6, 1864, expiration of service.

COLLIER, GEORGE G. Private Co. H, 50th Regiment Infantry, mustered Sept. 29, 1862, for nine months; discharged March 13, 1863, for disability.

COLLINS, FREDERICK. Corporal Co. M, 3d Regiment Heavy Artillery, mustered Aug. 23, 1864, for three years; discharged June 17, 1865, expiration of service.

COLLINS, JOSEPH. Unassigned recruit, 2d Regiment Cavalry, mustered May 6, 1865, for three years.

COLLINS, MICHAEL. Private Co. K, 3d Regiment Heavy Artillery, mustered May 12, 1864, for three years. Deserted July 6, 1864.

COLWELL, PATRICK. Private Co. F, 3d Regiment Heavy Artillery, mustered April 5, 1864, for three years; discharged Sept. 18, 1865, expiration of service.

COMPTON, JOSEPH. Private Co. H, 2d Regiment Infantry, mustered June 11, 1864, for three years. Deserted June 11, 1865.

CONANT, WALTER S. Private Co. C, 35th Regiment Infantry, mustered Aug. 19, 1862, for three years ; appointed Corporal Feb. 7, 1863; appointed Sergeant 1864; commissioned 2d Lieut., Nov. 29, 1864. Wounded near Petersburg, Va., March 31, 1865 ; discharged June 9, 1865, expiration of service.

CONHAM, WILLIAM O. Corporal Co. F, 2d Regiment Heavy Artillery, mustered Oct. 6, 1863, for three years. Died Nov. 13, 1864.

COUILLARD, ELIJAH. Private Co. C, 35th Regiment Infantry, mustered Aug. 19, 1862, for three years, appointed
. Corporal ; transferred to V. R. C., Jan. 16, 1864 ; discharged April 16, 1864.

CONLEY, JOHN. Unassigned recruit 2d Regiment Cavalry, mustered April 12, 1864, for three years.

CONLON, JOHN. General service U. S. A. mustered March 17, 1864.   .

CONN, JOSEPH. Private V. R. C., mustered July 22, 1864.

CONNORS, JAMES. Unassigned recruit 2d Regiment Cavalry, mustered Aug. 27, 1864, for three years.

CONNORS, JOHN. Private Co. A, 26th Regiment Infantry, mustered May 11, 1864, for three years ; discharged Aug. 26, 1865, expiration of service.

CONNORS, MARTIN. Private Co. M, 4th Regiment Cavalry, mustered March 1, 1864, for three years ; discharged Nov. 14, 1865, expiration of service.

CONWAY, MICHAEL. Private Co. K, 37th Regiment Infantry, mustered Sept. 2, 1862, for three years ; died of wounds May 5, 1863, at Falmouth, Va.

COOK, CHARLES E. Private Co. F, 44th Regiment Infantry, mustered Sept. 12, 1862, for nine months, discharged June 18, 1863, expiration of service.

COOK, GEORGE. Private Co. H, 42d Regiment Infantry, mustered Oct. 1, 1862, for nine months, deserted Oct. 1, 1862, at Readville, Mass.

COOK, JOHN F. Private Co. F, 44th Regiment Infantry, mustered Sept. 12, 1862, for nine months, discharged June 18, 1863, expiration of service.

COOK, JOSEPH S. 2d Lieutenant 23d Regiment Infantry, mustered Oct. 8, 1861 ; commissioned revoked Nov. 8, 1861.

COOTS, CHARLES. Private Co. K, 4th Regiment Heavy Artillery, mustered Aug. 18, 1864, for one year; discharged June 17, 1865, expiration of service.

COOTS, HENRY R. Private Co. F, 12th Regiment Infantry, mustered July 5, 1861, for three years; discharged July 1862.

COPELAND, ALBERT E. Private 4th Co. Unattached Infantry, mustered May 3, 1864, for ninety days ; discharged Aug. 6. 1864, expiration of service.

CORCUM, LEVI F. Private Co. G, 40th Regiment Infantry, mustered Sept. 5, 1862, for three years; discharged June 20, 1865, order War Department.

CORDIER, LOUIS. Private Co. I, 28th Regiment Infantry, mustered April 12, 1864, for three years; discharged June 30, 1865, expiration of service.

COREY, THOMAS S. Corporal 4th Co. Unattached Infantry, mustered May 3, 1864, for ninety days; discharged Aug. 6, 1864, expiration of service.

CORNELL, JOHN O. Private Co. F, 4th Regiment Cavalry, mustered Jan. 27, 1864, for three years ; discharged Nov. . 14, 1865, expiration of service.

CORNETT, JAMES H. Private Co. H, 2d Regiment Infantry, mustered May 6, 1864, for three years ; discharged July 14, 1865, expiration of service.

COSSETT, GEORGE F. Private Co. C, 35th Regiment Infantry, mustered Aug. 19, 1862, for three years. Killed Aug. 19, 1864, near Petersburg, Va.
.

COTTER, WILLIAM. Private Co. E, 19th Regiment Infantry, mustered Dec. 21, 1864, for three years ; discharged June 30, 1865, expiration of service.

COUCH, STILES. Private V. R. C., mustered June 20, 1864.

COX, FRANCIS. Private Co. E, 56th Regiment Infantry, mustered Jan. 12, 1864, for three years, discharged July 12, 1865, expiration of service. Absent, sick.

COYLE, JOHN. Private Co. H, 48th Regiment Infantry, mustered Sept. 25, 1862, for nine months; deserted Oct. 1, 1862.

COYNE, MICHAEL. Private Co. G, 40th Regiment Infantry, mustered Sept. 5, 1862, for three years, discharged June 16, 1865, expiration of service.

CRANDON, SANFORD. 1st Sergeant Co. H, 38th Regiment Infantry, mustered Aug. 20, 1862, for three years ; commissioned Oct. 26, 1864, 1st Lieutenant, discharged June 20, 1865, expiration of service.

CROCKETT, SAMUEL J. Corporal 4th Co. Unattached Infantry, mustered May 3, 1864, for ninety days, discharged Aug. 6, 1864, expiration of service.

CROMBIE, WALTER M. Corporal 29th Co. Unattached Heavy Artillery, mustered Aug. 20, 1864, for one year, discharged June 16, 1865, expiration of service.

CROOKER, ALFRED. Private Co. C, 35th Regt. Infantry; mustered August 19, 1862, for three years, wounded at Knoxville, Tenn., Nov. 1863, discharged June 9, 1865, expiration of service.

CROOKER, HENRY M. Private Co. G, 40th Regt. Infantry, mustered Sept. 5, 1862 for three years, transferred Jan. 1, 1865, to V. R. C. ; discharged July 7, 1865, expiration of service.

CROSS, HENRY. Private Co. H, 50th Regt. Infantry, mustered Sept. 29, 1862, for nine months ; discharged Aug. 24, 1863, expiration of service.

CROWELL, PHILANDER. Private Co. H, 1st Regt. Infantry, mustered May 23, 1861, for three years, wounded at Blackburn's Ford, Va., July 18, 1861, died same day.

CROWELL, THATCHER. Private 4th Co. Unattached Inf., mustered May 3, 1864, for ninety days, discharged Aug. 6, 1864, expiration of service.

CROWLEY, DANIEL. Private Co. C, 28th Regt. Infantry, mustered March 18, 1864, for three years; discharged June 30, 1865, expiration of service.

CUDWORTH, FRANK A. Private Co. H, 11th Regiment Infantry, mustered Oct. 17, 1861, for three years. Wounded near Manassas, Va., Aug. 29, 1862 ; died Oct. 23, 1862, Fairfax, Va.

CUDWORTH, JOHN F. Private Co. H, 1st Regiment Infantry, mustered May 23, 1861, for three years. Wounded at White Oak Swamp, Va., June 30, 1862 ; discharged Jan. 3, 1864, to re-enlist ; mustered Jan. 4, 1864, for three years. May 20, 1864, transferred to 11th Regiment Infantry, assigned to Co. A ; wounded at Cold Harbor, Va., June 3, 1864 ; transferred, Oct. 11, 1864, to Co. F, 10th Battalion V. R. C. ; discharged May 31, 1866, expiration of service.

CUDWORTH, RILEY F. Private 2d Co. Unattached Infantry, mustered May 3, 1864, for ninety days ; discharged Aug. 6, 1864, expiration of service ; re-enlisted same Company, Aug. 7, 1864, for 100 days ; discharged Nov. 15, 1864, expiration of service.

CUMMINGS, HENRY. Private Co. C, 35th Regiment Infantry, mustered Aug. 19, 1862, for three years; appointed Corporal Sept. 1, 1864 ; discharged June 9, 1865, expiration of service.

CUMMINGS, HORATIO N. Corporal Co. F, 24th Regiment Infantry, mustered Oct. 14, 1861, for three years ; discharged Oct. 14, 1864, expiration of service.

CUMMINGS, THOMAS. Private Co. B, 3d Regiment Cavalry, mustered March 17, 1864, for three years ; discharged Sept. 28, 1865, expiration of service.

CUMMINGS, WILLIAM R. S. Private Co. C, 35th Regiment Infantry, mustered Aug. 19, 1862, for three years ; transferred July 16, 1864, to V. R. C. ; discharged June 28, 1865, expiration of service.

CUNIGAN, THOMAS. Unassigned recruit 26th Regiment Infantry, mustered May 24, 1864, for three years.

CUNNINGHAM, JOHN. Private Co. H, 4th Regiment Cavalry, mustered Feb. 8, 1864, for three years ; discharged Nov. 14, 1865, expiration of service.

CURRAN, JOHN. Unassigned recruit 2d Regiment Cavalry, mustered Aug. 6, 1864, for three years.

CURLEIGH, WILLIAM. Private Co. E, 33rd Regiment Infantry, mustered Dec. 20, 1864, for three years ; transferred June 1, 1865, to 2d Regiment Infantry Co. D. ; discharged July 14, 1865, expiration of service.

CURRIER, CHARLES A. Private Co. G, 40th Regiment Infantry, mustered Sept. 5, 1862 ; appointed 1st Sergeant Sept. 16, 1862 ; commissioned 2d Lieut. Co. H, Sept. 1, 1863 ; commissioned 1st Lieut., March 26, 1864; wounded at the mine near Petersburg, Va., July 30, 1864 ; commissioned Capt., Jan. 5, 1865 ; assigned Co. G, May 1, 1865 ; discharged June 16, 1865.

CURRIER, LEWIS G. Private Co. E, 30th Regiment Infantry, mustered Dec. 20, 1861, for three years ; discharged Dec. 8, 1862, for disability. Mustered private Co. F. 3d Regiment Heavy Artillery, April 16, 1864, for three years ; discharged Sept. 18, 1865, expiration of service.

CURTIS, JOHN. General service U. S. A., mustered March 17, 1864.

CUSHING, HENRY. Private Co. I, 47th Regiment Infantry, mustered Oct. 24, 1862, for nine months ; discharged Sept. 1, 1863, expiration of service.

CUSHING, HOSEA G. JR. Private Co. C, 35th Regiment Infantry, mustered Aug. 19, 1862, for three years ; discharged Feb. 16, 1863, for disability. Mustered May 3, 1864, for ninety days, private 4th Co. Unattached Infantry ; discharged Aug. 6, 1864, expiration of service.

CUTTING, FREDERICK L. Corporal Co. G, 40th Regiment Infantry, mustered Sept. 5, 1862, for three years ; discharged June 16, 1865, expiration of service.

D

DADE, DAVID B. Private Co. H, 43d Regiment Infantry, mustered Sept. 26, 1862, for nine months; discharged July 30, 1863, expiration of service.

DAILEY, THOMAS. Private Co. G, 2d Regiment Heavy Artillery, mustered July 23, 1864, for three years; transferred Jan. 17, 1865, to Co. C, 17th Regiment Infantry; discharged July 11, 1865, expiration of service.

DALPE, JEAN B. Unassigned recruit 20th Regiment Infantry, mustered April 12, 1864, for three years.

DAM, BENJAMIN F. Private Co. B, 24th Regiment Infantry, mustered Sept. 20, 1861, for three years; discharged Jan. 2, 1862, for disability. Drowned Nov. 1862.

DAM, CHARLES E. Private Co. C, 35th Regiment Infantry, mustered Aug. 19, 1862, for three years. Wounded at Antietam, Md., Sept. 17, 1862; died of wound Dec. 27, 1862, at Chelsea.

DAMMERALL, WILLIAM H. H. Private Co. H, 2d Regiment Infantry, mustered May 25, 1861, for three years; prisoner at Fairfax Court House, Va., Aug. 1862; paroled and exchanged Dec. 19, 1862. Wounded at Chancellorsville, Va., May 4, 1863; discharged to re-enlist Dec. 30, 1864; mustered same day for three years; appointed Corporal Jan. 1864; discharged July 14, 1865, expiration of service.

DANIELS, JAMES. Private Co. M, 4th Regiment Cavalry, mustered March 1, 1864, for three years; discharged Nov. 14, 1865, expiration of service.

53

DANIELS, WILLIAM B. Private Co. G, 40th Regiment Infantry, mustered Sept. 5, 1862, for three years; discharged June 16, 1865, order of War Department. Died at Chelsea, April 17, 1869.

DANIELS, WILLIAM P. 2d Lieutenant Co. H, 50th Regiment Infantry, mustered Sept. 29, 1862, for nine months; discharged Aug. 24, 1863, expiration of service.

DANN, JOHN W. Unassigned recruit 28th Regiment Infantry, mustered May 13, 1864, for three years.

DANTE, EARNEST. Unassigned recruit 28th Regiment Infantry, mustered Aug. 22, 1864, for three years.

DAVIDSON, ROBERT C. Corporal Co. C, 35th Regiment Infantry, mustered Aug. 19, 1862, for three years; appointed Sergeant, Feb. 7, 1863. Wounded July 30, 1864; died at City Point, Va., Aug. 19, 1864, from wound.

DAVIDSON, THOMAS W. General service U. S. A., mustered March 17, 1864.

DAVIS EDWARD J. Private Co. L, 2d Regiment Cavalry, mustered May 10, 1864, for three years. Deserted Oct. 31, 1864.

DAVIS, GEORGE. Private 6th Light Battery, mustered Dec. 24, 1864, for three years. Deserted Feb. 21, 1865.

DAVIS, JOHN. Private Co. A, 35th Regiment Infantry, musterd Aug. 9, 1862, for three years; tranferred Jan. 5, 1864, to V. R. C.

DAVIS, JOHN. Private Co. H, 42d Regiment Infantry, mustered Sept. 24, 1862, for nine months; discharged Aug. 20, 1863, expiration of service.

54

DAVIS, LEWELLYN F. Private Co. B, 1st Regiment Infantry, mustered May 23, 1861, for three years. Deserted May 28, 1861.

DAVIS, NATHANIEL T. Private Co. H, 1st Regiment Infantry, mustered May 23, 1861, for three years; discharged May 24, 1864, expiration of service; appointed Pay-master's clerk U. S. Navy, May 1864.

DAVIS, WILLIAM. Unassigned recruit 3d Regiment Cavalry, mustered March 17, 1864, for three years. Deserted May 1864.

DAY, ALBERT J. Private 8th Light Battery, mustered May 30, 1862, for six months, on quota of Boston; discharged Nov. 29, 1862, expiration of service. Mustered private Co. I, 1st Regiment Cavalry, Dec. 5, 1863, for three years on Chelsea quota; discharged June 29, 1865, expiration of service.

DAY, JOHN. Unassigned recruit 26th Regiment Infantry, mustered May 24, 1864, for three years.

DAY, JOHN H. Private Co. B, 35th Regiment Infantry, mustered May 10, 1864, for three years ; transferred June 9, 1865, to 29th Regiment Infantry. Dropped as deserter.

DAY, JOHN W. Private Co. H, 1st Regiment Infantry, mustered May 23, 1861, for three years ; discharged Aug. 29, 1861, at Bladensburg, Va., disability. Re-enlisted in R. I. Cavalry, Nov. 30, 1861 ; taken prisoner June 1, 1863; released Sept. 1863; re-enlisted Jan. 4, 1864, for three years ; commissioned 2d Lieutenant 4th U. S. Cavalry, April 15, 1864.

DEAN, CHARLES. Private Co. H, 50th Regiment Infantry, mustered Sept. 29, 1862, for nine months; discharged Aug. 24, 1863, expiration of service.

DEARBORN, CHARLES H. Private Co. G, 40th Regiment Infantry, mustered Sept. 5, 1862, for three years; discharged April 2, 1863, disability.

DEARBORN, CHARLES L. Private Co. G, 40th Regiment Infantry, mustered Sept. 5, 1862, for three years. Died Jan. 27, 1864, at Hilton Head, S. C., chronic diarrhœa.

DEARBORN, GEORGE A. Private Co. C, 35th Regiment Infantry, mustered Aug. 19, 1862, for three years; discharged June 9, 1865, expiration of service.

DeLACY, PETER. Unassigned recruit 2d Regiment Infantry, mustered Oct. 16, 1864, for three years.

DELACONE, THOMAS. Unassigned recruit 2d Regiment Infantry, mustered Aug. 12, 1864, for three years.

DELANO, MARCUS. Private Co. C, 1st Battalion Heavy Artillery, mustered Nov, 25, 1863, for three years; discharged June 25, 1865, expiration of service.

DELANO, WILLIAM C. Private 11th Light Battery; mustered Jan. 2, 1864, for three years; discharged June 16, 1865, expiration of service.

DELILE, JEAN. Private 7th Light Battery, mustered Dec. 4, 1864, for three years; discharged Nov. 10, 1865, expiration of service.

DEMMING, PATRICK. Private V. R. C., mustered June 23, 1864.

DEMPSEY, JEREMIAH. Private Co. C, 35th Regiment Infantry, mustered Aug. 19, 1862, for three years. Died Aug. 24, 1863.

DEMPSEY, PATRICK. Private Co. H, 50th Regiment Infantry, mustered Sept. 29, 1862, for nine months ; discharged Aug. 24, 1863, expiration of service.

DENHAM, ROBERT H. Private Co. C, 35th Regiment Infantry, mustered Aug. 19, 1862, for three years ; discharged Jan. 16, 1863, disability. Died at Chelsea, Jan. 11, 1865.

DERBY, WILLIAM H. Corporal Co. A, 44th Regiment Infantry, mustered Sept. 12, 1862, for nine months ; discharged June 15, 1863, expiration of service.

DESSAWER, JOHN. Corporal Co. B, 3d Regiment Cavalry, mustered March 16, 1864, for three years ; discharged April 17, 1865, disability.

DEVINE, JOHN. Unassigned recruit 2nd Regiment Infantry, mustered May 18, 1864, for three years.

DEVLIN, JOHN. Unassigned recruit 1st Regiment Cavalry, mustered Dec. 29, 1863, for three years; rejected Jan. 5, 1864.

DILLAWAY, WILLIAM H. Private Co. H, 43d Regiment Infantry, mustered Oct. 11, 1862, for nine months ; discharged July 30, 1863, expiration of service.

DINSMORE, SANDFORD. Engineer Corps U. S. A., mustered Dec. 21, 1864.

DINSMORE, WILLIAM J. Private Co. H, 1st Regiment Infantry, mustered May 23, 1861, for three years. Wounded at Manassas, Va., Aug. 29, 1862 ; died in ambulance near Centreville, Va., Sept. 3, 1862.

DIXON, HORATIO. Private Co. H, 50th Regiment Infantry, mustered Sept. 29, 1862, for nine months; discharged Aug. 24, 1863, expiration of service.

DOANE, WALTER W. Musician 4th Co. Unattached Infantry, mustered May 3, 1864, for ninety days ; discharged Aug. 6, 1864, expiration of service.

DODGE, BENJAMIN F. Corporal Co. G, 40th Regiment Infantry, mustered Sept. 5, 1862, for three years ; appointed Sergeant, Sept. 16, 1862 ; transferred to Co. B, 9th Regiment V. R. C., Oct. 15, 1863 ; appointed Quarter-master's Sergeant, March 4, 1864 ; discharged Sept. 5, 1865 ; expiration of service.

DODGE, JAMES A. Quarter-master's Sergeant, Co. G, 4th Regiment Cavalry, mustered Jan. 27, 1864, for three years ; discharged Nov. 14, 1865, expiration of service.

DOHERTY, CORNELIUS. Private Co. I, 56th Regiment Infantry, mustered Feb. 4, 1864, for three years ; discharged July 12, 1865 ; absent, sick.

DOHERTY, JOHN. Private Co. I, 2d Regiment Infantry, mustered July 23, 1864, for three years. Deserted Aug. 1, 1864, at Atlanta, Ga.

DOHM, WILLIAM. Private Co. E, 19th Regiment Infantry, mustered Dec. 21, 1864, for three years; discharged June 28, 1865, order of War Department.

DONAGHY, JAMES. Private Co. G, 40th Regiment Infantry, mustered Sept. 5, 1862, for three years. Wounded at Drury's Bluff, Va., May 16, 1864; discharged March 31, 1865, disability from wound.

DONAHUE, EDWARD. Private Co. F, 56th Regiment Infantry, mustered Jan. 12, 1864, for three years. Deserted March 10 1864.

DOLAN, JAMES. Private Co. F, 56 Regiment Infantry, mustered Jan. 12, 1864, for three years. Deserted Jan. 25, 1864.

DOLE, CHARLES F. Private 4th Co. Unattached Infantry, mustered May 3, 1864, for ninety days; discharged Aug. 6, 1864, expiration of service.

DONKLE, SAMUEL. Private V. R. C., mustered June 7, 1864.

DONNELL, JOHN. Private 6th Light Battery, mustered Dec. 22, 1864, for three years. Deserted Jan. 28, 1865.

DONNELL, JOHN A. Private Co. G, 2d Regiment Cavalry, mustered May 11, 1864, for three years; discharged July 20, 1865, expiration of service.

DOUGLASS, COURTLAND H. Private Co. A, 30th Regiment Infantry, on quota of Boston; discharged Jan. 1, 1864, to re-enlist. Re-enlisted and mustered on quota of Chelsea, Jan. 2, 1864, as 1st Sergeant; appointed Hospital Steward, June 1, 1865; commissioned 2d Lieut., Jan. 25, 1866; discharged July 5, 1866, expiration of service.

59

DOUGLASS, EUGENE F. Private 4th Co. Unattached Infantry, mustered May 3, 1864, for 90 days; discharged Aug. 6, 1864, expiration of service.

DOW, JOSEPH E. Private 2d Light Battery, mustered July 31, 1861, for three years; discharged Oct. 18, 1862, for disability.

DOWNING, WASHINGTON J. Private 13th Light Battery, mustered Dec. 23, 1864, for three years; discharged July 28, 1865, expiration of service.

DOYLE, EDWARD. Private Co. I, 48th Regiment Infantry, mustered Oct. 18, 1862, for nine months. Deserted Dec. 4, 1862, at Readville, Mass.

DOYLE, PATRICK. Private Co. A. 35th Regiment Infantry, mustered Aug. 9, 1862, for three years. Wounded at Antietam, Md., Sept. 17, 1862; wounded near Petersburg, Va., Aug. 11, 1864; discharged June 9, 1865, expiration of service; absent, sick.

DOYLE, WILLIAM. Unassigned recruit 9th Regiment Infantry, mustered May 11, 1864, for three years; discharged May 12, 1864, rejected recruit.

DRAWBRIDGE, THOMAS N. Private Co. H, 1st Regiment Infantry, mustered May 25, 1861, for three years; discharged at Budd's Ferry, Md., March 15, 1862, for disability.

DREW, JOHN. 1st Sergeant Co. C, 1st Regiment Cavalry, mustered Sept. 17, 1861, for three years on quota of Boston ; discharged Dec. 31, 1863, to re-enlist. Mustered on Chelsea's quota Jan. 1, 1864, for three years ; commissioned 2d Lieut. Feb. 2, 1864 ; commissioned Capt., Sept. 2, 1864 ; discharged June 26, 1865, expiration of service.

DREW, STEPHEN C. 2nd Lieutenant 18th Regiment Infantry, mustered Dec. 1, 1862, for three years ; promoted 1st Lieut., May 3, 1863 ; discharged Sept. 2, 1864, expiration of service.

DRISCOLL, JOHN. Private Co. E, 24th Regiment Infantry, mustered March 19, 1864, for three years ; discharged Jan. 20, 1866, expiration of service.

DRUMMOND, WILLIAM A. Private 4th Co. Unattached Infantry, mustered May 3, 1864, for ninety days ; discharged Aug. 6, 1864, expiration of service.

DRURY, WILLIAM P. Corporal Co. H, 1st Regiment Infantry, mustered May 23, 1861, for three years ; appointed Sergt., Oct. 1, 1861 ; discharged for promotion, Sept. 8, 1862 ; commissioned 2d Lieut., assigned to Co. A, Jan. 1, 1863. Wounded at Gettysburg, Pa., July 3, 1863 ; promoted 1st Lieut., Sept. 22, 1865 ; discharged May 25, 1864, expiration of service. Sept. 22, 1864, mustered for one year ; Captain 61st Regiment Infantry; discharged April 28, 1865, for disability.

DROWN, THEODORE B. Private 4th Co. Unattached Infantry, mustered May 3, 1864, for ninety days ; discharged Aug. 6, 1864, expiration of service.

DUBOIS, RICHARD C. General service U. S. A., mustered March 26, 1864; discharged Oct. 9, 1865, to accept 2d Lieut. 14th Regiment U. S. Infantry.

DUCKRELL, WILLIAM J. Private Co. E, 5th Regiment Infantry, mustered May 1, 1861, for three months, on quota of Medford; discharged July 31, 1861, expiration of service. Mustered private Co. E, 40th Regiment Infantry, Sept. 16, 1862, for three years; not credited to any quota; discharged Dec. 15, 1864, order of War Department. Mustered Dec. 5, 1864, on quota of Chelsea, for one year, 2d Lieut. 61st Regiment Infantry; discharged July 16, 1865, expiration of service.

DUFRAINE, NAPOLEON. Private Co. G, 4th Regiment Cavalry, mustered Jan. 27, 1864, for three years; discharged Nov. 14, 1865, expiration of service.

DUGAL, THOMAS. Unassigned recruit 28th Regiment Infantry, mustered May 11, 1864, for three years.

DUMAS, EARNEST. Private Co. M, 4th Regiment Cavalry, mustered Dec. 21, 1864, for three years. Deserted April 4, 1865,

DUNDASS, JAMES. Private Co. F, 11th Regiment Infantry, mustered June 13, 1861, for three years. Wounded at Gettysburg, Pa., July 3, 1863; discharged Feb. 2, 1864, disability from wound. Died at Chelsea, Aug. 15, 1880.

DUNDASS, JOHN. Private 18th Co. Unattached Infantry, mustered Aug. 4, 1864, for 100 days; discharged Nov. 14, 1864, expiration of service.

DUNN, CALEB. Unassigned recruit 2d Regiment Cavalry, mustered May 24, 1864, for three years.

DUNN, JAMES. Private 13th Light Battery, mustered Nov. 29, 1862, for three years. Deserted Jan. 6, 1863.

DUNN, JOHN V. Private Co. G, 40th Regiment Infantry, mustered Sept. 5, 1862, for three years; discharged May 25, 1865, order of War Department.

DUNNING, JOHN A. Corporal Co. H, 50th Regiment Infantry, mustered Sept. 29, 1862, for nine months; discharged Aug. 24, 1863, expiration of service.

DUPEE, ALBERT E. Private Co. C, 12th Regiment Infantry, mustered June 26, 1861, for three years; taken prisoner March 25, 1862; discharged May 22, 1862. Mustered Corporal Co. E, 45th Regiment Infantry, Sept. 20, 1862, for nine months on quota of Wrentham; discharged July 7th, 1863, expiration of service.

DUREN, FREEMAN H. Private Co. B, 13th Regiment Infantry, mustered July 16, 1861, for three years; appointed Corporal, Sept. 1, 1862; appointed Sergeant, May 1, 1863; discharged Aug. 1, 1864, expiration of service.

DURFEE, WILLIAM. Private Co. F, 2d Regiment Cavalry, mustered Aug. 10, 1864, for three years; discharged July 20, 1865, expiration of service.

DURGIN, AUGUSTUS. Private Co. H, 50th Regiment Infantry, mustered Sept. 19, 1862, for nine months; discharged March 9, 1863, for disability.

EARLE, GEORGE W. Private Co. G, 40th Regiment Infantry, mustered Sept. 5, 1862, for three years. Wounded at Drury's Bluff, Va., May 16, 1864, died at Hampton, Va., May 19, 1864.

EASTERBROOK, KIMBALL JR. Private Co. G, 40th Regiment Infantry, mustered Sept. 5, 1862, for three years ; appointed Quarter-master's Sergeant, Oct. 21, 1863 ; discharged Dec. 28, 1864, for promotion ; commissioned 1st Lieut., Nov. 16, 1864 ; discharged June 16, 1865, expiration of service.

EASTMAN, CHARLES F. Corporal Co. H, 19th Regiment Infantry, mustered Dec. 10, 1861, for three years ; discharged July 20, 1862, for disability.

EDGECOMB, JOSEPH W. Private Co. H, 50th Regiment Infantry, mustered Sept. 29, 1862, for nine months ; discharged Feb. 4, 1863, for disability.

EDGERLY, HIRAM O. Private Co. D, 4th Regiment Cavalry, mustered Jan. 9, 1864, for three years ; appointed Sergeant, May 1, 1864 ; discharged Aug. 12, 1865, for promotion 2d Lieut. U. S. C. Troops.

EDMUNDS JOHN JR. 1st Sergeant Co. H, 43d Regiment Infantry, mustered Sept. 20, 1862, for nine months ; discharged July 30, 1863, expiration of service.

EDWARDS, EDWARD E. Private Co. A, 1st Regiment Cavalry, mustered Sept. 17, 1861, for three years ; discharged Oct. 24, 1861, rejected recruit. Mustered Sept. 2, 1862, for three years, private Co. G, 40th Regiment Infantry ; discharged June 16, 1865, expiration of service,

EDWARDS, GEORGE W. Private Co. K, 3d Regiment Heavy Artillery, mustered May 12, 1864, for three years; discharged Sept. 18, 1865, expiration of service.

EDWARDS, JOHN C. Private 15th Light Battery, mustered Jan. 27, 1864, for three years; discharged July 5, 1864, disability.

EHRENSTAN, MAX. Private Co. E, 43d Regiment Infantry, mustered Oct. 1, 1862, for nine months; discharged June 2, 1863; re-enlisted 2d Regiment Heavy Artillery, commissioned 2d Lieut. 2d Regiment Corps D'Afrique, Dec. 18, 1863.

ELDRIDGE, ELLERY W. Private 2d Light Battery, mustered July 31, 1861, for three years; discharged Aug. 16, 1864, expiration of service; Hospital Steward U. S. A., Sept. 1864.

ELDRIDGE, HORACE P. Sergeant Co. H, 43d Regiment Infantry, mustered Sept. 26, 1862, for nine months; discharged July 30, 1863, expiration of service.

ELFORD, WILLIAM R. Private Co. I, 26th Regiment Infantry, mustered Sept. 24, 1861, for three years; transferred April 6, 1864, to Co. H, 3d Regiment V. R. C.; discharged Oct. 17, 1864, expiration of service.

ELLERY, ALPHONSO. Private Co. G, 40th Regiment Infantry, mustered Sept. 12, 1862, for three years; discharged June 16, 1865, expiration of service.

ELWELL, JOHN B. General service U. S. A., mustered March 19, 1864.

EMERSON, GEORGE H. Private Co. H, 43d Regiment Infantry, mustered Sept. 20, 1862, for nine months; discharged July 30, 1863, expiration of service.

EMERSON, JOSEPH H. Unassigned recruit 3d Regiment
Cavalry, mustered Aug. 18, 1864, for three years.

EMERSON, STEPHEN G. Private Co. H, 1st Regiment Infantry, mustered July 31, 1862, for three years. Killed
May 3, 1863, at Chancellorsville, Va.

ENOS, JAMES. Private Co. A, 28th Regiment Infantry, mustered March 12, 1864, for three years. Deserted April
13, 1864.

EVANS, FRANK S. Private Co. H, 43d Regiment Infantry,
mustered Sept. 20, 1862, for nine months; discharged
July 30, 1863, expiration of service.

EVANS, JAMES F. Hospital Steward U. S. A., mustered
Jan. 15, 1864.

EVANS, JOEL W. P. Private Co. F, 17th Regiment Infantry, mustered Jan. 31, 1862, for three years; discharged
Jan. 30, 1865, expiration of service.

EVANS, THOMAS H. Private Co. H, 43d Regiment Infantry, mustered Sept. 20, 1862, for nine months; discharged
July 20, 1863, expiration of service.

EVERDEAN, CHARLES S. Private Co. H, 1st Regiment
Infantry, mustered May, 23, 1861, for three years; wounded near Manassas, Va., Aug. 29, 1862; discharged Nov.
5, 1862, disability from wound. Appointed Master's
Mate, Navy, Aug. 20, 1863; discharged May 31, 1868.

EVERDEAN, GEORGE W. Private Co. C, 35th Regiment Infantry, mustered Aug. 19, 1862, for three years; wounded at Antietam, Md., Sept. 17, 1862 ; discharged Jan. 5, 1863, disability from wound.

EVERDEAN, JOSEPH B. Private Co. G, 40th Regiment Infantry, mustered Sept. 5, 1862, for three years; discharged June 16, 1865, expiration of service.

EVERDEAN, WILBUR F. Private Co. H, 1st Regiment Infantry, mustered May 23, 1861, for three years ; discharged Feb. 25, 1863, for disability, at Falmouth, Va.

FARGO, HENRY C. Private Co. A, 12th Regiment Infantry, mustered June 26, 1861, for three years ; discharged July 8, 1864, expiration of service.

FARLEY, HENRY B. Private Co. C, 35th Regiment Infantry, mustered Aug. 19, 1862, for three years. Wounded at Antietam, Md., Sept. 17, 1862 ; discharged Nov. 2, 1863, to enlist in general service of U. S. A.; discharged 1864. Died Oct. 29, 1876, Taunton, Mass.

FARLEY, PATRICK. Private Co. B, 9th Regiment Infantry, mustered June 11, 1861, for three years ; discharged June 15, 1863, for disability.

FARMER, CHARLES. Private Co. E, 9th Regiment Infantry, mustered June 11, 1861, for three years ; appointed Sergeant, Oct. 29, 1862 ; discharged June 21, 1864, expiration of service ; re-enlisted on quota of Somerville, in Marine Corps, Aug. 17, 1864.

FARMER, CHARLES E. Private 6th Light Battery, mustered Jan. 16, 1862, for three years ; discharged Jan. 5, 1864, to re-enlist. Mustered Jan. 6, 1864, for three years ; discharged Feb. 6, 1865, expiration of service. Killed in Boston, Feb. 21, 1865.

FARMER, EDWARD. Private Co. F, 28th Regiment Infantry, mustered Jan. 2, 1862, for three years ; discharged Jan. 1, 1864, to re-enlist. Mustered Jan. 2, 1864, for three years. Deserted March 30, 1864.

FARMER, JOHN. Private V. R. C., mustered May 28, 1864.

FARMER, OWEN. Private 6th Light Battery, mustered Dec. 11, 1861, for three years. Died July 5, 1863, at Baton Rouge, La.

FARNSWORTH, ANDREW J. Private Co. K, 12th Regiment Infantry, mustered June 26, 1861, for three years. Wounded at Antietam, Md., Sept. 17, 1862 ; wounded at Fredericksburg, Va., Dec. 13, 1862 ; discharged Sept. 21, 1863, disability from wounds.

FELLOWS, CHARLES O. Private Co. H, 1st Regiment Infantry, mustered May 23, 1861, for three years ; discharged Jan. 17, 1862. Commissioned Dec. 13, 1861, 2d Lieut. Co. D, 17th Regiment Infantry ; commissioned 1st Lieut. Co. A, 17th Regiment Infantry, Aug. 13, 1862 ; commisioned Capt. Co. F, 17th Regiment, Aug. 4, 1864 ; discharged July 11, 1865, expiration of service.

FELLOWS, JOHN F. Lieut.-Col. 17th Regiment Infantry ; mustered Aug. 21, 1861 ; taken prisoner near Newbern, N. C., Feb. 1, 1864 ; discharged Aug. 3, 1864 ; commissioned Colonel, Oct. 9, 1864 ; not mustered.

FENNO, CHARLES F. Private 4th Co. Unattached Infantry, mustered May 3, 1864, for ninety days ; discharged Aug. 6, 1864, expiration of service.

FERRIS, JOB F. Private Co. K, 43d Regiment Infantry ; mustered Sept. 16, 1862, for nine months ; discharged July 30, 1863, expiration of service.

FICKETT, ALBERT A. Private 4th Co. Unattached Infantry, mustered May 3, 1864, for ninety days ; discharged Aug. 6, 1864, expiration of service.

FIELD, EDWIN. Private Co. B, 13th Regiment Infantry ; mustered July 16, 1861, for three years. Killed at Gettysburg, Pa., July 1, 1863.

FIELD, FREDERICK A. Private Co. A, 43d Regiment Infantry, mustered Oct. 11, 1862, for nine months ; discharged July 30, 1863, expiration of service.

FIELD, WARREN S. Private Co. G, 40th Regiment Infantry, mustered Sept. 5, 1862, for three years; discharged June 16, 1865, expiration of service.

FIFIELD, CALVIN S. Sergeant 16th Co. Unattached Infantry, mustered Aug. 6, 1864, for 100 days; discharged Nov. 14, 1864, expiration of service.

FINN, JOHN. Private 12th Light Battery, mustered Dec. 9, 1862, for three years; discharged July 25, 1865, expiration of service.

FISCHER, WILLIAM. Private Co. A, 2d Regiment Cavalry, mustered April 16, 1864, for three years. Deserted May 9, 1864.

FISHER, CHARLES R. Private Co. H, 43d Regiment Infantry, mustered Sept. 20, 1862, for nine months; discharged July 30, 1863, expiration of service.

FITZPATRICK, DAVID. Private Co. E, 24th Regiment Infantry, mustered Dec. 5, 1861, for three years. Wounded at Goldsborough, N. C., Dec. 1862; discharged Jan. 3, 1864, to re-enlist; mustered Jan. 4, 1864, for three years; discharged Jan. 20, 1866, expiration of service.

FITZSIMMONS, JOHN. Private Co. H, 42d Regiment Infantry, mustered Sept. 24, 1862, for nine months. Deserted Sept. 25, 1862, at Readville, Mass.

FLANAGAN, THOMAS. Private Co. G, 3d Regiment Cavalry, mustered Jan. 14, 1864, for three years; absent without leave since June 1865.

FLANIGAN, JOHN. Private Co. H, 42d Regiment Infantry, mustered Sept. 24, 1862, for nine months. Deserted Sept. 30, 1862, at Readville, Mass.

FLEMMING, JAMES. Unassigned recruit 2d Regiment Infantry, mustered July 22, 1864, for three years.

FLETCHER, JOHN W. 2d Lieutenant Co. K, 43d Regiment
Infantry, mustered Sept. 16, 1862, for nine months; discharged July 30, 1863, expiration of service. Commissioned Capt., July 14, 1863, 2d Regiment, Wilde's African
Brigade; resigned May 14, 1864.

FLYNN, CHARLES. Private V. R. C., mustered Sept. 7, 1864;
discharged Nov. 30, 1865, order of War Department.

FLYNN, PATRICK. Private Co. H, 56th Regiment Infantry,
mustered Jan. 27, 1864, for three years; taken prisoner.
Died July 24, 1864, at Andersonville, Ga.

FOLEY, JAMES. Private Co. D, 2d Regiment Infantry, mustered July 23, 1864, for three years; died June 24, 1865,
Washington, D.C.

FOLEY, MICHAEL. Private 12th Light Battery, mustered
Jan. 15, 1864, for three years; discharged July 25, 1865,
expiration of service.

FOLSOM, JOHN A. Private 9th Light Battery, mustered
Aug. 10, 1862, for three years; discharged June 20, 1863,
for disability.

FOLSOM, WILLIAM J. Private Co. H, 43d Regiment Infantry, mustered Sept. 20, 1862, for nine months; discharged
July 30, 1863, expiration of service. Mustered private
4th Co. Unattched Infantry, May 3, 1864, for ninety days;
discharged Aug. 6, 1864, expiration of service.

FORD, JOSEPH. Unassigned Recruit 2d Regiment Infantry,
mustered Aug. 18, 1864, for three years.

FORD, MICHAEL. Private Co. F, 28th Regiment Infantry,
mustered Dec. 13, 1861, for three years; deserted Sept.
8, 1862.

FORMAN, GEORGE. Private Co. I, 2d Regiment Cavalry, mustered Aug. 9, 1864, for three years; discharged July 20, 1865, expiration of service.

FORREST, HENRY. Private Co. H, 43d Regiment Infantry, mustered Sept. 20, 1862, for nine months; deserted Sept. 29, 1862, Readville, Mass.

FORSAITH, JAMES L. Corporal Co. H, 50th Regiment Infantry, mustered Sept. 29, 1862, for nine months; discharged Aug. 24, 1863, expiration of service.

FOSTER, HENRY A. General Service U. S. A.; mustered April 20, 1864.

FOSTER, PETER. Private Co. D, 17th Regiment Infantry, mustered Jan. 27, 1862, for three years; deserted Feb. 1862.

FOWLER, STEPHEN D. Private Co. E, 5th Regiment Infantry, mustered May 1, 1861, for three months; discharged July 31, 1861, expiration of service. Mustered Aug. 19, 1862, for three years, 1st Sergeant Co. C, 35th Regiment Infantry; discharged June 9, 1865, expiration of service.

FRACKER, JOHN W. Private Co. H, 43d Regiment Infantry, mustered Sept. 20, 1862, for nine months; discharged July 30, 1863, expiration of service.

FRANCIS, JOSEPH H. Private V. R. C. mustered June 20, 1864.

FRANKLIN, THOMAS. Unassigned recruit 2d Regiment Infantry, mustered May 13, 1864, for three years.

FRANELLO, ANGELLO. Private Co. I, 2d Regiment Heavy Artillery, mustered Dec. 11, 1863, for three years; discharged Sept. 3, 1865, expiration of service.

FRAWLEY, THOMAS. Private Co. K, 3d Regiment Heavy Artillery, mustered May 12, 1864, for three years; discharged Sept. 18, 1865, expiration of service.

FRAZIER, HUGH. Private Co. H, 48th Regiment Infantry, mustered Sept. 25, 1862, for nine months; discharged Sept. 3, 1863, expiration of service.

FREELAND, ROBERT. Private V. R. C., mustered June 20, 1864.

FRENCH, JAMES. Private Co. H, 20th Regiment Infantry, mustered April 12, 1864, for three years; discharged July 16, 1865, expiration of service.

FREY, JAMES. Private Co. G, 2d Regiment Infantry, mustered June 13, 1864, for three years: discharged July 5, 1865, for disability.

FROST, CHARLES H. Private Co. C, 2d Regiment Heavy Artillery, mustered Oct. 8, 1863, for three years; discharged Sept. 3, 1865, expiration of service.

FROST, JONATHAN J. Corporal Co. H, 1st Regiment Infantry, mustered May 21, 1861, for three years; discharged Oct. 16, 1862, at Chelsea, for disability.

FUHRMANN, GEORGE. Private Co. G, 2d Regiment Infantry, mustered May 17, 1864, for three years; discharged July 14, 1865, expiration of service.

FULLER, CHARLES E. Private 4th Co: Unattached Infantry, mustered May 3, 1864, for ninety days; discharged Aug. 6, 1865, expiration of service.

FULLER, HARRISON. Private Co. I. 1st Regiment Infantry, mustered Dec. 4, 1861, for three years; discharged May 25, 1864, expiration of service.

GAFFNEY, EDWARD E. Corporal Co. L, 2d Regiment Heavy Artillery, mustered Dec. 25, 1863, for three years ; discharged Aug. 19, 1865, expiration of service.

GAGE, EDWARD M. Musician 4th Co. Unattached Infantry, mustered May 3, 1864, for ninety days ; discharged Aug. 6, 1864, expiration of service.

GALLAGHER, CHARLES W. Private 4th Co. Unattached Infantry ; mustered May 3, 1864, for ninety days ; discharged Aug. 6, 1864, expiration of service.

GALLAGHER, DANIEL. Private Co. E, 28th Regiment Infantry, mustered March 24, 1864, for three years ; discharged June 30, 1865, expiration of service.

GALLAGHER, JAMES F. Private Co. L, 3d Regiment Cavalry, mustered Nov. 19, 1861, for three years ; discharged Dec. 27, 1865, expiration of service.

GALLAGHER, JOHN. Private V. R. C., mustered July 23, 1864.

GALUSHA, FLORILLA B. Private Co. G, 40th Regiment Infantry, mustered Sept. 5, 1862, for three years ; discharged June 16, 1865, expiration of service.

GARDNER, WARREN H. Private Co. I, 1st Regiment Infantry, mustered May 24, 1861, for three years ; wounded near Richmond, Va., June 25, 1862, died July 5, 1862, on his passage home.

GANNON, MARTIN. General Service U. S. A., mustered April 8, 1864, for three years ; discharged April 8, 1867, expiration of service.

GARLAND, IRA S. Wagoner, Co. C, 1st Battalion Heavy Artillery, mustered Nov. 21, 1863, for three years ; discharged Oct. 20, 1865, expiration of service.

GARMAN, FELIX D. P. Private Co. D, 2d Regiment Infantry, mustered Dec. 20, 1864, for three years ; discharged July 14, 1865, expiration of service.

GARVIN, JAMES A. Private Co. A, 26th Regiment Infantry, mustered Sept. 14, 1861, for three years ; discharged Dec. 31, 1863, to re-enlist ; mustered Jan. 1, 1864, on Lowell quota ; discharged Aug. 26, 1865, expiration of service.

GEARY, GEORGE W. Private Co. H, 43d Regiment Infantry, mustered Sept. 20, 1862, for nine months ; discharged July 30, 1863, expiration of service.

GEOGHAN, JOHN. Unassigned recruit 2d Regiment Infantry, mustered May 14, 1864, for three years.

GERRISH, ISRAEL H. Corporal Co. G, 40th Regiment Infantry, mustered Sept. 5, 1862 ; appointed Sergeant, June 1, 1863 ; transferred May 31, 1864, to V. R. C. ; discharged June 29, 1865, expiration of service.

GERRISH, JAMES R. Sergeant Co. H, 1st Regiment Infantry, mustered May 23, 1861, for three years ; discharged Oct. 5, 1862, for disability.   ·

GERRISH, WILLIAM. Private Co. H, 1st Regiment Infantry, mustered May 23, 1861, for three years ; discharged July 22, 1861, for disability. Commissioned 1st Lieut. 20th Regiment U. S. C. T., Jan. 28, 1864 ; resigned Aug. 1864.

GIBBY, WILLIAM H. Private Co. G, 40th Regiment Infantry, mustered Sept. 5, 1862, for three years ; transferred to V. R. C., Feb. 20, 1864 ; discharged Dec. 6, 1864.

GIBBY, WILLIAM H. JR. Private Co. C, 1st Regiment Cavalry, mustered Jan. 5, 1864, for three years; discharged June 9, 1865, expiration of service.

GIBLER, WILLIAM. General service U. S. A., mustered March 17, 1864.

GIBSON, FREDERICK M. Private Co. G, 40th Regiment Infantry, mustered Sept. 5, 1862, for three years; discharged June 16, 1865, expiration of service.

GIBSON, WILLIAM. Private Co. A, 44th Regiment Infantry, mustered Sept. 12, 1862, for nine months. Deserted Oct. 8, 1862, at Readville, Mass.

GIFFORD, ALBERT D. Private Co. H, 50th Regiment Infantry, mustered Sept. 29, 1862, for nine months; discharged Aug. 24, 1863, expiration of service.

GILBERT, CHARLES. Private Co. H, 1st Regiment Infantry, mustered May 23, 1861, for three years; discharged July 22, 1861, for disability. Re-enlisted on quota of Boston, Oct. 24, 1862; wounded at Gettysburg, Pa., July 3, 1863; discharged Oct. 23, 1863, disability from wounds. Died in Marine Hospital, Chelsea.

GILBERT, GEORGE B. Private Co. B, 2d Regiment Heavy Artillery, mustered July 29, 1863, for three years. Killed March 8, 1865, near Kinston, N. C.

GILES, JOHN H. Private Co. H, 50th Regiment Infantry, mustered Sept. 29, 1862, for nine months; discharged Aug. 24, 1863, expiration of service.

GILLISPIE, ROBERT. Private Co. C, 12th Regiment Infantry, mustered June 26, 1861, for three years; appointed Corporal, Dec. 25, 1861. Wounded at Antietam, Md., Sept. 17, 1862; discharged Feb. 21, 1863, disability from wound.

GILLING, WILLIAM F. Private Co. H, 43d Regiment Infantry, mustered Sept. 20, 1862, for nine months; discharged July 30, 1863, expiration of service.

GILLINGS, GEORGE C. Private Co. C, 35th Regiment Infantry, mustered Aug. 19, 1862, for three years; discharged June 9, 1865, expiration of service.

GILLETT, PERRIN T. Private Co. I, 22d Regiment Infantry, mustered Sept. 6, 1861, for three years; appointed Corporal, Oct. 10, 1862. Wounded at Fredericksburg, Va., Dec. 13, 1862; transferred to V. R. C., July 16, 1863; discharged Oct. 7, 1864, expiration of service. Mustered Corporal Co. G, 61st Regiment for one year, Nov. 19, 1864, on quota of Cambridge; discharged July 16, 1865, expiration of service.

GILMAN, CHARLES W. Private Co. C, 35th Regiment Infantry, mustered Aug. 19, 1862, for three years; wounded May 18, 1864. Killed near Petersburg, Va., Dec, 27, 1864.

GILMAN, JAMES E. Corporal Co. A, 43d Regiment Infantry, mustered Oct. 11, 1862, for nine months; appointed Sergeant-Major, Nov. 3, 1862; discharged May 28, 1863, disability.

GILMAN, LEVI. Private 11th Light Battery, mustered Dec. 20, 1864, for three years. Died, May 14, 1865, at Washington, D. C.

GILMORE, GEORGE. Private Co. G, 2d Regiment Heavy Artillery, mustered Aug. 16, 1864, for three years; discharged, Sept. 3, 1865, expiration of service.

GIPSON, MONTGOMERY. Private Co. C, 35th Regiment Infantry, mustered Aug. 19, 1862, for three years. Wounded at South Mountain, Md., Sept. 14, 1862 ; discharged Nov. 28th, 1862, disability from wound.

GIRAGHTY, JOHN F. Private Co. H, 43d Regiment Infantry, mustered Sept. 20, 1862, for nine months. Deserted Nov. 3, 1862, at Readville, Mass.

GLAZIER, LOUIS. Private Co. G, 2d Regiment Infantry, mustered Nov, 30, 1864, for three years ; discharged July 14, 1865, expiration of service.

GLEASON, MATTHEW R. Private Co. H, 48th Regiment Infantry, mustered Sept. 25, 1862, for nine months ; discharged Sept. 3, 1863, expiration of service.

GLOVER, BENJAMIN T. Private Co. G, 40th Regiment Infantry, mustered Sept. 5, 1863, for three years. Wounded at Drury's Bluff, Va., May 16, 1864 ; appointed Corporal Oct. 8, 1864 ; discharged May 24, 1865, disability from wounds.

GLOVER, MORTON E. Private Co. L, 3d Regiment Heavy Artillery, mustered May 30, 1865, for three years ; discharged Sept. 18, 1865, expiration of service.

GODDING, GILBERT H. Private Co. I, 1st Regiment Cavalry, mustered Jan. 14, 1864, for three years. Deserted Jan. 1, 1865, from Co. C.

GOFF, THOMAS M. Unassigned recruit 2d Regiment Infantry, mustered May 17, 1864, for three years.

GOLDING, WILLIAM H. Private 4th Co. Unattached Infantry, mustered May 3, 1864, for ninety days ; discharged Aug. 6, 1864, expiration of service.

78

GOODING, GEORGE. Private Co. H, 43d Regiment Infantry, mustered Sept. 20, 1862, for nine months ; discharged July 30, 1863, expiration of service.

GOODRICH, J. HENRY. Private Co. C, 35th Regiment Infantry, mustered Aug. 19, 1864, for three years ; appointed Corporal Dec. 1, 1864 ; discharged June 9, 1865, expiration of service.

GOODWIN, CLEMENT F. Private Co. H, 43d Regiment Infantry, mustered Sept. 20, 1862, for nine months ; discharged July 30, 1863, expiration of service.

GOODRIDGE, SIDNEY S. Private Co. K, 20th Regiment Infantry, mustered July 23, 1861, for three years ; discharged Sept. 13, 1862, for disability.

GORMAN, FELIX D. D. Private Co. E, 33d Regiment Infantry, mustered Dec. 20, 1864, for three years ; transferred Jan. 1, 1865, to 2d Infantry ; discharged July 14, 1865.

GOULD, AUGUSTUS L. 2d Lieutenant Co. H, 42d Regiment Infantry, mustered Sept. 24, 1862, for nine months ; Acting Assistant Quarter-master Engineer's department, Jan. 15, 1862 ; discharged Aug. 20, 1863, expiration of service. Commissioned Capt. 1st Regiment La. (colored,) Engineers, Sept. 10, 1863. Died August 25, 1872, at Everett.

GOULD, JESSE, JR. Private 4th Co. Unattached Infantry, mustered May 3, 1864, for ninety days ; discharged Aug. 6, 1864.

GOULDING, JOSEPH M. Private Co. C, 35th Regiment Infantry, mustered Aug. 19, 1862, for three years. Killed Sept. 17, 1862, at Antietam, Md.

GRADY, MICHAEL A. Unassigned recruit 3d Regiment Cavalry, mustered March 18, 1864, for three years.

GRAFF, HENRY. Unassigned recruit 2d Regiment Cavalry, mustered Dec. 24, 1864, for three years.

GRAHAM, JOHN. Private Co. C, 17th Regiment Infantry, mustered Feb. 10, 1862, for three years; appointed Corporal, Sept. 1862 ; discharged Feb. 11, 1865, expiration of service. Died at Chelsea, Jan. 17, 1866, disease contracted in the service.

GRANT, CHARLES H. Private 4th Co. Unattached Infantry, mustered May 3, 1864, for ninety days; discharged Aug. 6, 1864, expiration of service. Mustered Jan. 2, 1865, private Co. D, 1st Battalion Front. Cavalry, for one year on quota of Dedham ; discharged June 30, 1865, expiration of service.

GRANT, JAMES S. Sergeant Co. H, 50th Regiment Infantry, mustered Sept. 29, 1862, for nine months; discharged Feb. 25, 1863, for disability.

GRANT, JOSEPH H. Sergeant Co. H, 50th Regiment Infantry, mustered Sept. 29, 1862, for nine months; discharged Aug. 24, 1863, expiration of service.

GRANT, MELVILLE C. Private Co. C, 5th Regiment Infantry, mustered May 1, 1861, for three months; discharged July 31, 1861, expiration of service. Re-enlisted U. S. Corps Engineers private Co. C ; appointed Corporal, Dec. 1, 1862; Sergeant, June 5, 1863; discharged Oct. 24, 1864, expiration of service.

GRAY, JOHN. Private Co, K, 3d Regiment Heavy Artillery, mustered May 12, 1864, for three years. Deserted July 3, 1865.

GRAY, WILLIAM F. Private Co. G, 1st Regiment Infantry, mustered May 23, 1861, for three years; taken prisoner at Williamsburg, Va., May 5, 1862; exchanged, discharged May 22, 1862, order of War Department.

GREEN, HENRY. Private Co. H, 50th Regiment Infantry, mustered Sept. 29, 1862, for nine months; discharged Aug. 24, 1863, expiration of service.

GREEN, JOHN. Sergeant Co. G, 40th Regiment Infantry, mustered Sept. 5, 1862, for three years; discharged Dec. 13, 1862, for disability.

GREEN, MARTIN S. Private Co. E, 26th Regiment Infantry, mustered May 12, 1864, for three years. Deserted June 30, 1865.

GREENWOOD, JAMES W. Sergeant Co. K, 29th Regiment Infantry, mustered May 22, 1861, for three years; appointed 1st Sergeant, Sept. 1862; discharged Dec. 26, 1862, for disability.

GREGORY DANIEL V. 1st Sergeant Co. C, 2nd Regiment Cavalry, mustered April 16, 1864, for three years; discharged July 20, 1865, expiration of service.

GREISSENGER, ADOLPH. Unassigned recruit 2d Regiment Cavalry, mustered Aug. 6, 1864, for three years.

GRENENHARST, WILLIAM. Unassigned recruit 28th Regiment Infantry, mustered April 15, 1864, for three years.

GRIFFIN, ALFRED S. Private 11th Light Battery, mustered Jan. 2, 1862, for three years; discharged June 16, 1865, expiration of service.

GRIFFIN, JACOB E. Private Co. H, 50th Regiment Infantry, mustered Sept. 29, 1862, for nine months; discharged Aug. 24, 1863, expiration of service.

GRIFFIN, JOHN. Unassigned recruit 2d Regiment Infantry, mustered May 17, 1864, for three years.

GRIMES, MICHAEL. Private Co. E, 9th Regiment Infantry, mustered Aug. 22, 1862, for three years; discharged June 21, 1864, expiration of service.

GROFFAN, ALONZO. Private Co. I, 2d Regiment Heavy Artillery, mustered Dec. 11, 1863, for three years. Deserted July 10, 1865.

GROGAN, JAMES. Unassigned recruit 2d Regiment Cavalry, mustered May 17, 1864, for three years.

GROSS, CYRUS. Private Co. L, 3d Regiment Heavy Artillery, mustered May 30, 1864, for three years; discharged Sept. 18, 1865, expiration of service.

GROVER, SAMUEL H. Private 4th Co. Unattached Infantry, mustered May 3, 1864, for ninety days; discharged Aug. 6, 1864, expiration of service.

GROVER, THOMAS. Private Co. H, 50th Regiment Infantry, mustered Sept. 29, 1862, for nine months; discharged Aug. 24, 1863, expiration of service. Mustered private 4th Co. Unattached Infantry, May 3, 1864, for ninety days; discharged Aug. 6, 1864, expiration of service.

GURNEY, GEORGE B. Private 4th Co. Unattached Infantry, mustered May 3, 1864, for ninety days; discharged Aug. 6, 1864, expiration of service.

GUARED, THOMAS. Private 6th Light Battery, mustered Dec. 20, 1864, for three years; discharged Aug. 7, 1865, expiration of service.

GUELPA, JOHN B. Private Co. H, 50th Regiment Infantry, mustered Sept. 29, 1862, for nine months; discharged Aug. 24, 1863, expiration of service.

82

GUILLETTE, HYACINTHA. Private Co. H, 59th Regiment Infantry, mustered March 12, 1864, for three years ; transferred June 1, 1865, to 57th Regiment Infantry; discharged July 30, 1865, from 57th Regiment, expiration of service ; absent, wounded.

H

HACKET, JOHN H. Private Co. K, 5th Regiment Cavalry, mustered July 22, 1864, for three years. Deserted May 13, 1865.

HADLEY, ALBERT F. Private Co. K, 43d Regiment Infantry, mustered Oct. 28, 1862, for nine months ; discharged July 30, 1864, expiration of service.

HADLEY, DANIEL. Private Co. C, 24th Regiment Infantry, mustered Oct. 9, 1861, for three years ; deserted Dec. 8, 1861.

HADLEY, EDWARD F. Private Co. H, 1st Regiment Infantry, mustered May 23, 1861, for three years; discharged May 25, 1864, expiration of service. Mustered Private Co. E, 61st Regiment Infantry, on Cambridge quota: discharged June 4, 1865, expiration of service.

HADLOCK, CHARLES W. Wagoner Co. D, 3d Regiment Heavy Artillery, mustered Aug. 4, 1863, for three years ; discharged Sept. 18, 1865, expiration of service.

HAGAN, JAMES. Unassigned Recruit 19th Regiment Infantry, mustered March 21, 1864, for three years.

HAGGART, JAMES. Unassigned Recruit 24th Regiment Infantry, mustered July 29, 1862, for three years.

HAGLAN, CHARLES. Private Co. C, 2d Regiment Cavalry, mustered May 6, 1864, for three years; discharged July 20, 1865, expiration of service.

HALEY, JOHN P. Sergeant Co. E, 30th Regiment Infantry, mustered Dec. 31, 1861, for three years; appointed 1st Sergeant March 21, 1862; discharged for promotion Sept. 12, 1862, mustered 2d Lieutenant Sept. 12, 1862. Killed Sept. 19, 1864, at Berryville, Va.

HALL, SAMUEL R. Corporal Co. H, 50th Regiment Infantry, mustered Sept. 29, 1862, for nine months; discharged Aug. 24, 1863, expiration of service.

HALL, THEODORE. Private Co. L, 5th Regiment Cavalry, mustered July 22, 1864, for three years; deserted May 13, 1865.

HALL, WILLIAM H. General Service U. S. A., mustered March 17, 1864.

HALLETT, BARNABAS. Private Co. G, 4th Regiment Cavalry, mustered Jan. 27, 1864, for three years; discharged Nov. 14, 1865, expiration of service.

HALLGREEN, HENRY J. Captain Co. A, 43d Regiment Infantry, mustered Oct. 11, 1862, for nine months; discharged July 30, 1863, expiration of service.

HALLGREEN, ROBERT P. Private Co. H, 1st Regiment Infantry, mustered Sept. 12, 1861, for three years; wounded at Yorktown, Va., April 26, 1862; transferred to 1st Regiment, U. S. Cavalry, Dec. 10, 1862; appointed Corporal, 1863.

HALLGREEN, WILLIAM C. Private Co. H, 1st Regiment Infantry, mustered Sept. 12, 1861, for three years; discharged Sept. 22, 1862, for disability.

HAMILTON, CHARLES M. Sergeant Co. A, 22d Regiment Infantry, mustered Sept. 2, 1861, for three years; discharged for promotion, June 28, 1862, mustered same day, 2d Lieutenant; promoted 1st Lieutenant, Sept. 26, 1862'; dismissed Feb. 18, 1863. Served on quota of Boston, Private Co. K, 6th Regiment Infantry, for three months, mustered April 22, 1861; discharged Aug. 2, 1861, expiration of service.

HAMMOND, FRANK. Private Co. G, 40th Regiment Infantry, mustered Sept. 5, 1862, for three years; discharged June 16, 1865, expiration of service.

HAMMOND, JAMES R. Private Co. H, 50th Regiment Infantry, mustered Sept. 29, 1862, for nine months; discharged Aug. 24, 1863, expiration of service.

HANCOCK, THOMAS. Musician Co. B, 17th Regiment Infantry, mustered Feb. 15, 1864, for three years; discharged July 11, 1865, expiration of service.

HANCLEM, FELIX. Private Co. K, 2d Regiment Cavalry, mustered May 10, 1864, for three years; deserted June 14, 1864.

HANEY, THOMAS. Private Co. B, 43d Regiment Infantry, mustered Oct. 11, 1862, for nine months; deserted Oct. 11, 1862, at Readville, Mass.

HANEY, THOMAS. Private Co. H, 43rd Regiment Infantry, mustered Sept. 20, 1862, for nine months. Deserted Sept. 25, 1862, at Readville, Mass.

HANLAN, PETER. Ordinance Corps, U. S. A., mustered April 18, 1864.

HANLON, JOHN. Private Co. F, 11th Regiment Infantry, mustered June 13, 1861, for three years ; discharged June 24, 1864, expiration of service.

HANNIFORD, JAMES. Unassigned recruit 2d Regiment Infantry, mustered June 9, 1864, for three years ; discharged June 27, 1864, rejected recruit.

HANOVER, GEORGE B. Captain Co. H, 43d Regiment Infantry, mustered Sept. 20, 1862, for nine months ; discharged July 10, 1863, expiration of service.

HARDING, THOMAS. Sergeant Co. H, 1st Regiment Infantry, mustered May 23, 1861, for three years. Killed July 18, 1861, at Blackburn's Ford, Va.

HARLOW, DEXTER. Private Co. H. 43d Regiment Infantry, mustered Sept. 20, 1862, for nine months ; discharged July 30, 1863, expiration of service.

HARPER, WILLIAM. Private Co. H, 48th Regiment Infantry, mustered Sept. 22, 1862, for nine months. Deserted Oct. 16, 1862.

HARRINGTON, CHARLES H. Private Co. H, 2d Regiment Infantry, mustered July 30, 1864, for three years ; discharged July 2, 1865, expiration of service.

HARRINGTON, JOHN C. JR. Private 8th Light Battery, mustered May 30, 1862, for six months ; discharged Nov. 29, 1862, expiration of service.

HARRIS, THEODORE Unassigned recruit 2nd Regiment Infantry, mustered May 13, 1864, for three years.

HARRISON, JOHN L. Private Co. H, 43d Regiment Infantry, mustered Sept. 20, 1862, for nine months ; discharged July 30, 1863, expiration of service. Re-enlisted Private 4th Co. Unattached Infantry, mustered May 3, 1864, for ninety days; discharged Aug. 6, 1864, expiration of service. Re-enlisted Corporal Co. K, 4th Regiment Heavy Artillery, mustered Aug. 18, 1864, for one year; discharged June 17, 1865, expiration of service.

HART, JOHN. Private Co. D, 28th Regiment Infantry, mustered March, 18, 1864. Died at Andersonville, Ga., June 1, 1864.

HARTMAN, JOHN. Unassigned recruit 2d Regiment Cavalry, mustered May 15, 1864, for three years.

HARVEY, JOHN. Corporal Co. H, 1st Regiment Infantry, Mustered May 23, 1861, for three years ; appointed Sergeant, Oct. 1, 1861 ; discharged Sept. 17, 1863, for disability.

HARWOOD, OTIS F. Private Co. H, 43d Regiment Infantry, mustered Oct, 11, 1862, for nine months. Deserted Nov. 3, 1862, at Readville, Mass.

HASELTINE, HIRAM R. Private V. R. C., mustered Dec. 20, 1864; discharged Nov. 15, 1865, order of War Department.

HASKELL, CLARENCE G. Private Co. F, 2d Regiment Heavy Artillery, mustered Oct. 8, 1863, for three years ; died March 30, 1865, at Newbern, N. C. .

HASKELL, FRANK H. Private 4th Co. Unattached Infantry, mustered May 3, 1864, for ninety days ; discharged Aug. 6, 1864, expiration of service.

HASKELL, MARCUS M. Private Co. C, 35th Regiment Infantry, mustered Aug. 17, 1862, for three years; wounded
Sept. 17, 1862, at Antietam, Md.; wounded Dec, 13, 1862,
at Fredericksburg, Va.; wounded May 24, 1864 at North
Anna River Va.; wounded Aug. 19, 1864, near Weldon R.
R.; wounded Sept. 30, 1864, Poplar Grove Church, Va.;
appointed Sergeant, Dec. 1, 1864; wounded March 26,
1865, near Petersburg, Va.; discharged June 9, 1865,
expiration of service.

HASKELL, THEODORE F. Private Co. H, 1st Regiment
Infantry, mustered May 23, 1861, for three years; dis-
charged July 24, 1862, for disability. Died at Chelsea,
June 22, 1871, of consumption, contracted in the service.

HATCH, CHARLES H. Private Co. H, 50th Regiment Infantry, mustered Sept. 29, 1862, for nine months; discharged Aug. 24, 1863, expiration of service.

HATCH, ISAAC J. JR. Private Co. G, 40th Regiment In-
fantry, mustered Sept. 5, 1862, for three years; appointed
Corporal June 1, 1863; died Oct. 30, 1863, at Folly
Island, S. C., of chronic diarrhœa.

HATCH, WILLIAM W. Private Co. A, 3d Regiment Cavalry, mustered Nov. 28, 1863, for three years; wounded
Oct., 1864; transferred to Co. I, 10th Regiment V. R. C.;
discharged Oct. 5, 1865, expiration of service.

HATFIELD, JOHN. Private Co. A, 28th Regiment Infantry,
mustered April 16, 1864, for three years; absent, wounded since May 5, 1864.

HATHAWAY, WILLIAM R. Private Co. H, 20th Regiment
Infantry, mustered July 31, 1861, for three years; wound-
ed at Ball's Bluff, Va., Oct. 21, 1861 ; died at Poolesville,
Md., Nov. 27, 1861.

HAWES, AUGUSTUS W. Private Co. H, 50th Regiment Infantry, mustered Sept. 29, 1862, for nine months; discharged Aug. 24, 1863, expiration of service. Re-enlisted in 29th Regiment, Maine, Nov., 1863.

HAWKES, HARRISON. Private Co. H, 50th Regiment Infantry, mustered Sept. 29, 1862, for nine months; discharged Aug. 24, 1863, expiration of service

HAWKINS, PATRICK. Private Co. H, 48th Regiment Infantry, mustered Sept. 25, 1862, for nine months; deserted Nov. 20, 1862.

HAYES, RICHARD. Private Co. K, 3d Regiment Heavy Artillery, mustered May 12; 1864, for three years; discharged Sept. 18, 1865, expiration of service.

HAYES, CHARLES E. Private Co. G, 2nd Regiment Cavalry, mustered April 9, 1863, for three years. Deserted May 14, 1863.

HAYDEN, CHARLES. Private Co. C, 2d Regiment Infantry mustered May 17, 1864, for three years; discharged July 14, 1865, expiration of service.

HAYDEN, JOHN. Private Co. H, 43d Regiment Infantry, mustered Sept. 20, 1862, for nine months; discharged July 30, 1863, expiration of service.

HEAD, GUY C. Wagoner, Co. E, 24th Regiment Infantry, mustered Oct. 7, 1861, for three years; discharged Oct. 8, 1864, expiration of service.

HEALEY, JAMES. Private Co. H, 42d Regiment Infantry, mustered Sept. 24, 1862, for nine months; discharged Aug. 20, 1863, expiration of service.

HEARNE, DENNIS C. General service U. S. A., mustered March 28, 1864.

HEAVENER, CHURCHILL. Private 4th Co. Unattached Infantry, mustered May 3, 1864, for ninety days; discharged August 6th, 1864, expiration of service.

HEENAN, JOHN. Private Co. G, 40th Regiment Infantry, mustered Sept. 5, 1862, for three years; discharged June 1, 1865, expiration of service.

HEISTANCE, WILLIAM H. Hospital Steward U. S. A., mustered March 29, 1864.

HEMMENWAY, GEORGE S. H. Private Co. H, 43d Regiment Infantry, mustered Sept. 20, 1862, for nine months; discharged July 30, 1863, expiration of service.

HENNER, GEORGE W. Private Co. A, 30th Regiment Infantry, mustered May 22, 1862, for three years, at New Orleans, La.; discharged May 1, 1864, to re-enlist. Mustered on quota of Chelsea, Jan. 2, 1864, for three years; discharged May 22, 1865, expiration of service.

HENNESEY, CHARLES. Unassigned recruit 3d Regiment Cavalry, mustered March 29, 1864.

HENNESEY, JAMES F. Private Co. A, 9th Regiment Infantry, mustered June 11, 1861, for three years; discharged Aug. 18, 1861, disability from wound.

HENRY, PATRICK. Private Co. I, 2d Regiment Infantry, mustered June 10, 1864, for three years. Deserted June 24, 1865.

HENRY, WILLIAM S. Corporal Co. H, 50th Regiment Infantry, mustered Sept. 29, 1862, for nine months; discharged Aug. 24, 1863, expiration of service.

HERSEY, HARRISON D. Private Co. C, 12th Regiment
Infantry, mustered Feb. 18, 1863, for three years ; wounded at Gettysburg, Pa., July 2, 1863; transferred June 25,
1864, to 39th Regiment Infantry; discharged Aug. 2,
1865, expiration of service.

HEYWOOD, WILLIAM. Private Co. G, 19th Regiment Infantry, mustered March 29, 1864, for three years; discharged June 30, 1865, expiration of service.

HICKS, WILLIAM H. Private Co. C, 35th Regiment Infantry, mustered Aug. 19, 1862, for three years ; discharged
Nov. 26, 1862.

HIGGINS, ELISHA A. Private Co. E, 43d Regiment Infan-
try, mustered Oct. 1, 1862, for nine months ; discharged
June 2, 1863 ; re-enlisted 2d Regiment Heavy Artillery,
June 2, 1863, unassigned recruit.

HIGGINS, JOHN. Private Co. H, 42d Regiment Infantry,
mustered Sept. 24, 1862, for nine months. Deserted Nov.
1, 1862, at Readville, Mass.

HIGGINS, JOHN. Private V. R. C., mustered May 28, 1864.

HIGHT, HENRY W. Private Co. H, 50th Regiment Infantry, mustered Sept. 29, 1862, for nine months ; discharged
March 13, 1863, disability.

HILBOURN, ALPHEUS J. Captain 4th Co. Unattached Infantry, mustered May 3, 1864, for ninety days ; discharged
Aug. 6, 1864, expiration of service.

HILL, FRANK A. Private Co. I, 35th Regiment Infantry,
mustered May 10, 1864, for three years. Died Aug. 5,
1864, at Portland, Me.

HILL, GEORGE A. Unassigned recruit 3d Regiment Infantry, mustered Jan. 13, 1864, for three years; discharged May 13, 1864, rejected recruit.

HILL, JOHN. Private Co. A, 19th Regiment Infantry, mustered March 15, 1864, for three years; wounded May 12, 1864.

HILL, JOHN. Unassigned recruit 2d Regiment Infantry, mustered June 13, 1864, for three years.

HILTON, HIRAM F. Wagoner, Co. A, 43d Regiment Infantry, mustered Oct. 11, 1862, for nine months; discharged July 30, 1863. expiration of service.

HINCKLEY, CHARLES E. Private Co. H, 50th Regiment Infantry, mustered Sept. 29, 1862, for nine months; discharged Aug. 24, 1863, expiration of service. Mustered on quota of Boston, Sergeant Co. C, 56th Regiment Infantry, Dec. 28, 1863. Killed April 2, 1865, near Petersburg, Va.

HINCKLEY, DAVID F. Private 4th Co. Unattached Infantry, mustered May 3, 1864, for ninety days; discharged Aug. 6, 1864, expiration of service.

HINCKLEY, JAMES C. Private 11th Light Battery, mustered Dec. 20, 1864, for three years; discharged June 16, 1865, expiration of service.

HINDS, WILLIAM A. Corporal Co. H, 42d Regiment Infantry, mustered Sept. 24, 1862, for nine months; discharged Aug. 20, 1863, expiration of service.

HOBBS, CYRUS. Captain Co. H, 50th Regiment Infantry, mustered Sept. 29, 1862, for nine months; discharged Aug. 24, 1863, expiration of service.

HODGES, JOHN W.   Private Co. C, 35th Regiment Infantry, mustered Aug. 19, 1862, for three years.   Killed Dec. 13, 1862, at Fredericksburg, Va.

HODGKINS, FRANCIS P.   Private Co. H, 50th Regiment Infantry, mustered Sept. 29, 1862, for nine months.   Deserted Dec. 10, 1862, at New York.

HODGKINS, WILLIAM H.   Private Co. G, 40th Regiment Infantry, mustered Sept. 5, 1862, for three years; wounded at Olustee, Fla., Feb. 20, 1864; wounded at Cold Harbor, Va., June 3, 1864; discharged June 16, 1865, expiration of service.

HOFFMAN, FREDERICK.   Private 13th Light Battery, mustered Dec. 20, 1863, for three years.   Deserted Jan. 9, 1863.

HOFFMAN, JOHN HENRY.   Private Co. C, 1st Regiment Infantry, mustered Aug. 13, 1862, for three years; discharged May 25, 1864, expiration of service.

HOGAN, THOMAS M.   Private Co. E, 24th Regiment Infantry, mustered March 18, 1864, for three years; discharged Jan. 20, 1866, expiration of service.

HOLBROOK, JOHN W.   Private Co. H, 50th Regiment Infantry, mustered Sept. 29, 1862, for nine months; discharged Aug. 24, 1863, expiration of service.

HOLDEN, HORACE G.   Private Co. H, 50th Regiment Infantry, mustered Sept. 29, 1862, for nine months; discharged Aug. 24, 1863, expiration of service.

HOLDEN, LEVERETT D.   Private Co. H, 1st Regiment Infantry, mustered Sept. 10, 1861, for three years; discharged May 25, 1864, expiration of service.

HOLDER, JAMES. Unassigned recruit 20th Regiment Infantry, mustered April 4, 1864, for three years.

HOLLAND ADELBERT. Private Co. H, 50th Regiment Infantry, mustered Oct. 13, 1862, for nine months ; discharged Aug. 24, 1863, expiration of service.

HOLLAND, CHARLES. Private Co. A, 2d Regiment Infantry, mustered July 20, 1864, for three years ; discharged July 14, 1865, expiration of service.

HOLMAN, LIBERTY. Private Co. G, 4th Regiment Cavalry, mustered Jan. 27, 1864, for three years ; discharged May 8, 1865, disability.

HOLMES, GEORGE W. Private Co. F, 5th Regiment Cavalry, mustered June 11, 1864, for three years ; discharged Oct. 31, 1865, expiration of service.

HOLMES, HENRY T. 1st. Lieutenant Co. H, 50th Regiment Infantry, mustered Sept. 29, 1862, for nine months ; discharged Aug. 24, 1863, expiration of service.

HOLMES, JOHN W. Private Co. H, 50th Regiment Infantry, mustered, Sept. 29, 1862, for nine months ; discharged Aug. 24, 1863, expiration of service. Mustered Corporal Co. D, 1st Battalion Heavy Artillery, Sept. 30, 1863, for three years ; discharged Sept. 12, 1865, expiration of service.

HOLMES, SIDNEY. Private Co. C, 35th Regiment Infantry, mustered Aug. 19, 1862, for three years. Died Dec. 7, 1863, Portsmouth Grove Hospital, R. I.

HOLMES, THOMAS G. Unassigned recurit 28th Regiment Infantry, mustered March 28, 1864, for three years.

HOLT, CHARLES. Unassigned recruit 26th Regiment Infantry, mustered May 24, 1864, for three years.

HOLT, JAMES E. Private 4th Co. Unattached Infantry, mustered May 3, 1864, for ninety days ; discharged Aug. 6, 1864, expiration of service.

HOPKINS, LAWRENCE W, Private V. R. C., mustered June 20, 1864 ; discharged Dec. 27, 1865, order of War Department.

HORTON, HENRY D. Private 4th Co. Unattached Infantry, mustered May 3, 1864, for ninety days ; discharged Aug. 6th, 1864, expiration of service.

HOWARD, CHARLES A. Private Co. G, 40th Regiment Infantry, mustered Sept. 5, 1862, for three years ; discharged June 16, 1865, expiration of service.

HOWARD, NOAH P. Private Co. C, 35th Regiment Infantry, mustered Aug. 19, 1862, for three years ; transferred to V. R. C., July 25, 1864, discharged July 29, 1865.

HOWARD, THOMAS F. Corporal Co. K, 4th Regiment Cavalry, mustered March 1, 1864, for three years ; appointed Sergeant, Sept. 25, 1864 ; discharged Nov. 14, 1865, expiration of service.

HOWE, CHARLES H. Private Co. I, 58th Regiment Infantry, mustered May 13, 1864, for three years ; discharged July 14, 1865, expiration of service.

HOWE, FRANK T. Private Co. G, 40th Regiment Infantry, mustered Sept. 5, 1862, for three years ; discharged March 31, 1864, order of War Department ; enlisted U. S. A. same day ; discharged Aug. 22, 1864, order of War Department.

HOWE. ALONZO C. Private Co. K, 58th Regiment Infantry, mustered Dec. 21, 1864, for three years ; discharged July 14, 1865, expiration of service.

HOWLETT, JAMES. Private Co. A, 2d Regiment Cavalry, mustered March 19, 1864, for three years; discharged May 27, 1865, disability.

HOYT, CHARLES H. Private Co. H, 43d Regiment Infantry, mustered Oct. 13, 1862, for nine months; deserted Oct. 13, 1862, Readville, Mass.

HUBBARD, CHARLES H. Private Co. G, 40th Regiment Infantry, mustered Sept. 5, 1863, for three years. Killed June 3, 1864, at Cold Harbor, Va.

HULLS, JAMES. Private Co. I, 55th Regiment Infantry, mustered Aug. 16, 1864, for three years; discharged Aug. 29, 1865, expiration of service.

HUMPHREY, CHARLES L. Musician Co. H, 43d Regiment Infantry, mustered Sept. 20, 1862, for nine months; discharged July 30, 1863, expiration of service.

HUMPHREY, EDWARD W. Private Co. K, 4th Regiment Cavalry, mustered March 1, 1864, for three years; discharged Nov. 14, 1865, expiration of service.

HUMPHREY, WILLIAM H. Private Co. B, 12th Regiment Infantry, mustered June 26, 1861; appointed Corporal Nov. 26, 1862; wounded at Fredericksburg, Va., Dec. 13, 1862; appointed Sergeant Jan. 1, 1864; discharged July 8, 1864, expiration of service.

HUNNEMAN, JOHN. Private Co. C, 1st Regiment Infantry, mustered May 27, 1861, for three years; discharged Dec. 1, 1862, for disability.

HUNNEWELL, RICHARD. Private Co. H, 50th Regiment Infantry, mustered Sept. 29, 1862, for nine months; discharged Aug. 24, 1863, expiration of service.

HUNT, JOHN R. Private Co. D, 1st Regiment Cavalry, mustered Feb. 20, 1864, for three years; discharged June 29, 1865, expiration of service.

HUNTER, ALVAH F. Signal Corps U.S.A., mustered April 10, 1864.

HURD, FRANK. Private 4th Co. Unattached Infantry, mustered May 3, 1864, for ninety days; discharged Aug. 6, 1864, expiration of service.

HURLEY, DANIEL F. Private Co. G, 40th Regiment Infantry, mustered Sept. 5, 1862, for three years; transferred Aug. 6, 1864, to 13th Regiment V. R. C.; discharged Oct. 26, 1864, for disability.

HURLEY, JOHN W. Sergeant Co. H, 50th Regiment Infantry, mustered Sept. 29, 1862, for nine months; discharged Aug. 24, 1863, expiration of service. Died in Chelsea, Nov. 11, 1863.

HURST, WILLIAM. Private Co. K, 43d Regiment Infantry, mustered Sept. 16, 1862, for nine months; discharged July 30, 1863, expiration of service.

HUSE, NELSON S. Private Co. H, 1st Regiment Infantry, mustered May 23, 1861, for three years; wounded at Blackburn's Ford, Va., July 18, 1861; discharged at Budd's Ferry, Md., March 30, 1862, disability from wound.

HUTCHINS, ISAIAH M. Private Co. G, 40th Regiment Infantry, mustered Sept. 5, 1862, for three years; discharged June 16, 1865, expiration of service.

HUTCHINS, LEVI. Corporal Co. G, 40th Regiment Infantry, mustered Sept. 5, 1862, for three years; appointed Sergeant Dec. 10, 1863; commissioned 1st Lieutenant April 21, 1864; wounded June 1, 1864, at Cold Harbor, Va.; discharged Jan. 1, 1865, disability from wound.

HUTCHINS, SAMUEL, Jr. Private 4th Co. Unattached Infantry, mustered May 3, 1864, for ninety days; discharged Aug. 6, 1864, expiration of service.

HUTCHINSON, ALLEN. Corporal Co. C, 35th Regiment Infantry, mustered Aug. 19, 1862, for three years. Deserted Oct. 6, 1862.

HYDE, WILLIAM H. Private Co. K, 43d Regiment Infantry, mustered Oct. 7, 1862, for nine months; discharged July 20, 1863, expiration of service.

I

ILSLEY, DANIEL P. Sergeant Co. H, 43d Regiment Infantry, mustered Sept. 20, 1862, for nine months; discharged July 30, 1863, expiration of service.

ILSLEY, HOSEA Jr. Private Co. C, 35th Regiment Infantry, mustered Aug. 19, 1862, for three years; appointed Corporal May 21, 1864; discharged June 9, 1865, expiration of service. Died Dec. 23, 1873.

ILSLEY, JONATHAN C. Private Co. H, 1st Regiment Infantry, mustered May 23, 1861, for three years; discharged July 22, 1861, for disability; enlisted in Navy, Nov. 12, 1861; discharged Nov. 29, 1864.

ILSLEY, PHILIP G. Corporal 4th Co. Unattached Infantry, mustered May 3, 1864, for ninety days; discharged Aug. 6, 1864, expiration of service.

IRISH, CORNELIUS. Private Co. L, 3d Regiment Cavalry, mustered Nov. 28, 1861, for three years; appointed Corporal Jan. 1, 1862; appointed Sergeant Dec. 1, 1862; appointed Quarter Master Sergeant May 1, 1863; discharged April 15, 1864, for promotion; commissioned 2d Lieutenant 1st La. Cavalry, April 15, 1864.

IRWIN, GEORGE. Unassigned recruit 28th Regiment Infantry, mustered March 26, 1864, for three years; transferred April 23, 1864, to Navy.

J

JACKSON, CHARLES A. Private Co. H, 1st Regiment Infantry, mustered May 23, 1861, for three years; discharged Aug. 23, 1862, for promotion; mustered Aug. 23, 1862, 2d Lieutenant 39th Regiment Infantry; promoted 1st Lieutenant Co. F, 40th Regiment Infantry, Aug. 27, 1862; transferred Sept. 1, 1862, to 41st Regiment (3d Cavalry); Sept. 2, 1862, promoted Captain Co. E, 40th Regiment Infantry; resigned and discharged June 8, 1863.

JACOBS, WILLIAM. Unassigned recruit 2d Regiment Cavalry, mustered April 18, 1864, for three years.

JAMES, WILLIAM A. Private Co. L, 1st Regiment Cavalry, mustered Jan. 6, 1864, for three years; appointed Corporal, July 1, 1864; died Oct. 22, 1864, at Washington, D.C.

JAMES, WILLIAM H. Private 4th Co. Unattached Infantry, mustered May 3, 1864, for ninety days; discharged Aug. 6, 1864, expiration of service.

JAMES, JOHN M. Private Co. H, 1st Regiment Infantry, mustered Sept. 10, 1861, for three years; discharged Feb. 18, 1863, for disability. Died at Chelsea, Feb. 11, 1865.

JELLISON, GREENLEAF S. Private Co. C, 35th Regiment Infantry, mustered Aug. 19, 1862, for three years; discharged Jan. 10, 1863, disability.

JELLSON, WILLIAM. Artillery U. S. A., mustered March 15, 1864.

JENKINS, GEORGE. Private Co. K, 3d Regiment Heavy Artillery, mustered May 12, 1864, for three years. Deserted Oct. 1, 1864.

JENKINS, HORATIO, JR. Private Co. I, 5th Regiment Infantry, mustered May 1, 1861, for three months; discharged July 31, 1861, expiration of service. Commissioned 1st Lieut. Co. G, 40th Regiment Infantry, Aug. 12, 1862; promoted Capt. Co. H, 40th Regiment Infantry; commissioned Major April 20, 1864, taken prisoner at Drury's Bluff, Va., May 16, 1864, escaped from rebel prison December, 1864; promoted Lieut. Colonel June 2, 1864; discharged Feb. 18, 1865; commissioned Lieut. Colonel 4th Regiment Cavalry, Feb. 4, 1865; commissioned Colonel April 23, 1865, wounded and taken prisoner at High Bridge, Va., April, 1865; discharged Nov. 14, 1865, expiration of service, Brevet Brig. Gen'l.

JENNINGS, PHILIP M. Private Co. H, 50th Regiment Infantry, mustered Sept. 29, 1862, for nine months, discharged Aug. 24, 1863, expiration of service.

JENNINGS, STEPHEN E. Private Co. H, 1st Regiment Infantry, mustered May 23, 1861, for three years, discharged May 25, 1864, expiration of service; mustered Aug. 31, 1864, for three years, private 2d Light Battery on quota of Chicopee, discharged June 11, 1865, expiration of ser-' vice.

JEWETT, DEXTER. Private 4th Co. Unattached Infantry, mustered May 3, 1864, for ninety days, discharged Aug. 6, 1864, expiration of service; re-enlisted private Co. G, 13th Regiment, Maine, September 29, 1864, transfered to 30th Maine, 1864.

JEWETT, GEORGE O. Corp. Co. H, 1st Regiment Infantry, mustered May 23, 1861, for three years, discharged July 22, 1861, for disability; mustered private Co. D, 17th Regiment Infantry, Mar. 25, 1862, for three years on quota of Boston; transferred to 13th Regiment V. R. C. February 1, 1864, appointed 1st Sergeant Sept. 1864, discharged May 1, 1865, expiration of service.

JEWETT, WILLIAM M. Private Co. H, 1st Regiment Infantry, mustered May 23, 1861, for three years; discharged July 22, 1861, for disability; mustered 1st Sergeant Co. H, 42d Regiment Infantry, Sept. 24, 1862, for nine months; discharged Aug. 20, 1863, expiration of service.

JOHNSON, CHARLES. Private Co. D, 24th Regiment Infantry, mustered Dec. 20, 1864, for three years. Deserted Aug. 17, 1865.

JOHNSON, FREDERICK. Private 12th Light Battery, mustered Nov. 28, 1862, for three years; discharged July 25, 1865, expiration of service.

JOHNSON, GEORGE H. Private Co. G, 40th Regiment Infantry, mustered Sept. 5, 1862, for three years; discharged June 10, 1865, expiration of service.

JOHNSON, GUSTAVUS. Unassigned recruit 20th Regiment Infantry, mustered April 12, 1864, for three years.

JOHNSON, HENRY. Private Co. H, 1st Regiment Infantry, mustered May 23, 1861, for three years; discharged Jan. 8, 1863, for disability.

JOHNSON, JAMES. Private Co. F, 2d Regiment Infantry, mustered May 11, 1864, for three years. Deserted from Hospital at Nashville, Tenn.

JOHNSON, JOHN. Unassigned recruit 2d Regiment Infantry, mustered May 24, 1864, for three years.

JOHNSON, JOSEPH. Private Co. H, 48th Regiment Infantry, mustered Sept. 25, 1862, for nine months. Deserted Oct. 1, 1862.

JOHNSON, ROBERT. Private 13th Light Battery, mustered Nov. 26, 1862, for three years. Deserted Jan. 16, 1863.

JOHNSON, THOMAS. Private 8th Light Battery, mustered June 9, 1862, for six months. Deserted June 9, 1862.

JOHNSON, THOMAS. Private Co. L, 4th Regiment Cavalry, mustered July 8, 1864, for three years; discharged Nov. 14, 1865, expiration of service.

JOHNSON, THOMAS J. Private V. R. C., mustered May 28, 1864.

JONES, CHARLES. Private 6th Light Battery, Dec. 1, 1864, for three years, discharged Aug. 7, 1865, expiration of service.

JONES, CHARLES. Unassigned recruit 2d Regiment Infantry, mustered June 13, 1864, for three years.

JONES, DAVID. Unassigned recruit 2d Regiment Infantry, mustered July 7, 1864, for three years.

JONES, EDWARD L. Corp. Co. H, 1st Regiment Infantry, mustered May 23, 1861, for three years ; discharged, Sept. 6, 1862, for disability; mustered Sergeant Co. H, 42d Regiment Infantry, October 1, 1862, for nine months, discharged May 23, 1863, for promotion ; commissioned Captain Co.· E, 1st Regiment, La., April 10, 1863, Engineers ; transferred Sept. 1863, to U. S. C. Vol. Engineer Corps.

JONES, GEORGE. Private Co. G, 28th Regiment Infantry, mustered April 15, 1864, for three years. Deserted May 2, 1864.

JONES, HENRY. Private Co. H, 50th Regiment Infantry, mustered Sept. 29, 1862, for nine months; discharged Aug. 24, 1863, expiration of service. Private 10th Light Battery, mustered Jan. 5, 1864, for three years ; discharged June 9, 1865, expiration of service.

JONES, JOHN. Private Co. K, 3d Regiment Heavy Artillery, mustered, May 12, 1864, for three years ; deserted July 5, 1864.

JONES, JOHN F. Private Co. H, 43d Regiment Infantry, mustered Sept. 20, 1862, for nine months ; discharged July 30, 1863, expiration of service.

JONES, JOHN F. Private Co. H, 56th Regiment Infantry, mustered Jan. 27, 1864, for three years. Died Nov. 28, 1864, at Waitfield, Vt.

JONES, JOHN P. Private Co. H, 1st Regiment Infantry, mustered May 23, 1861, for three years, appointed Corporal Jan. 1, 1864; wounded at Wilderness, May 4, 1864. Died at Chelsea, April 27, 1870.

JONES, PAUL. Private 6th Light Battery, mustered Dec. 24, 1864, for three years. Deserted Jan. 25, 1865, at New Orleans, La.

JONES, THOMAS. Private Co. H, 50th Regiment Infantry, mustered Sept. 29, 1862, for nine months; discharged Aug. 24, 1863, expiration of service.

JONES, THOMAS. Private Co. I, 2d Regiment Infantry, mustered June 9, 1864, for three years. Deserted July 15, 1864.

JONES, WILLIAM W. Private Co. A, 40th Regiment Infantry, mustered Aug. 23, 1862, for three years; discharged Sept. 21, 1863, for disability.

JORDAN, GEORGE E. N. Private V. R. C., mustered June 15, 1864.

JOYCE, GEORGE W. Unassigned recruit 2d Regiment Infantry, mustered May 11, 1864, for three years. Discharged, May 12, 1864, rejected recruit.

JUDKINS, HIRAM. Private Co. H, 43d Regiment Infantry, mustered Sept. 20, 1862, for nine months; discharged March 8, 1863, for disability.

JUDSON, WALTER H. 2d Lieutenant Co. C, 13th Regiment Infantry, mustered July 16, 1861, for three years; taken prisoner, paroled, dismissed Nov. 22, 1862. Died March 1863.

KANE, THOMAS. Unassigned recruit 2d Regiment Heavy Artillery, mustered July 16, 1864, for three years.

KEARVIN, JOHN. Private Co. F, 29th Regiment Infantry, mustered Dec. 6, 1861, for three years. Deserted Aug. 28, 1862, at Alexandria, Va.

KEEFE, JOHN. Private 6th Light Battery, mustered Dec, 22, 1864, for three years; discharged Aug. 7, 1865, expiration of service.

KEEGAN, FRANK. Private Co. G, 2d Regiment Infantry, mustered July 22, 1864, for three years. Died June 5, 1865, at Savannah, Ga.

KEEGAN, MICHAEL. Unassigned recruit 2d Regiment Infantry, mustered July 22, 1864, for three years.

KELLEY, JAMES. Unassigned recruit 28th Regiment Infantry, mustered April 15, 1864, for three years.

KELLEY, JAMES. Private Co. H, 2d Regiment Heavy Artillery, mustered Aug. 10, 1864, for three years; discharged, June 26, 1865, expiration of service.

KELLY, GEORGE W. Private V. R. C., mustered May 28, 1864.

KELLY, JOHN. Private Co. K, 2d Regiment Cavalry, mustered May 7, 1864, for three years. Deserted June 25, 1864.

KELLY, LAWRENCE H. Private Co. H, 1st Regiment Infantry, mustered Aug. 12, 1861, for three years; taken prisoner near Manassas, Va., Aug. 29, 1862 ; paroled, exchanged Nov. 1, 1862. Killed July 2, 1863, at Gettysburg, Pa.

KELLY, PATRICK. Private Co. A, 2d Regiment Cavalry, mustered Aug. 20, 1864, for three years ; discharged July 26, 1865, expiration of service.

KENDALL, LEROY. Private 4th Co. Unattached Infantry, mustered May 3d, 1864, for ninety days ; discharged Aug. 6, 1864, expiration of service.

KENDRICK, GEORGE C. Unassigned recruit 20th Regiment Infantry, mustered April 12, 1864, for three years.

KENDRICK, NATHAN P. Private Co. D, 20th Regiment Infantry, mustered April 12, 1864, for three years ; discharged July 16, 1865, expiration of service.

KENNEFICK, JOHN. Private Co. H, 50th Regiment Infantry, mustered Sept. 29, 1862, for nine months. Deserted Nov. 18, 1862, at Boxford, Mass.

KENNEY, CHARLES. Private Co. H, 42d Regiment Infantry, mustered Sept. 24, 1862, for nine months. Deserted Oct. 18, 1862, at Readville, Mass.

KENNISON, FREDERICK L. Private 9th Light Battery, mustered Aug. 10, 1862, for three years ; discharged June 6, 1865, expiration of service.

KEON, MICHAEL. Unassigned recruit 2d Regiment Cavalry, mustered Aug. 18, 1864, for three years.

KEOUGH, HENRY J. Private Co. K, 43d Regiment Infantry, mustered Sept. 16, 1862, for nine months ; discharged July 30, 1863, expiration of service.

KERRIGAN, PATRICK. Private Co. C, 45th Regiment Infantry, mustered Sept. 26, 1862, for nine months. Deserted Oct. 1, 1862, at Readville, Mass.

KERSE, PATRICK. Private Co. C, 2d Regiment Heavy Artillery, mustered Aug. 4, 1863, for three years; discharged Aug. 10, 1863, by civil authority.

KILBRIDE, BERNARD. Private Co. D, 2d Regiment Heavy Artillery, mustered Aug. 18, 1864, for three years; discharged June 26, 1865, expiration of service.

KILLAM, MARK. Private V. R. C., mustered June 22, 1864.

KIMBALL, GEORGE. Private Co. C, 2d Regiment Cavalry, mustered May 13, 1864, for three years; discharged July 20, 1865, expiration of service.

KIMBALL, JAMES H. Private Co. H, 43d Regiment Infantry, mustered Sept. 20, 1862, for nine months; discharged July 30, 1863, expiration of service. Mustered Jan. 4, 1864, for three years, private Co. E, 3d Regiment Cavalry. Died Sept. 30, 1864, at New Orleans, La.

KING, GEORGE. Unassigned recruit 2d Regiment Cavalry, mustered Dec. 3, 1864, for three years.

KING, JAMES P. Corporal Co. C, 2d Regiment Cavalry, mustered March 17, 1864, for three years; discharged July 20, 1865, expiration of service.

KING, MICHAEL. Private Co. M, 4th Regiment Cavalry, mustered Dec. 21, 1864, for three years; discharged Nov. 14, 1865, expiration of service.

KING, THOMAS JR. Corporal Co. H, 43d Regiment Infantry, mustered Sept. 20, 1863, for nine months; discharged July 30, 1863, expiration of service.

KINNEVAN, PATRICK. General service U. S. A., mustered March 1, 1864.

KIRBY, JOHN. Private Co. C, 35th Regiment Infantry, mustered June 14, 1864, for three years; never joined Regiment.

KNAPP, ARTHUR M. Private Co. F, 44th Regiment Infantry, mustered Sept. 12, 1862, for nine months; discharged June 18, 1863, expiration of service.

KNAPP, TIMOTHY T. Private Go. F, 44th Regiment Infantry, mustered Sept. 12, 1862, for nine months; discharged June 18, 1863, expiration of service.

KNELL, GEORGE H. Private Co. I, 16th Regiment Infantry, mustered July 12, 1861, for three years. Deserted Dec. 20, 1862.

KNIGHT, NOAH M. Private Co. I, 4th Regiment Cavalry, mustered Jan. 1, 1864, for three years. Deserted Aug. 10, 1865.

KNOWLES, BENJAMIN F. Private Co. G, 40th Regiment Infantry, mustered Sept. 5, 1862, for three years; discharged June 16, 1865, expiration of service.

KNOWLES, HENRY F. Private Co. H, 43d Regiment Infantry, mustered Sept. 20, 1862, for nine months; discharged July 30, 1863, expiration of service.

KNOX, CHARLES V. Private Co. H, 19th Regiment Infantry, mustered Aug. 28, 1861, for three years; wounded and taken prisoner near Richmond, Va., June 26, 1862; paroled, discharged, Feb. 28, 1863, for disability; (transferred to Co. I.)

KNANDHIN, JOHN. Private V. R. C., mustered May 28, 1864.

KUCHLAND, CARL. Unassigned recruit 2d Regiment Infantry, mustered May 13, 1864.

KURTZ, ISRAEL H. Hospital Steward U. S. A., mustered March 29, 1864.

LAKE, CHARLES H. General service U. S. A., mustered March 17, 1864.

LALLEY, MICHAEL. Unassigned recruit 2d Regiment Cavalry, mustered May 6, 1864, for three years.

LAMONT, JOHN C. Private Co. K, 1st Regiment Cavalry, mustered Jan. 29, 1862, for three years ; transferred to Co. K, 4th Regiment Cavalry. Killed March 1, 1864, at McGurth's Creek, Fla.

LAMON, JAMES. Private C. H, 48th Regiment Infantry, mustered Sept. 25, 1862, for nine months. Deserted Oct. 27, 1862.

LAMOS, HORACE A. Private Co. H, 1st Regiment Infantry, mustered May 23, 1861, for three years ; wounded April 26, 1862, at Yorktown, Va. ; discharged Sept. 25, 1862, disability from wound.

LAND, NICHOLAS L. Private 4th Co. Unattached Infantry, mustered May 3, 1864, for ninety days ; discharged Aug. 6, 1864, expiration of service.

LANDRACHS, GEORGE. Private Co. C, 28th Regiment Infantry, mustered April 16, 1864, for three years. Died Dec. 17, 1864, at Washington, D. C.

LANE, ARTHUR F. Private 4th Co. Unattached Infantry, mustered May 3, 1864, for ninety days : discharged Aug. 6, 1864, expiration of service.

LANE, CHARLES L. Private Co. A, 2d Regiment Cavalry, mustered May 10, 1864, for three years. Deserted June 9, 1864.

LANE, DANIEL. Private Co. B, 23d Regiment Infantry, mustered Oct. 21, 1861, for three years; discharged Dec. 2, 1863, to re-enlist. Mustered Dec. 3, 1863, same Regiment and Company for three years; discharged June 25, 1865, expiration of service.

LANE, FREDERICK T. Private Co. C, 1st Battalion Heavy Artillery, mustered April 22, 1863, for three years, dis- Oct. 20, 1865, expiration of service.

LANE, JOHN A. Private Co. C, 35th Regiment Infantry, mustered Aug. 19, 1862, for three years. Killed Sept. 17, 1862, at Antietam, Md.

LANE, THOMAS J. Signal Corps U. S. A., mustered March 18, 1864.

LANE, WILLIAM H. Private Co. H, 1st Regiment Infantry, mustered May 23, 1861, for three years; wounded July 18, 1861, at Blackburn's Ford, Va.; wounded April 26, 1862, at Yorktown, Va.; discharged Oct. 20, 1862, disability from wounds; mustered on quota of Rockport, Corporal Co. A, 3d Heavy Artillery, Jan. 10, 1863, for three years; discharged September 18, 1865, expiration of service.

LANGLEY, ASAPH. Private Co. I, 32d Regiment Infantry, mustered Aug. 12, 1862, for three years; transferred Sept. 15, 1863, to 6th Regiment 2d Battalion V.R.C.; discharged April 14, 1865, disability.

LANMAN, J. F. General Service U. S. A., mustered March 17, 1864.

LARKINS, JOHN. Private Co. H, 2nd Regiment Infantry, mustered June 10, 1864, for three years. Deserted Nov. 13, 1864.

LARKINS, JOHN W. Private Co. D, 33d Regiment Infantry, mustered June 10, 1864, for three years. Deserted Aug. 16, 1864.

LARVIN, WILLIAM. Unassigned recruit 28th Regiment Infantry, mustered January 15, 1864, for three years, discharged Jan. 17, 1864, rejected recruit.

LASLIE, CHARLES. Private Co. K, 29th Regiment Infantry, mustered May 22, 1861, for three years ; wounded May 6, 1864, at Wilderness, Va.; discharged Aug. 19, 1864, disability from wound.

LATURE, JOSEPH. Private Co. I, 1st Regiment Cavalry, mustered Jan. 14, 1864, for three years. Deserted Mar. 26, 1864.

LAWLER, MICHAEL. Private Co. G, 22d Regiment Infantry, mustered Sept. 12, 1861, for three years ; discharged Oct. 23, 1863, for disability.

LAWRENCE, ALBERT B. Private Co. K, 4th Regiment Cavalry, mustered March 1, 1864, for three years; discharged Nov. 14, 1865, expiration of service.

LAWRENCE, WALTER. Private Co. A, 15th Regiment Infantry, mustered March 28, 1864, for three years ; transferred July 27, 1864, to Co. G, 20th Regiment Infantry ; transferred to V. R. C. ; discharged July 27, 1865.

LAWSON, EDWARD. Private Co. G, 4th Regiment Infantry, mustered Jan. 27, 1864, for three years ; discharged April 11, 1865, expiration of service.

LAWTON, GEORGE B. Private 4th Co. Unattached Infantry, mustered May 3, 1864, for ninety days ; discharged Aug. 6, 1864, expiration of service.

LAWTON, WILLIAM H.   Private Co. G, 40th Regiment Infantry, mustered Sept. 5, 1862, for three years; transferred Sept. 1, 1864, to V. R. C.; discharged Sept. 5, 1864.

LEARNED, GEORGE G.   Private Co. H, 1st Regiment Infantry, mustered May 23, 1861, for three years, wounded July 18, 1861, at Blackburn's Ford, Va., discharged Jan. 17, 1862, disability from wound.

LEARNED, SAMUEL F. H.   Private Co. H, 1st Regiment Infantry, mustered May 23, 1861, for three years, discharged March 27, 1863, for promotion; commissioned 2d Lieut. March 27, 1863, 9th Regiment Ullman's Brigade, Corps D'Afrique.

LEARY, MARTIN.   Unassigned recruit 2d Regiment Cavalry, mustered Nov. 30, 1864, for three years.

LEAVIS, GEORGE.   Private Co. F, 28th Regiment Infantry, mustered March 28, 1864, for three years, wounded May 12, 1864, at Wilderness, died from wound June 3, 1864.

LEAVITT, JOHN W.   Private 4th Company Unattached Infantry, mustered May 3, 1864, for ninety days, discharged Aug. 6, 1864, expiration of service.

LeBAR, NELSON.   Private V. R. C., mustered June 16, 1864.

LeBLANC, REMI.   Private Co. H, 43d Regiment Infantry, mustered Sept. 20, 1862, for nine months, discharged July 30, 1863, expiration of service.   Entered Navy 1864.

LEE, CHARLES H.   Unassigned recruit 26th Regiment Infantry, mustered July 7, 1864.

LEE, JOHN.   Private Co. G, 28th Regiment Infantry, mustered March 16, 1864, for three years.   Died Oct. 16, 1864, at Philadelphia, Pa.

LEE, JOHN. Unassigned recruit 2d Regiment Infantry, mustered July 22, 1864, for three years.

LEGG, CHARLES A. Corporal Co. C, 1st Regiment Cavalry, mustered Sept. 17, 1861, for three years on quota of Auburn ; discharged Dec. 31, 1864, to re-enlist. Mustered Jan. 1, 1864, for three years on Chelsea quota ; appointed Sergeant, May 14, 1864 ; discharged June 29, 1865, expiration of service.

LEIZ, PETER. Private Co. A, 20th Regiment Infantry, mustered April 12, 1864, for three years ; discharged July 16, 1865, expiration of service.

LEONARD, DAVID A. Private Co. D, 40th Regiment Infantry, mustered Sept. 3, 1862, for three years ; discharged June 16, 1865, expiration of service.

LEONARD, LAWRENCE. Private Co. M, 2nd Regiment Heavy Artillery, mustered Aug. 20, 1864, for three years, discharged May 25, 1865, expiration of service.

LEONARD, THOMAS. Private Co. I, 2d Regiment Cavalry, mustered June 10, 1864, for three years. Deserted July 10, 1864.

LEVERATT, JOHN. Private Co. C, 35th Regiment Infantry, mustered Aug. 19, 1862, for three years, scalded by bursting of locomotive at Nicholasville, Ky., June 6, died June 7, 1863.

LEWIS, CHARLES G. Private Co. G, 20th Regiment Infantry, mustered April 12, 1864, for three years.

LEWIS, GEORGE. Private Co. G, 4th Regiment Cavalry, mustered Jan. 27, 1864, for three years. Deserted Aug. 18, 1865.

LEWIS, GEORGE A. Musician Co. G, 40th Regiment Infantry, mustered Sept. 5, 1862, for three years. Died Jan. 28, 1864, at Beaufort, S. C., of chronic diarrhœa.

LINCOLN, CHARLES S. Quarter-Master Sergeant Co. I, 1st Regiment Cavalry, mustered Jan. 14, 1864, for three years; discharged June 26, 1865, expiration of service.

LINEHAN, CORNELIUS. Private Co. E, 28th Regiment Infantry, mustered Dec. 13, 1861, for three years; wounded Sept. 17, 1862, at Antietam, Md.; discharged June 8, 1863, disability from wounds.

LINEHAN, TIMOTHY. Private Co. H, 42d Regiment Infantry, mustered Sept. 24, 1862, for nine months. Deserted Oct. 18, 1862, at Readville, Mass.

LINGAN, PIERCE. Unassigned recruit 28th Regiment Infantry, mustered May 6, 1864, for three years; discharged May 10, 1864, rejected recruit.

LINN, WILLIAM H. Private Co. K, 3d Regiment Heavy Artillery, mustered May 12, 1864, for three years. Deserted June 29, 1864.

LINSCOTT, BENJAMIN H. Private Co. G, 40th Regiment Infantry, mustered Sept. 5, 1862, for three years; appointed Corporal Sept. 16, 1862 ; appointed 1st Sergeant Oct., 1863 ; commissioned 1st Lieutenant Jan. 27, 1864 ; commissioned Captain Sept. 7, 1864 ; discharged June 16, 1865, expiration of service.

LISCHENE, JOHN. Unassigned recruit 2d Regiment Infantry, mustered Aug. 16, 1864, for three years.

LISSETT, MAXIMO. Private Co. E, 28th Regiment Infantry, mustered March 31, 1864, for three years; discharged June 30, 1865, expiration of service.

LITTLE, FREDERICK R. Private 4th Co. Unattached Infantry, mustered May 3, 1864, for ninety days; discharged Aug. 6, 1864, expiration of service.

LITTLE, JOHN J. General service U. S. A., mustered Jan. 18, 1864.

LITTLE, WILLIAM H. Private V. R. C., mustered June 16, 1864.

LOFTUS, F. B. General service U. S. A., mustered March 17, 1864.

LOMBARD, GEORGE E. Private Co. H. 43d Regiment Infantry, mustered Sept. 20, 1862, for nine months; discharged July 30, 1863, expiration of service. Died Sept. 14, 1872, Chelsea, of consumption contracted in the service.

LORD, CHARLES A. Private Co. H, 1st Regiment Infantry, mustered Sept. 24, 1861, for three years; appointed Corporal, Aug. 1, 1863; discharged May 25, 1864, expiration of service.

LORD, GEORGE F. Sergeant Co. H, 50th Regiment Infantry; mustered Sept. 29, 1862, for nine months. Died June 17, 1863, at Baton Rouge, La.

LORD, GEORGE F. Private Co. H, 43d Regiment Infantry, mustered Sept. 20, 1862, for nine months; discharged July 30, 1863, expiration of service. Re-enlisted private 4th Co. Unattached Infantry, May 3, 1864, for ninety days; discharged Aug. 6, 1864, expiration of service. Re-enlisted Private Co. M, 3d Regiment Cavalry, on quota of Cambridge, Dec. 30, 1864, for one year; discharged Sept. 28, 1865, expiration of service.

LORENZ, FRANZ. Private Co. A, 2d Regiment Infantry, mustered Aug. 16, 1864, for three years; discharged July 14, 1865, expiration of service.

LOUCH, JAMES W. Private Co. H, 43d Regiment Infantry, mustered Sept. 20, 1862, for nine months; discharged July 30, 1863, expiration of service. Mustered Dec. 12, 1863, for three years, unassigned recruit 1st Regiment Cavalry; transferred to Navy April 23, 1864.

LOUD, NATHAN N. Private Co. H, 1st Regiment Infantry, mustered May 23, 1861, for three years; discharged Jan. 4, 1864, to re-enlist. Mustered Jan. 5, 1864, for three years; May 24, 1864, transferred to 11th Regiment Infantry, appointed Corporal. Killed Oct. 27, 1864, at Hatcher's Run, Va.

LOVERING, JOHN D. Private 4th Co. Unattached Infantry, mustered May 3, 1864, for ninety days; discharged Aug. 6, 1864, expiration of service.

LOWELL, AMOS T. Private Co. A, 3d Regiment Heavy Artillery, mustered Jan. 10, 1863, for three years; discharged Jan. 5, 1864, for disability.

LUCAS, CHARLES H. Corporal Co. H, 50th Regiment Infantry, mustered Sept. 29, 1862, for nine months; discharged Aug. 24, 1863, expiration of service.

LUCAS, JOHN. Private V. R. C., mustered Aug. 15, 1864; discharged Nov. 21, 1865, order of War Department.

LUDLOW, JOHN R. Private Co. A, 28th Regiment Infantry, mustered April 16, 1864, for three years; absent, wounded since May 11, 1864.

LUKE, JOHN A. Private Co. H, 1st Regiment Infantry, mustered Sept. 18, 1861, for three years ; taken prisoner near Manassas, Va., Aug. 29, 1862 ; exchanged Nov. 1, 1862; wounded on road to Gettysburg, Pa., July, 1863 ; discharged May 25, 1864, expiration of service.

LULL, SAMUEL E. Private Co. G, 42d Regiment Infantry, mustered Sept. 12, 1862, for nine months. Deserted Oct. 1, 1862, at Readville, Mass.

LYMAN, WILLIAM. Private Co. M, 1st Regiment Heavy Artillery, mustered March 7, 1862. Wounded May 19, 1864, at Wilderness, Va. ; died May 20, 1864, at Fredericksburg, Va.

LYNCH, JOHN B. General service U. S. A., mustered Jan. 18, 1864, for three years ; discharged Feb. 20, 1867, expiration of service.

LYNCH, MAURICE. Private Co. A, 9th Regiment Infantry, mustered June 11, 1861, for three years ; appointed Corporal Aug. 1, 1861. Wounded June 27, 1862, near Richmond, Va. ; died July 5, 1862.

LYONS, CHARLES. Private V. R. C., mustered Aug. 11, 1864 ; discharged Nov. 17, 1865, order of War Department.

M

MABIE, EDWARD. Private Co. K, 3d Regiment Heavy Artillery, mustered May 12, 1864, for three years. Deserted June 29, 1864.

MACE, JOHN. Unassigned recruit 2d Regiment Infantry, mustered May 27, 1864, for three years.

MADERT, JACOB. General service U. S. A., mustered March 25, 1864; discharged Nov. 1, 1865, order of War Department.

MADDOX, STEPHEN H. Corporal Co. A, 55th Regiment Infantry, mustered May 31, 1863, for three years. Died Jan. 31, 1864, at Folly Island, S. C.

MAGEE, HENRY. Corporal Co. K, 1st Regiment Cavalry, N. B., mustered Dec. 29, 1863, for three years ; transferred April 27, 1864, to Navy.

MAHONEY, EDWARD. Private Co. H, 42d Regiment Infantry, mustered Sept. 24, 1862, for nine months ; discharged Aug. 20, 1863, expiration of service. Mustered Jan. 12, 1864, for three years, private Co. E, 56 Regiment Infantry. Died Feb. 26, 1864, at Chelsea.

MALONE, PATRICK. Private Co. H, 42d Regiment Infantry, mustered Sept. 24, 1862, for nine months. Deserted Oct. 10, 1862, at Readville.

MALONEY, EDWARD. Private Co. E, 25th Regiment Infantry, mustered Jan. 8, 1864, for three years ; discharged July 13, 1865, expiration of service.

MALONEY, PATRICK J. Private 15th Light Battery, mustered Jan. 27, 1864, for three years ; transferred Aug. 22, 1864, to Navy.

MANDERVILLE, JOHN M. Corporal Co. H, 1st Regiment Infantry, mustered May 23, 1861, for three years; appointed 1st Sergeant, Sept, 1, 1861; discharged for promotion July 17, 1862; mustered 1st Lieut., July 17, 1862. Aug. 29, 1862, killed in action at Manassas, Va.

MANN, BARNABAS N. 1st Lieutenant and Adjutant 17th Regiment Infantry, mustered Aug. 21, 1861, for three years; assigned to Co. D, Nov. 1862. Wounded Dec. 17, 1862, at Goldsboro', N. C.; wounded and taken prisoner Feb. 1, 1864, near Newbern, N. C.; died Oct. 8, 1864, in rebel prison at Charleston, S. C.

MANN, HENRY C. Private Co. K, 6th Regiment Infantry, mustered April 22, 1861, for three months; discharged Aug. 2, 1861, expiration of service. Mustered Oct. 11, 1862, for nine months on quota of Boston, 1st Sergeant Co. C, 42d Regiment Infantry; discharged Aug. 20, 1863, expiration of service.

MANNING, JAMES C. Private Co. B, 1st Regiment Cavalry, mustered Sept. 12, 1861, for three years; discharged Sept. 8, 1864, expiration of service.

MANSTON, HAZEN. Private Co. M, 4th Regiment Infantry, mustered March 23, 1864, for three years. Deserted Aug. 18, 1865.

MANTON, ELIJAH JR. Corporal 4th Co. Unattached Infantry, mustered May 3, 1864, for ninety days; discharged Aug. 6, 1864, expiration of service.

MAPHIN, JAMES. Private 2d Light Battery, mustered Jan. 8, 1864, for three years; transferred Feb. 2, 1864, to 28th Regiment Infantry.

MARDEN, CHARLES M. Corporal Co. H, 42 Regiment Infantry, mustered Sept. 24, 1862, for nine months; discharged Aug. 30, 1863, expiration of service.

MARSH, GEORGE W. Private 11th Light Battery, mustered Aug. 25, 1862, for nine months; discharged May 25, 1863, expiration of service. Mustered Jan. 2, 1864, for three years, Artificer 11th Light Battery; discharged June 16, 1865, expiration of service.

MARSH, SAMUEL H. Unassigned recruit 15th Regiment Infantry, mustered April 9, 1864, for three years. Deserted April 20, 1864.

MARSHALL, GEORGE E. Private Co. C, 13th Regiment Infantry, mustered July 16, 1861, for three years; appointed Corporal, July 29, 1861; appointed 1st Sergeant, Feb. 1, 1862; wounded Aug. 30, 1862, near Manassas, Va.; discharged Aug. 15, 1862; commissioned same date Capt. Co. G, 4th Regiment Infantry; commissioned Major, March 10, 1864; commissioned Lieut.-Col., April 20, 1864. Killed June 1, 1864, at Cold Harbor, Va.

MARSHALL, HENRY W. Private 2d Light Battery, mustered July 8, 1864, for three years; discharged Aug. 11, 1865, expiration of service.

MARSHALL, JOHN. Private 6th Light Battery, mustered Dec. 23, 1864, for three years; discharged Aug, 7, 1865, expiration of service.

MARSTEN, GEORGE. Private Co. K, 2d Regiment Cavalry, mustered May 11, 1864, for three years. Deserted June 2, 1864.

MARTIN, JAMES. Corporal Co. K, 3d Regiment Heavy Artillery, mustered May 12, 1864, for three years; discharged Sept. 18, 1865, expiration of service.

MARTIN, JOHN W. Corporal 12th Light Battery, mustered Nov. 26, 1862, for three years; discharged July 25, 1865, expiration of service.

MARTIN, PATRICK. Private Co. G, 2d Regiment Infantry, mustered Aug. 20, 1864, for three years ; discharged July 11, 1865, expiration of service.

MASON, CHARLES H. Private 13th Light Battery, mustered Jan, 21, 1863, for three years ; discharged Jan. 30, 1864, for disability.

MASON, GEORGE A. Private Co. A, 6th Regiment Infantry, mustered July 15, 1864, for 100 days ; discharged Oct. 27, 1864, expiration of service.

MASON, HENRY JR. Private Co. H, 1st Regiment Infantry, mustered May 23, 1861, for three years ; wounded Aug. 29, 1862, near Manassas ; March 15, 1864, transferred to V. R. C. ; discharged April 23, 1864, disability from wounds.

MASON, N. EMMONS. Private Co. H, 1st Regiment Infantry, mustered May 23, 1861, for three years ; discharged Dec. 26, 1862, for disability.

MASON, ROBERT E. Sergeant Co. C, 3d Regiment Cavalry, mustered March 16, 1864, for three years ; discharged Sept. 28, 1865, expiration of service.

MASON, WALTER. Private Co. H, 43d Regiment Infantry, mustered Sept. 20, 1864, for nine months ; discharged July 30, 1863, expiration of service.

MASON, WILLIAM J. Private Co. C, 35th Regiment Infantry, mustered Aug. 19, 1862, for three years ; appointed Corporal, Nov. 1, 1862 ; wounded at Fredericksburg, Va., Dec. 12, 1862 ; discharged April 8, 1863, disability from wound.

MATTER, ARTHUR. Unassigned recruit 2nd Regiment Infantry, mustered Aug. 18, 1864, for three years.

MATTESON, WILLIAM E.   Private Co. E, 2d Regiment Infantry, mustered May 24, 1864, for three years ; discharged July 14, 1865, expiration of service.

MATTHEWS, WILLIAM H.   Sergeant Co. C, 35th Regiment Infantry, mustered Aug. 19, 1862, for three years.   Died Feb. 7, 1863.

MAXFIELD, DANIEL.   Private Co. G, 19th Regiment Infantry, mustered March 28, 1864, for three years.   Died June 23, 1864, at Baltimore, Md.

MAYNARD, CORNELIUS D.   Private Co. H, 43d Regiment Infantry, mustered Sept. 20, 1862, for nine months ; discharged July 30, 1863, expiration of service ; re-enlisted 29th Regiment Maine Infantry, Dec. 1863.

MAYO, BENJAMIN H.   Private Co. G, 40th Regiment Infantry, mustered Sept. 5, 1862, for three years ; appointed Corporal, Dec. 1862 ; taken prisoner at Drury's Bluff, Va., May 16, 1864.   Died Feb. 23, 1865, at Florence, S. C., from starvation.

MAYO, RICHARD G.   Private Co. A, 17th Regiment Infantry, mustered July 21, 1861, for three years ; appointed Corporal, Feb. 9, 1862 ; discharged Oct. 13, 1862, disability.

McCANN, JOHN.   Private Co. F, 19th Regiment Infantry, mustered Aug. 28, 1861, for three years ; taken prisoner near Richmond, July 1. 1862 ; exchanged.   Wounded Sept. 17, 1862, at Antietam, Md. ; discharged May 4, 1863, disability from wound.

McCANN, JOHN.   Unassigned recruit 2d Regiment Infantry, mustered May 13, 1864, for three years.

McCARTY, BARTHOLOMEW. Private 12th Light Battery, mustered Nov. 15, 1862, for three years; discharged May 15, 1863, disability.

McCARTY, CHARLES. Unassigned recruit 3d Regiment Cavalry, mustered Aug. 20, 1864, for three years.

McCARTY, JOHN. Private Co. F, 16th Regiment Infantry, mustered July 12, 1861, for three years. Died Aug. 17, 1862, at Philadelphia, Pa.

McCARTY, TIMOTHY. Unassigned recruit 20th Regiment Infantry, mustered Sept. 6, 1862, for three years.

McCLANE, WILLIAM. Private V. R. C., mustered May 28, 1864.

McCONNAUGHTY, JOHN K. General service U. S. A., mustered Feb. 20, 1864, for three years ; discharged Feb. 20, 1867, expiration of service.

McCONNELL, WILLIAM. Private Co. H, 1st Regiment Infantry, mustered Sept. 24, 1861, for three years; wounded Aug. 29, 1862, near Manassas, Va.; discharged March 8, 1863, disability from wound.

McCONOLOGUE, JAMES S. Private Co. G, 61st Regiment Infantry, mustered Nov. 11, 1864, for one year; discharged July 16, 1865, expiration of service.

McCORMACK, JOSEPH. 3d Artillery U. S. A., mustered March 8, 1864.

McCORMY, JAMES. Unassigned recruit 2d Regiment Cavalry, mustered May 6, 1864, for three years.

McCRACKEN, JAMES T. Sergeant Co. L, 1st Regiment Cavalry, mustered Jan. 6, 1864, for three years ; discharged June 26, 1865, expiration of service.

McCULLOCH, ROBERT. Corporal Co. C, 35th Regiment
Infantry, mustered Aug. 19, 1862, for three years ; appointed Sergeant, March 25, 1863. Killed Oct. 1, 1864,
accidently, near Petersburg, Va.

McDAVITT, HUGH. Private Co. A, 43d Regiment Infantry, mustered Oct. 11, 1862, for nine months ; discharged
July 30, 1863, expiration of service.

McDONALD, CHARLES. Private Co. C, 19th Regiment Infantry, mustered March 21, 1864, for three years ; discharged June 30, 1865, expiration of service.

McDONALD, DONALD. Private Co. B, 9th Regiment Infantry, mustered June 11, 1861, for three years; discharged
Jan. 6, 1863, disability.

McDONALD, JAMES. Private Co. L, 2d Regiment Cavalry,
mustered March 27, 1864, for three years. Deserted
April 16, 1864.

McDONALD, PATRICK. Unassigned recruit 32d Regiment
Infantry, mustered Dec. 22, 1864, for three years.

McDONOUGH, JOHN. Private Co. B, 28th Regiment Infantry, mustered Jan. 10, 1862, for three years; discharged
Jan. 1, 1864, to re-enlist. Mustered Jan. 2, 1864, for
three years. Deserted April 1, 1864.

McFADDEN, THOMAS. Private Co. B, 2d Regiment Heavy
Artillery, mustered Aug. 18, 1864, for three years; discharged June 28, 1865, expiration of service.

McGUINISS, PATRICK. Private Co. F, 1st Regiment Heavy
Artillery, mustered Nov. 25, 1864, for three years ; discharged Aug. 16, 1865, expiration of service.

McGOWAN, JAMES. Corporal Co. H, 42d Regiment Infantry, mustered Sept. 24, 1862, for nine months; discharged Aug. 20, 1863, expiration of service. Mustered June 19, 1864, for three years, on quota of Milton; Sergeant Co. A, 28th Regiment Infantry; discharged June 30, 1865, expiration of service.

McGOWAN, THOMAS. Private Co. H, 42d Regiment Infantry, mustered Oct. 9, 1862, for nine months; discharged Aug. 20, 1863, expiration of service.

McGRATH, MICHAEL L. Unassigned recruit 3d Regiment Heavy Artillery, mustered May 12, 1864, for three years; discharged May 31, 1864, rejected recruit.

McGUIRE, MICHAEL. Private Co. I, 9th Regiment Infantry, mustered June 11, 1861, for three years; wounded June 27, 1862, at Gaines' Mills, Va. Deserted July 5, 1863.

McINTYRE, JAMES. Private Co. H, 43d Regiment Infantry, mustered Sept 20, 1862, for nine months; discharged July 30, 1863, expiration of service.

McINTYRE, JAMES F. Private Co. L, 1st Regiment Cavalry, mustered Jan. 6, 1864, for three years; discharged June 26, 1865, expiration of service.

McKEE, JOHN. Private Co. B, 3d Regiment Cavalry, mustered Dec. 9, 1863, for three years; appointed Sergeant, Aug. 5, 1865; appointed Com. Sergeant, Aug. 25, 1865; commissioned 1st Lieut. Oct. 5, 1865, not mustered; discharged Oct. 8, 1865, expiration of service.

McKEEVER, JAMES. Private 11th Light Battery, mustered Dec. 20, 1864, for three years; discharged June 16, 1865, expiration of service.

McKENDRY, WALLACE. General service U. S. A., mustered Jan. 1864.

McKENNY, ALFRED H. Private Co. G, 40th Regiment Infantry, mustered Sept. 5, 1862, for three years; discharged Nov. 12, 1862, disability.

McKENZIE, WILLIAM. Private Co. H, 43d Regiment Infantry, mustered Sept. 26, 1862, for nine months; discharged July 30, 1863, expiration of service.

McKINNEY, WILLIAM H. Private Co. M, 1st Regiment Cavalry, mustered Jan. 14, 1864, for three years.

McLANE, THOMAS. Private 18th Co. Unattached Infantry, mustered Aug. 6, 1864, for 100 days; discharged Nov. 14, 1864, expiration of service.

McLAUGHLIN, CHARLES. Private Co. H, 42d Regiment Infantry, mustered Sept. 24, 1862, for nine months; discharged Aug. 20, 1863, expiration of service; mustered May 19, 1864, on quota of Boston, private Co. K, 3d Regiment Heavy Artillery; discharged Sept. 13, 1865, expiration of service.

McLAUGHLIN, JAMES. Private Co. G, 40 Regiment Infantry, mustered Sept. 2, 1862, for three years; discharged June 16, 1865, expiration of service.

McLAUGHLIN, JOHN. Unassigned recruit 3rd Regiment Heavy Artillery, mustered May 10, 1864, for three years, discharged May 13, 1864, rejected recruit.

McLEOD, JOHN T. Private Co. B, 1st Regiment Infantry, mustered May 23, 1861, for three years; discharged July 20, 1861, disability.

McMAHAN, JOHN. Private 13th Light Battery, mustered Dec. 30, 1862, for three years. Deserted Jan. 3, 1863.

McMAHAN, THOMAS. Private Co. A, 9th Regiment Infantry, mustered June 11, 1861, for three years ; wounded May 5, 1864, Wilderness, Va. ; discharged June 21, 1864, expiration of service.

McPOLAND, JOHN. Private Co. F, 3d Regiment Cavalry, mustered Oct. 27, 1862, for three years. Deserted Nov. 3, 1862.

McQUADE, CHARLES. Private Co. B, 1st Regiment Cavalry, mustered Jan. 1, 1864, for three years ; transferred to Navy, May 3, 1864.

McQUEENEY, THOMAS J. Private Co. K, 3d Regiment Heavy Artillery, mustered Nov. 9, 1864, for three years ; discharged Sept. 18, 1865, expiration of service.

McRAE, CHRISTOPHER. Private Co. I, 20th Regiment Infantry, mustered April 12, 1864, for three years ; discharged July 16, 1865, expiration of service.

MEARS, DANIEL P. Corporal 42d Regiment, N. Y. ; dis-. charged Nov. 1861 : re-enlisted private Co. I, 1st Regiment Infantry, mustered Dec. 28, 1861, for three years ; June 1862, taken prisoner. Died July 18, 1862, at Richmond, Va.

MEARS, GEORGE. Private Co. H, 43d Regiment Infantry, mustered Sept. 20, 1862, for nine months ; discharged July 30, 1863, expiration of service.

MERRIAM FRANCIS J. Private Co. K, 59th Regiment Infantry, mustered April 21, 1864, for three years ; transferred June 1, 1863, to 57th Regiment Infantry ; discharged from 57th Regiment July 7, 1865 for disability.

MERRIAM, WILLIAM N. Private Co. D, 17th Regiment Infantry, mustered Jan. 31, 1862, for three years ; Feb. 1, 1864, taken prisoner near Newburn, N. C. Died May 24, 1864, at Andersonville, Ga.

MERRILL, CHARLES. Corporal 2d Light Battery, mustered Mar. 4, 1864, for three years ; discharged Aug. 11, 1865, expiration of service.

MERRILL, ISRAEL H. Private Co. G, 40th Regiment Infantry, mustered Sept. 5, 1862, for three years ; discharged June 16, 1865, expiration of service.

MERRITT, HENRY A. 2d Lieut. 2d Regiment Heavy Artillery, mustered Aug. 23, 1863 ; discharged for promotion Aug. 17, 1864 ; mustered Aug. 17, 1864, 1st Lieut. on quota of Salem ; discharged Sept. 3, 1865, expiration of service.

MERRITT, MARTIN. Private Co. H, 43d Regiment Infantry, mustered Sept. 20, 1862, for nine months ; discharged July 30, 1863, expiration of service. Mustered Mar. 11, 1864, for three years, private 16th Light Battery ; discharged June 27, 1865, expiration of service.

MERRITT, THOMAS T. Private 4th Co. Unattached Infantry, mustered May 3d, 1864, for ninety days ; discharged Aug. 6, 1864, expiration of service.

MERTZ, JACOB. Private Co. H, 2d Regiment Infantry, mustered May 27, 1864, for three years. Deserted July 3, 1864.

MESERVE, CHARLES. Private Co. E, 4th Regiment Cavalry, mustered January 27, 1864, for three years ; discharged Nov. 14, 1865, expiration of service.

MESSER, CHARLES. Private V. R. C., mustered May 28, 1864.

METZKI, HENRY. Private Co. H, 2d Regiment Infantry, mustered June 9, 1864, for three years. Deserted Aug. 2, 1864.

MEYER, CARL. Private Co. G, 2d Regiment Cavalry, mustered Aug. 19, 1864, for three years. Deserted March 5, 1865.

MILES, JOHN. Private Co. A, 2d Regiment Cavalry, mustered June 9, 1864, for three years ; discharged July 20, 1865, expiration of service.

MILLER, CHARLES. Sergeant Co. E, 28th Regiment Infantry, mustered April 5, 1864, for three years ; discharged June 30, 1865, expiration of service.

MILLER, CHARLES. Private Co. D, 28th Regiment Infantry, mustered April 5, 1864, for three years ; transferred June 15, 1865, to V. R. C.

MILLER, CHARLES A. Private Co. D, 28th Regiment Infantry, mustered Mar. 17, 1864, for three years ; transferred April 1, 1865, to V. R. C.; discharged July 25, 1865.

MILLER, JARED, Private Co. I, 33d Regiment Infantry, mustered Dec. 20, 1864, for three years.

MILLER, JOHN. Private V. R. C., mustered July 22, 1864.

MILLER, JOHN. Private Co. A, 2d Regiment Infantry, mustered June 11, 1864, for three years. Deserted Sept. 18, 1864.

MILLER, JOHN. Private Co. H, 2d Regiment Infantry, mustered May 24, 1864, for three years; discharged July 26, 1865, expiration of service.

MILLER, JOHN. Private Co. K, 2d Regiment Infantry, mustered Jan. 13, 1864, for three years; discharged July 14, 1865, expiration of service.

MILLIKEN, ALFRED A. Private 8th Light Battery, mustered May 30, 1862, for six months; appointed Corporal, Sept. 1862 ; discharged Nov. 29, 1862, expiration of service. ·

MINARD, NELSON C. Private Co. K, 13th Regiment Infantry, mustered Aug. 1, 1862, for three years; discharged March 31, 1864, to re-enlist. Mustered, April 1, 1864, for three years ; transferred July 13, 1864, to 39th Regiment Infantry ; transferred June 2, 1865, to 32d Regiment Infantry ; discharged July 12, 1865, by order of War Department.

MITCHELL, GEORGE L. Private 4th Co. Unattached Infantry, mustered May 3, 1864, for ninety days ; discharged Aug. 6, 1864, expiration of service. Mustered Jan. 2, 1865, for one year, on quota of Cambridge, private Co. D, 1st Regiment Cavalry ; discharged June 30, 1865, expiration of service.

MITCHELL, HENRY. Unassigned recruit 2d Regiment Infantry, mustered May 17, 1864, for three years.

MITCHELL, JACOB, JR. Private 4th Co. Unattached Infantry, mustered May 3, 1864, for ninety days ; discharged Aug. 6, 1864, expiration of service.

MITCHELL, PATRICK. Private Co. F, 28th Regiment Infantry, mustered Dec. 13, 1861, for three years. Killed Sept. 1, 1862, at Chantilly. Va.

MITCHELL, WILLIAM J. Private Co. F, 56th Regiment Infantry, mustered Jan. 12, 1864, for three years. Wounded near Petersburg, Va. ; died of wounds, June 17, 1864.

MONROE, JAMES. Private 12th Light Battery, mustered Nov. 29, 1862, for three years. Deserted, Dec. 27, 1863.

MONROE, JOHN JR. Musician Co. K, 2d Regiment Infantry, mustered May 25, 1861, for three years on quota of Charlestown ; discharged to re-enlist, Dec. 30, 1863. Mustered Dec. 31, 1863, Chelsea's quota, for three years ; discharged Jan. 14, 1865, expiration of service.

MONTAGUE, FRANCIS. Private 10th Light Battery, mustered June 11, 1864, for three years ; discharged June 9, 1865, expiration of service.

MONTAGUE, WILLIAM H. Private Co. H, 1st Regiment Infantry, mustered Sept. 24, 1861, for three years; wounded at Yorktown, Va., April 26, 1862 ; discharged Oct. 22, 1862, disability from wound. Died, May 12, 1864, at Chelsea.

MONTO, GEORGE. Private Co. G, 2d Regiment Heavy Artillery, mustered Aug. 5, 1864, for three years ; discharged Sept. 3, 1865, expiration of service.

MOODY, FRANCIS O. Private Co. H, 1st Regiment Infantry, mustered May 23, 1861, for three years ; discharged Feb. 4, 1863, for disability.

MOONEY, FELIX. Private 12th Light Battery, mustered Jan. 15, 1864, for three years. Died, July 8, 1864, at Port Hudson, La.

MOORE, THOMAS. Private Co. I, 2d Regiment Infantry, mustered July 22, 1864, for three years. Deserted, August 7, 1864.

MORAN, JOEL W. Hospital Steward U. S. A., mustered March 30, 1864.

MORAN, JOHN. Private Co. F, 19th Regiment Infantry, mustered Aug. 28, 1861, for three years ; discharged Oct. 25, 1862, to enlist in U. S. Artillery.

MORAN, MARTIN. Private Co. I, 9th Regiment Infantry, mustered June 11, 1861, for three years ; appointed Corporal, Jan. 26, 1862. Deserted, Aug. 28, 1862.

MORAN, THOMAS. Unassigned recruit 2d Regiment Cavalry, mustered June 11, 1864, for three years.

MORAN, THOMAS F. Private 6th Light Battery, mustered Sept. 12, 1864, for three years ; discharged June 19, 1865, expiration of service.

MOREY, GEORGE A. Private Co. E, 4th Regiment Cavalry, mustered Jan. 27, 1864, for three years ; discharged Nov. 14, 1865, expiration of service.

MORGAN, WILLIAM. Private Co. I, 2d Regiment Cavalry, mustered June 10, 1864, for three years. Deserted, May 31, 1865.

MORINI, FRANK. Unassigned recruit 3d Regiment Cavalry, mustered March 16, 1864, for three years. Deserted May, 1864.

MORO, JOSEPH. Private Co. A, 2d Regiment Infantry, mustered May 6, 1864, for three years ; discharged May 30, 1865, expiration of service.

MORRILL, BENJAMIN. Private Co. C, 35th Regiment Infantry, mustered Aug. 19, 1862, for three years ; discharged Nov. 3, 1862, for disability.

MORRILL, FRANCIS L. Private Co. D, 42d Regiment Infantry, mustered Oct. 4, 1862, for nine months ; taken prisoner Jan. 1, 1863, exchanged July 22, 1864.

MORRILL, GEORGE E. Private Co. H, 43d Regiment Infantry, mustered Sept. 20, 1862, for nine months; discharged July 30, 1863, expiration of service.

MORRILL, HENRY. Private Co. D, 42d Regiment Infantry, mustered Oct. 10, 1862, for nine months. Deserted, Dec. 3, 1862, at Readville, Mass.

MORRIS, JOHN. Private Co. A, 43d Regiment Infantry, mustered Oct. 11, 1862, for nine months; discharged July 30, 1863, expiration of service.

MORRISON, RICHARD L. Private Co. H, 1st Regiment Infantry, mustered May 23, 1861, for three years; discharged July 22, 1861, for disability.

MORTON, GEORGE A. Unassigned recruit 2nd Regiment Infantry, mustered May 10, 1864, for three years.

MOSSEY, JOSEPH. Private Co. L, 3d Regiment Heavy Artillery, mustered May 30, 1864, for three years; discharged Sept. 18, 1865, expiration of service.

MULLER, JOHN. Unassigned recruit 28th Regiment Infantry, mustered March 17, 1864, for three years; transferred April 2, 1864, to Navy.

MULLIGAN, THOMAS. Unassigned recruit 2d Regiment Infantry, mustered May 17, 1864, for three years.

MURPHY, JAMES H. Private Co. H, 1st Regiment Infantry, mustered May 23, 1861, for three years. Killed July 18, 1861, at Blackburn's Ford, Va.

MURPHY, JOHN. Private Co. H, 2d Regiment Infantry, mustered July 22, 1864, for three years. Deserted, Aug. 7, 1864.

MURPHY, JOSEPH. Unassigned recruit 2d Regiment Infantry, mustered June 10, 1864, for three years.

MURPHY, SAMUEL. Private 18th Co. Unattached Infantry, mustered Aug. 6, 1864, for 100 days; discharged Nov. 14, 1864, expiration of service.

MURRAY, JAMES. Private 12th Light Battery, mustered Dec. 8, 1862, for three years; discharged July 25, 1865, expiration of service.

MURRAY, JOHN. Private Co. B, 4th Regiment Cavalry, mustered Dec. 22, 1864, for three years. Deserted, May 17, 1865.

MURRAY, WILLIAM C. Private 1st Light Battery, mustered July 23, 1864, for three years. Deserted, Aug. 22, 1864, at Gallop's Island.

MYERS, CHARLES. Unassigned recruit 2d Regiment Infantry, mustered July 8, 1864, for three years.

MYERS, FRANCIS. General Service U. S. A., mustered March 17, 1864.

MYERS, JOHN H. Private Co. E, 44th Regiment Infantry, mustered Sept. 12, 1862, for nine months; discharged June 8, 1863, expiration of service; mustered Feb. 8, 1864, for three years Sergeant Co. H, 4th Regiment Cavalry, on quota of North Chelsea; discharged Nov. 14, 1865, expiration of service.

MYRICK, FRANKLIN B. 2d Lieut. Co. C, 35th Regiment Infantry, mustered Aug. 13, 1862; promoted 1st Lieut. Jan. 1, 1863; promoted Captain June 24, 1863, wounded Nov. 19, 1863, at Knoxville, Tenn.; promoted Major Nov. 14, 1864; discharged June 9, 1865, expiration of service.

N

NALLY, JOHN. Private 13th Light Battery, mustered Dec. 30, 1862, for three years. Deserted Jan. 9, 1863.

NASON, CHARLES E. Private Co. M, 1st Regiment Heavy Artillery, mustered Mar. 4, 1862, for three years; discharged Mar. 3, 1865, expiration of service.

NEAL, JOHN. Private Co. K, 58th Regiment Infantry, mustered Dec. 1, 1864, for three years; discharged Jan. 14, 1865, expiration of service.

NEEDHAM, THOMAS. Private Co. H, 1st Regiment Infantry, mustered May 23, 1861, for three years, wounded at Bull Run, Va., July 18, 1861. Died Aug. 1, 1861, at Culpepper, Va.

NEELEY, JAMES. Unassigned recruit 2d Regiment Infantry, mustered July 8, 1864, for three years.

NEILD, SAMUEL N. Quarter-Master Sergeant Co. C, 1st Regiment Cavalry, mustered Jan. 1, 1864, for three years; discharged June 29, 1865, expiration of service.

NELSON, ALONZO R. Private Co. B, 11th Regiment Infantry, mustered June 13, 1861, for three years; wounded June 29, 1862, near Richmond, Va.; discharged June 24, 1864, expiration of service.

NEVILLE, PATRICK. Private Co. A, 2d Regiment Infantry, mustered, June 11, 1864, for three years. Deserted, Sept. 17, 1864, at Atlanta, Ga.

NEWELL, EDWARD K. Private 4th Co. Unattached Infantry, mustered May 3, 1864, for ninety days; discharged Aug. 6, 1864, expiration of service.

NEWLAND, JAMES. Private 12th Light Battery, mustered Jan. 15, 1864, for three years ; discharged July 25, 1865, expiration of service.

NEWLAND, THOMAS. Private 12th Light Battery, mustered Jan. 15, 1864, for three years ; discharged July 25, 1865, expiration of service.

NEWLING, JOHN H. Private Co. H, 1st Regiment Infantry, mustered May 23, 1861, for three years ; appointed Corporal, Oct. 1, 1861 ; discharged Dec. 31, 1862, for disability.

NICHOLS, JOSEPH A. Private Co. H, 50th Regiment Infantry, mustered Sept. 29, 1862, for nine months ; discharged Aug. 24, 1863, expiration of service.

NICHOLSON, FRANCIS N. Corporal Co. G, 28th Regiment Infantry, mustered Jan. 6, 1862, for three years. Killed, Sept. 17, 1862, at Antietam, Md.

NILAND, PATRICK J. Private Co. H, 50th Regiment Infantry, mustered Sept. 29, 1862, for nine months ; discharged Aug. 24, 1863, expiration of service.

NILAND, THOMAS. Private Co. G, 40th Regiment Infantry, mustered, Sept. 5, 1862, for three years ; appointed Corporal, Nov. 1, 1863 ; appointed Sergeant, Jan. 1, 1865 ; discharged June 16, 1865, expiration of service.

NORCROSS, CHARLES W. Private Co. M, 4th Regiment Cavalry, mustered March 1, 1864, for three years. Deserted, Aug. 9, 1865.

NORRIS, GEORGE. Sergeant 4th Co. Unattached Infantry, mustered May 3, 1864, for ninety days ; discharged Aug. 6, 1864, expiration of service.

NORRIS, GEORGE G. S. Private Co. I, 1st Regiment Infantry, mustered Dec. 27, 1861, for three years; transferred to V. R. C.. 1863; discharged Dec. 12, 1864, disability. Died Dec. 12, 1864, at Lowell.

NORRIS, JEREMIAH. Private 4th Co. Unattached Infantry, mustered May 3, 1864, for ninety days; discharged Aug. 6, 1864, expiration of service.

NORTH, JAMES N. Private Co. B, 1st Regiment Infantry, mustered Dec. 15, 1861, for three years; discharged July, 1863; 2d Lieut. Sept. 1, 1863, 35th Regiment U. S. C. T., 1st Regiment Wilde's African Brigade; commissioned 1st Lieut. and Adjutant 1st U. S. C. Cavalry, Dec. 7, 1863; Jan. 25, 1864, commissioned 1st Lieut. and Quarter-Master 24th Regiment Infantry, resigned Oct. 7, 1865.

NORTON, HANNIBAL D. 3d Lieutenant Co. C, 5th Regiment Infantry, mustered May 1, 1861, for three years; discharged July 31, 1861, expiration of service. Mustered July 28, 1862, Captain 32d Regiment Infantry; resigned and discharged Mar. 18, 1863, Brevet-Major, V. R. C., June 15, 1863; promoted Major V. R. C., March, 1865.

NOYES, GEORGE A. Private Co. H, 1st Regiment Infantry, mustered May 23, 1861, for three years. Killed April 26, 1862, at Yorktown, Va.

NUGENT, JOHN. Private Co. A, 43d Regiment Infantry, mustered Oct. 11, 1862, for nine months. Deserted Oct. 25, 1862, at Readville.

NYMAN, EDGAR A. Private Co. H, 50th Regiment Infantry, mustered Sept. 29, 1862, for nine months; discharged Jan. 14, 1863, for disability.

OAKMAN, WILLIAM C. Private Co. C, 35th Regiment Infantry, mustered Aug. 19, 1862 ; appointed Corporal Nov. 1, 1862 ; appointed Sergeant Sept. 12, 1863 ; wounded Sept. 30, 1864, near Petersburg, Va., taken prisoner, died Oct. 7, 1864, on exchange boat.

O'BRIEN, DENNIS A. Sergeant Co. H, 42d Regiment Infantry, mustered Sept. 24, 1862, for nine months ; discharged Aug. 20, 1863, expiration of service.

O'CONNELL, PATRICK. Unassigned recruit 28th Regiment Infantry, mustered May 10, 1864, for three years.

O'CONNOR, PATRICK. Private 2d Light Battery, mustered Dec. 31, 1863, for three years ; discharged Aug. 11, 1865, expiration of service.

O'DONNELL, JAMES. Private Co. C, 1st Battery Heavy Artillery, mustered April 22, 1863, for three years. Deserted Oct. 18, 1864.

O'DONNELL, MICHAEL. Private Co. I, 11th Regiment Infantry, mustered June 13, 1861, for three years ; discharged March 21, 1863, for disability. Mustered Jan. 2, 1865, 1st Battery Frontier Cavalry private Co. D, for one year on quota of Dover ; discharged June 30, 1865, expiration of service.

O'MALLEY, CHARLES. Private Co. G, 2d Regiment Infantry, mustered Aug. 12, 1864, for three years. Deserted, Sept. 11, 1864.

O'NEIL, CHARLES. Unassigned recruit 2d Regiment Cavalry, mustered Aug. 25, 1864, for three years.

O'NEIL, JAMES M. Private Co. H, 58th Regiment Infantry, mustered April 18, 1864, for three years ; transferred to V. R. C., April 1, 1865.

O'NEIL, JOHN. Private Co. B, 2d Regiment Infantry, mustered June 9, 1864, for three years. Deserted, Aug. 1, 1864, at Atlanta, Ga.

O'NEIL, PATRICK. Private Co. H, 2d Regiment Heavy Artillery, mustered Aug. 13, 1864, for three years ; transferred Jan. 17, 1865, to 17th Regiment Infantry ; discharged July 11, 1865, for disability.

ORCUTT, JOHN. Private Co. C, 53d Regiment Infantry, mustered Nov. 6, 1862, for nine months. Deserted, Nov. 20, 1862, at Groton, Mass.

OSGOOD, JOSIAH A. Corporal Co. C, 24th Regiment Infantry, mustered Oct. 18, 1861, for three years ; discharged Oct. 31, 1863, for promotion. Commissioned Capt. Co. K, 47th Regiment Infantry, Oct. 31, 1862, for nine months ; discharged Sept. 1, 1863, expiration of service.

OWENS, JOHN. Private Co. A, 28th Regiment Infantry, mustered April 13, 1864, for three years. Killed, June 3, 1864, at Cold Harbor, Va.

P

PAGE, AMBROSE M. Private Co. D, 35th Regiment Infantry, mustered Aug. 16, 1862, for three years; discharged Sept. 9, 1864, for promotion.

PAGE, GEORGE J. Corporal 14th Light Battery, mustered Feb. 27, 1864, for three years; discharged June 15, 1865, expiration of service.

PAINE, EDWIN R. Private Co. C, 35th Regiment Infantry, mustered Aug. 19, 1862, for three years; discharged June 9, 1865, expiration of service.

PAINE, WILLIAM W. 1st Sergeant Co. G, 33d Regiment Infantry, mustered Aug. 5, 1862, for three years. Died of wounds May 23, 1864, at Resaca, Ga.

PANCOAST, JOSIAH. General service U. S. A., mustered March 17, 1864.

PARK, EDWARD. Private Co. I, 44th Regiment Infantry, mustered Sept. 12, 1862, for nine months; discharged June 18, 1863, expiration of service.

PARKHURST, EUGENE D. C. Private Co. G, 40th Regiment Infantry, mustered Sept. 5, 1862, for three years. Died, Oct. 3, 1863, at Folly Island, S. C., of chronic diarrhœa.

PARKER, ALEXANDER. Private Co. H, 48th Regiment Infantry, mustered Sept. 25, 1862, for nine months; discharged Sept. 3, 1863, expiration of service.

PARKER, NATHAN W. Private Co. G, 40th Regiment Infantry, mustered Sept. 5, 1862, for three years; discharged June 16, 1865, expiration of service. Died at Chelsea. March 2, 1875, of typhoid pneumonia.

PARKER, WILLIAM L. Private Co. D, 35th Regiment Infantry, mustered Aug. 16, 1862, for three years. Deserted Dec. 16, 1862.

PARSONS, STEPHEN S. Private 12th Light Battery, mustered, Nov. 26, 1862, for three years. Died, Feb 19, 1863, at New Orleans, La.

PARSONS, WILLIAM H. Private Co. C, 56th Regiment Infantry, mustered Dec. 28, 1863, for three years; discharged July 12, 1865, expiration of service; absent, sick.

PATNOT, JOSEPH. Private Co. C, 35th Regiment Infantry, mustered Jan. 7, 1864, for three years; transferred June 9, 1865, to 29th Regiment Infantry; discharged July 29, 1865, expiration of service.

PATRICK, ALBERT E. Private Co. H, 43d Regiment Infantry, mustered Sept. 20, 1862, for nine months; discharged July 30, 1863, expiration of service.

PATTAN, GEORGE H. Private 11th Light Battery, mustered March 15, 1864, for three years; discharged June 16, 1865, expiration of service.

PAUL, EDWIN F. Hospital steward U. S. A., mustered April 5, 1864.

PEABODY, JAMES A. Private 11th Light Battery, mustered Jan. 2, 1864 for three years, discharged June 16, 1865, expiration of service.

PEABODY, JAMES W. Private 4th Co. Unattached Infantry, mustered May 3, 1864, for ninety days; discharged Aug. 6, 1864, expiration of service.

PEARSON, REUBEN. Private Co. H, 50th Regiment Infantry, mustered Sept. 29, 1862, for nine months; discharged Aug. 24, 1863, expiration of service.

PEARSON, SAMUEL F. Private Co. G, 40th Regiment Infantry, mustered Sept. 5, 1862, for three years ; discharged Jan. 8, 1864, for disability.

PEARSON, WILLIAM E. Corporal Co. H, 50th Regiment Infantry, mustered Sept. 29, 1862, for nine months ; discharged Aug. 24, 1863, expiration of service.

PERLEY, ELBRIDGE G. Private Co. H, 1st Regiment Infantry, mustered May 23, 1861, for three years ; discharged July 22, 1861, disability. Mustered Sept. 19, 1862, for nine months, private Co. D, 5th Regiment Infantry; discharged July 2, 1863, expiration of service.

PERKINS, CHARLES W. Private Co. H, 43d Regiment Infantry, mustered Sept. 20, 1862, for nine months ; discharged July 30, 1863, expiration of service.

PERRY, ALMON. Private Co. H, 43d Regiment Infantry, mustered Sept. 20, 1862, for nine months; discharged July 30, 1863, expiration of service.

PERRY, ALBERT D. Signal Corps U. S. A., mustered March 28, 1864.

PERRY, GEORGE. Unassigned recruit 28th Regiment Infantry, mustered May 10, 1864, for three years.

PERRY, JOHN H. Sergeant Co. H, 43d Regiment Infantry, mustered Sept. 20, 1862, for nine months ; discharged July 30, 1863, expiration of service.

PETERSON, JOHN. Private Co. C, 35th Regiment Infantry, mustered Aug. 19, 1862, for three years. Wounded Sept. 17, 1862, at Antietam, Md. ; discharged Jan. 26, 1863, for disability from wounds. Mustered same Regiment and Co., Jan. 4, 1864, for three years ; transferred June 9, 1865, to 29th Regiment Infantry; discharged July 29, 1865, expiration of service.

PETERSON, PETER A. Private Co. I, 11th Regiment Infantry, mustered June 13, 1861, for three years; transferred March 1, 1864, to V. R. C.

PHALEN, JOHN. Private Co. A, 28th Regiment Infantry, mustered Dec. 30, 1861, for three years. Drowned, Aug. 14, 1862, in the Potomac River.

PHELAN, JOHN E. Corporal Co. I, 19th Regiment Infantry, mustered Aug. 28, 1861, for three years; transferred Sept. 12, 1863, to V. R. C.; discharged July 29, 1864. Mustered Aug. 18, 1864, for one year, private Co. K, 4th Regiment Heavy Artillery; discharged June 17, 1865, expiration of service.

PHELPS, EDWARD A. Private Co. A, 1st Battery Heavy Artillery, mustered Feb. 26, 1862, for three years; discharged Feb. 27, 1865, expiration of service.

PHELPS, WILLIAM J. Private Co. D, 24th Regiment Infantry, mustered Nov. 13, 1861, for three years; wounded Aug. 16, 1864, at Deep Run, Va.; discharged Nov. 3, 1864, expiration of service.

PHILLIPS, LIONEL D. Corporal Co. H, 1st Regiment Infantry, mustered May 23, 1861, for three years; appointed Sergeant, Nov. 1, 1862; appointed 1st Sergeant, April 1, 1863. Wounded and taken prisoner July 2, 1863, at Gettysburg, Pa.; paroled, exchanged Sept. 1, 1863; discharged May 25, 1864, expiration of service. Mustered private Co. F, 61st Regiment Infantry, Sept. 9, 1864, for one year on quota of Ashland; discharged Jan. 6, 1865, expiration of service. Commissioned 2d Lieut. 6th Regiment U. S. C. T., Dec. 1864.

PICKFORD, HENRY. Private Co. H, 43, Regiment Infantry, mustered Sept. 20, 1862, for nine months; discharged July 30, 1863, expiration of service.

PICKERING, EDWARD N. Sergeant Co. D, 35th Regiment Infantry, mustered Aug. 16, 1862, for three years; discharged July 25, 1864; promotion U. S. C. T.

PIERCE, CHARLES A. Musician Co. C, 35th Regiment Infantry, mustered Aug. 19, 1862, for three years; discharged May 15, 1863, incompetency.

PIERCE, EDWARD F. Sergeant Co. E, 4th Regiment Cavalry, mustered Jan. 27, 1864, for three years; discharged Nov. 14, 1865, expiration of service.

PIERCE, JOHN. Private Co. C, 3d Regiment Heavy Artillery, mustered Aug. 14, 1863, for three years; discharged Sept. 18, 1865, expiration of service.

PIERCE, WILLIAM H. Private Co. A, 44th Regiment Infantry, mustered Sept. 12, 1862, for nine months; discharged June 18, 1863, expiration of service.

PIERCY, HENRY A. Private Co. E, 30th Regiment Infantry, mustered Oct. 9, 1861, for three years. Died, Nov. 12, 1862, at New Orleans, La.

PILKINGTON, GEORGE. Private V. R. C., mustered May 28, 1864.

PINKHAM, THEODORE. Private Co. I, 44th Regiment Infantry, mustered Sept. 12, 1862, for nine months; discharged June 18, 1863, expiration of service.

PITMAN, JOHN T. Private Co. M, 1st Regiment Cavalry, mustered Sept. 25, 1861, for three years; discharged April 29, 1862, for disability. Mustered Corporal Co. H, 43d Regiment Infantry, Sept. 20, 1862, for nine months; discharged July 30, 1863, expiration of service.

PLUMMER, JOSEPH. Private Co. G, 40th Regiment Infantry, mustered Sept. 5, 1862, for three years. Killed, May 16, 1864, at Drury's Bluff, Va.

POMROY, GEORGE K. Private Co. B, 13th Regiment Infantry, mustered Aug. 1, 1861, for three years; discharged July 17, 1863. Commissioned 2d Lieut. 3d Regiment U. S. Infantry; wounded July 2, 1863, at Gettysburg, Pa.; commissioned 1st Lieut., Sept. 20, 1863; resigned and discharged in 1865.

POOK, WATERMAN. Private 11th Light Battery, mustered Dec. 22, 1864, for three years; discharged June 16, 1865, expiration of service.

POOLE, GEORGE W. Private 5th Light Battery, mustered Sept. 29, 1861, for three years; discharged Dec. 11, 1863, to re-enlist. Mustered Dec. 12, 1863, on quota of Malden for three years; discharged June 12, 1865, expiration of service.

POOR, JAMES W. Private 5th Regiment Infantry, mustered July 18, 1864, for 100 days; discharged Nov. 16, 1864, expiration of service.

POOST, CHARLES. Private Co. G, 2d Regiment Cavalry, mustered April 12, 1864, for three years; discharged June 25, 1864, for disability.

PORTER, JOHN. Unassigned recruit 2d Regiment Infantry, mustered June 10, 1864, for three years.

POWELL, JOHN S. Private Co. F, 44th Regiment Infantry, mustered Sept. 12, 1863, for nine months; discharged June 18, 1863, expiration of service.

POWERS, FREDERICK E. Private 4th Co. Unattached Infantry, mustered May 3, 1864, for ninety days ; discharged Aug. 6, 1864, expiration of service.

PRATT, GEORGE W. Private Co. H, 43d Regiment Infantry, mustered Sept 20, 1862, for nine months ; discharged July 30, 1863, expiration of service.

PRATT, JOSEPH T. Private Co. C, 35th Regiment Infantry, mustered Aug. 19, 1862, for three years. Killed, Sept. 17, 1862, at Antietam, Md.

PRATT, JOSHUA H. Private 1st Light Battery, mustered May 18, 1861, for three months ; discharged Aug. 2, 1861, expiration of service.

PRATT, OLIVER D. Private Co. L, 1st Regiment Cavalry, mustered Nov. 11, 1861, for three years; transferred to Co. L, 4th Regiment Cavalry ; discharged April 20, 1864, to re-enlist. Mustered Co. L, 4th Cavalry, April 21, 1864, for three years; discharged Nov. 14, 1865, expiration of service.

PRATT, REUBEN A. Private Co I, 2d Regiment Infantry, mustered May 25, 1861, for three years ; discharged Jan. 15, 1862, disability.

PRATT, THOMAS W. Private Co. K, 43d Regiment Infantry ; mustered Sept. 16, 1862, for nine months ; discharged July 30, 1863, expiration of service.

PRAY, WILLIAM W. Private V. R. C., mustered Aug. 10, 1864 ; discharged Nov. 21. 1865, order of War Department.

PRENCHARD, THOMAS. Musician, 1st Regiment Cavalry, mustered Jan. 6, 1862, for three years; discharged Aug. 16, 1862, order of War Department.

PRESBREY, ALFRED A. Corporal Co. K, 43d Regiment Infantry, mustered Sept. 16, 1862, for nine months; discharged July 30, 1863, expiration of service.

PRESCOTT, FRANCIS H. Private 4th Co. Unattached Infantry, mustered May 3, 1864, for ninety days; discharged June 27, 1864, disability.

PRINCE, JOSEPH B. Jr. 1st Lieutenant Co. A, 30th Regiment Infantry, mustered Feb. 20, 1862, for three years; promoted Capt., Nov. 26, 1863; discharged Nov. 7, 1864, expiration of service.

PROCTOR, GEORGE. Private Co. H, 50th Regiment Infantry, mustered Sept. 29, 1862, for nine months; discharged Aug. 24, 1863, expiration of service.

PROCTOR, JAMES H. Sergeant Co. H, 50th Regiment Infantry, mustered Sept. 29, 1862, for nine months; discharged Aug. 24, 1863, expiration of service.

PROUDFOOT, JOHN. Private V. R. C., mustered May 28, 1864.

PROUTY, ALBERT B. Private Co. F, 5th Regiment Infantry, mustered July 16, 1864, for 100 days; discharged Nov. 16, 1864, expiration of service.

PRUDEN, FRANCIS A. Private Co. E, 18th Regiment Infantry, mustered Aug. 24, 1861, for three years; discharged April 3, 1863, for disability.

PUTNAM, FREELAND. Private 4th Co. Unattached Infantry, mustered May 3, 1864, for ninety days; discharged Aug. 6, 1864, expiration of service. Mustered Sergeant Co. D, 1st Battery Frontier Cavalry on quota of Cambridge, Jan. 2, 1865. for one year; discharged June, 30, 1865.

PUTNAM, GEORGE W. R. Private Co. D, 5th Regiment Infantry, mustered July 18, 1864, for 100 days; discharged Nov. 16, 1864, expiration of service. Mustered Jan. 5, 1865, for one year, private Co. H, 61st Regiment Infantry on quota of Hingham; discharged July 16, 1865, expiration of service.

Q

QUINN, CHARLES. Private Co. H, 50th Regiment Infantry, mustered, Sept. 29, 1862, for nine months; discharged Aug. 24, 1863, expiration of service.

QUINN, JOHN. Private Co. K, 2d Regiment Infantry, mustered June 13, 1864, for three years; discharged July 26, 1865, expiration of service.

R

RACKLIFF, BENJAMIN. Private Co. H, 43d Regiment Infantry, mustered Sept. 20, 1862, for nine months ; discharged July 30, 1863, expiration of service.

RAND, DANIEL. Private Co. A, 1st Regiment Cavalry, mustered June 29, 1864, for three years ; discharged June 25, 1865, expiration of service.

RANDALL, JOSEPH. Private V. R. C., mustered June 22, 1864 ; discharged Nov. 14, 1865, order of War Department.

RANDALL, THOMAS. Private Co. G, 2d Regiment Heavy Artillery, mustered Dec. 7, 1863, for three years ; discharged July 11, 1865, expiration of service.

RANDOLPH, JAMES L. Private Co. E, 2nd Regiment Infantry, mustered June 10, 1864, for three years. Deserted Oct. 22, 1864.

RANSON, ROBERT C. Private Co. C, 35th Regiment Infantry, mustered Aug. 19, 1862, for three years. Wounded at South Mountain, Md., Sept. 14, 1863 ; discharged Jan. 26, 1863, for disability from wound.

RAVEN, JOHN. Unassigned recruit 2d Regiment Infantry, May 7, 1864, for three years ; transferred June 6, 1864, to Navy.

RAWLIN, THOMAS. Private Co. B, 28th Regiment Infantry, mustered April 5, 1864, for three years ; discharged June 15, 1865, for disability.

RAYMOND, ALFRED. Private Co. H, 50th Regiment Infantry, mustered Sept. 29. 1862, for nine months ; discharged Aug. 4, 1863, expiration of service.

READMAN, CARL. Private Co. H, 2d Regiment Cavalry, mustered May 13, 1864, for three years. Died of wounds Nov. 2, 1864, at Winchester, Va.

REED, GEORGE H. Private Co. C, 35th Regiment Infantry, mustered Aug. 19, 1862, for three years. Wounded Sept. 17, 1862, at Antietam, Md.; discharged Feb. 28, 1863, disability from wound.

REED, HARRISON T. Private Co. E, 44th Regiment Infantry, mustered Sept. 12, 1862, for nine months ; discharged June 18, 1863, expiration of service.

REED, FREEMAN H. Private Co. C, 5th Regiment Infantry, mustered May 1, 1861, for three months ; discharged July 31, 1861, expiration of service. Enlisted in U. S. Cavalry, April 26, 1862, transferred to 4th U. S. Artillery, May 1862. Died, Oct. 30, 1862, at Nashville, Tenn.

REED, LUTHER A. Private Co. H, 50th Regiment Infantry, mustered Sept. 29, 1862, for nine months ; discharged March 20, 1863, disability.

REGAN, THOMAS. Private Co. F, 2d Regiment Infantry, mustered May 24, 1864, for three years. Wounded at Averysboro', N. C., March 16, 1865 ; discharged July 14, 1865, expiration of service ; absent, wounded.

REICHART, EDWIN. Private V. R. C., mustered June 7, 1864.

REID, WILLIAM. Unassigned recuit 2d Regiment Infantry, mustered July 7, 1864, for three years.

REILEY, EDWIN J. Private V. R. C., mustered June 7, 1864.

REIMER, ROBERT. Private Co. A, 2d Regiment Cavalry, mustered April 15, 1864, for three years. Deserted, May 24, 1864.

REMICK, CLARK H. Corporal Co. C. 35th Regiment Infantry, mustered Aug. 19, 1862, for three years ; discharged Jan. 21, 1863, disability. Commissioned 1st Lieut. 35th U. S. C. T., May 1863 ; wounded Feb. 20, 1864, near Sanderson, Fla.

REMICK, FRANK C. Private 4th Co. Unattached Infantry, mustered May 3, 1864, for ninety days; discharged Aug. 6, 1864, expiration of service.

RIBERO, JOSEPH W. Private Co. G, 40th Regiment Infantry, mustered Sept. 5, 1862, for three years; transferred Jan. 1, 1864, to 117th Co. 2d Battalion V. R. C. ; discharged Aug. 13. 1865.

RICE, JOHN. Unassigned recruit 2d Regiment Cavalry, mustered Aug. 6, 1864, for three years.

RICHARDS, CHARLES H. Private Co. D, 5th Regiment Infantry, mustered July 18, 1864, for 100 days ; discharged Nov. 16, 1864, expiration of service.

RICHARDS, FRANCIS D. Private Co. C, 35th Regiment Infantry, mustered Aug. 19, 1862, for three years. Wounded Sept. 17, 1862, at Antietam, Md. ; discharged March 4, 1863, disability from wound.

RICHARDS, FRANKLIN. Private 12th Light Battery, mustered Nov. 20, 1862, for three years ; discharged July 25, 1865, expiration of service.

RICHARDS, GEORGE H. Hospital Steward U. S. A., mustered March 26, 1864.

RICKER, ALPHEUS E. Private 12th Light Battery, mustered Nov. 15, 1862, for three years ; discharged July 25, 1865, expiration of service.

RICKER, HORACE S. Sergeant Co. C, 35th Regiment Infantry, mustered Aug. 19, 1862, for three years; discharged Oct. 30, 1862, for disability. Died, Feb. 3, 1864.

RIDER, WILLIAM H. H. Private Co. A, 43d Regiment Infantry, mustered Oct. 11, 1862, for nine months; discharged July 30, 1863 expiration of service.

RIDLON, JOSEPH H. Private Co. C, 35th Regiment Infantry, mustered Aug. 19, 1862, for three years. Wounded Sept. 17, 1862, at Antietam, Md.; discharged Feb. 28, 1863, disability from wounds.

RIGBY, WILLIAM H. Private Co. G, 40th Regiment Infantry, mustered Sept. 5, 1862, for three years; discharged June 9, 1865, by order of War Department.

RILEY, JOHN. Private Co. K, 20th Regiment Infantry, mustered Aug. 26, 1861, for three years. Killed, Sept. 17. 1862, at Antietam, Md.

RILEY, PATRICK. Private Co. B, 28th Regiment Infantry, mustered Jan. 10, 1862, for three years; appointed Sergeant Sept. 1, 1862. Killed, Dec. 13, 1862, at Fredericksburg, Va.

RILEY, PETER. Private Co. E, 3d Regiment Heavy Artillery, mustered Aug. 27, 1863, for three years; discharged Sept. 18, 1865, expiration of service.

RING, CHARLES T. Private Co. G, 40th Regiment Infantry, mustered Sept. 5, 1862, for three years. Wounded June 3, 1864, Cold Harbor, Va.; appointed Corporal, Sept. 1, 1864; discharged June 16, 1865, expiration of service.

RIPLEY, ROBERT. Private Co. H, 50th Regiment Infantry. mustered Sept. 29, 1862, for nine months; discharged Aug. 4, 1863, expiration of service.

ROACH, THOMAS. 3d U. S. Artillery, mustered March 8, 1864.

ROBERTS, ALBERT H. Private 4th Co. Unattached Infantry, mustered May 3, 1864, for ninety days; discharged Aug. 6, 1864, expiration of service.

ROBBINS, CHARLES T. 2d Lieutenant 3d Regiment Heavy Artillery, mustered Sept. 9, 1863, for three years ; promoted and mustered Sept. 2, 1864, 1st Lieutenant ; discharged Sept. 18, 1865, expiration of service. Mustered private Co. D, 13th Regiment Infantry, July 29, 1861, for three years on quota of Boston. Wounded Aug. 28, 1862, at Throughfare Gap, Va.; discharged Oct. 3, 1862, disability from wound.

ROBBINS, JOHN. General service U. S. A., mustered March 19, 1864.

ROBERTS, GEORGE T. Private 11th Light Battery, mustered Jan. 2, 1864, for three years. Wounded June 19, 1864, near Petersburg, Va.; discharged March 3, 1865, disability from wound.

ROBERTS, HORATIO. 1st Sergeant Co. H, 1st Regiment Infantry, mustered May 23, 1861, for three years ; discharged Oct. 12, 1861, for promotion. Commissioned 2d Lieutenant, Oct. 12, 1861 ; commissioned 1st Lieutenant, July 24, 1862. Wounded Aug. 29, 1862, near Manassas, Va., discharged; Feb. 5, 1864, resigned. Commissioned 2d Lieutenant V. R. C., Jan. 29th, 1864 ; discharged June 30, 1866.

ROBERTS, MYRON C. Private Co. H, 50th Regiment Infantry, mustered Sept. 29, 1862 for nine months ; discharged Aug. 24, 1863, expiration of service.

ROBERTS, SAMUEL. Private Co. I, 61st Regiment Infantry, mustered Dec. 19, 1864, for one year; discharged July 16, 1865, expiration of service.

ROBERTS, THOMAS. Private Co. B, 2d Regiment Infantry, mustered July 7, 1864, for three years. Deserted, Aug. 13, 1864, at Atlanta, Ga.

ROBERTS, WILLIAM. Unassigned recurit 20th Regiment Infantry, mustered April 13, 1864, for three years; transferred May 17, 1864, to Navy.

ROBERTS, WILLIAM. Private V. R. C., mustered July 23, 1864.

ROBINSON, CHARLES. Unassigned recruit 2d Regiment Infantry, mustered July 22, 1861, for three years.

ROBINSON, CHARLES G. Private Co. F, 24th Regiment Infantry, mustered Oct. 22, 1861, for three years; appointed Corporal, June 15, 1862 ; discharged Oct. 22, 1864, expiration of service.

ROBINSON, CURTIS B. Private Co. I, 3d Regiment Cavalry, mustered Dec. 2, 1863, for three years ; discharged Aug. 19, 1864, for disability.

ROBINSON, WILLIAM. Unassigned recurit 28th Regiment Infantry, mustered April 15, 1864, for three years.

RODGERS, JAMES. Unassigned recruit 3d Regiment Cavalry, mustered March 22, 1864, for three years. Deserted, May 1864.

RODGERS, JAMES. Unassigned recruit 28th Regiment Infantry, mustered May 10, 1863, for three years.

ROGERS, EDWARD H. Private Co. H, 43d Regiment Infantry, mustered Sept. 20, 1862, for nine months; discharged July 30, 1863, expiration of service.

ROGERS, FRANK H. Private Co. H, 1st Regiment Infantry, mustered Sept. 24, 1861, for three years; discharged April 29, 1864, for disability.

ROGERS, FREDERICK E. Private Co. D, 13th Regiment Infantry, mustered March 17, 1862, for three years; discharged Jan. 4, 1864, to re-enlist. Mustered Jan. 5, 1864, for three years; discharged Feb. 4, 1864, for promotion.· Mustered 2d Lieutenant 54th Regiment Infantry, Feb. 4, 1864; resigned and discharged June 12, 1865.

ROGERS, JAMES C. Captain Co. H, 48th Regiment Infantry, mustered Sept. 25, 1862, for nine months; discharged Sept. 3, 1863, expiration of service.

ROGERS, SAMUEL D.. Private Co. K, 4th Regiment Heavy Artillery, mustered Aug. 18, 1864, for one year; discharged June 17, 1865, expiration of service.

ROSS, CHARLES H. Private Co. C, 35th Regiment Infantry, mustered Aug. 19, 1862, for three years; discharged June 9, 1865, expiration of service.

ROWE, EDWARD F. 1st Sergeant Co. C, 13th Regiment Infantry, mustered July 16, 1861, for three years; discharged May 18, 1862; transferred to Navy, April 15, 1862.

ROWELL, HARRIFF. Private Co. B, 1st Regiment Infantry, mustered May 23, 1861, for three years; discharged July 31, 1861, disability.

RUSSELL, EDWARD K. 1st Sergeant 2d Light Battery, mustered July 31, 1861, for three years; discharged Oct. 22, 1862, for promotion. Mustered 2d Lieutenant, Oct. 22, 1862; discharged Oct. 3, 1863, for promotion. Mustered Oct. 3, 1863, 1st Lieutenant 6th Light Battery, for three years; discharged Dec. 30, 1864, for promotion. Mustered Dec. 30, 1864, Capt. 6th Light Battery; discharged Aug. 7, 1865, expiration of service.

RUSSELL, WILLIAM O. Saddler, Co. C, 1st Regiment Cavalry, mustered Jan. 1, 1864, for three years; discharged June 30, 1865, expiration of service. Served on quota of Boston, Sept. 19, 1861, to Dec. 31, 1863.

RYAN, JOHN. Unassigned recruit 2d Regiment Infantry, mustered July 22, 1864, for three years.

RYAN, JOHN. Private Co. E, 2d Regiment Cavalry, mustered Nov. 30, 1864, for three years; discharged July 20, 1865, expiration of service.

RYAN, JOHN H. Private Co. F, 2d Regiment Infantry, mustered June 11, 1864, for three years. Deserted, Aug. 9, 1864.

S

SALE, JOHN. Private Co. H, 50th Regiment Infantry, mustered Sept. 29, 1862, for nine months; discharged Aug. 24, 1863, expiration of service.

SALE, JOHN A. Private Co. A, 3d Regiment Cavalry, mustered private Jan. 4, 1864, for three years; discharged Sept. 28, 1865, expiration of service.

SAMPSON, EDEN. Private Co. H, 50th Regiment Infantry, mustered Sept. 29, 1862, for nine months; discharged Aug. 24, 1863, expiration of service.

SAMPSON, HENRY G. Private V. R. C., mustered June 20, 1864.

SAMUELS, JOSEPH. Private Co. C, 32d Regiment Infantry, mustered Oct. 31, 1861, for three years ; discharged Jan. 4, 1863, for disability. Mustered Sergeant Co. K, 4th Regiment Heavy Artillery, Aug. 18, 1864, for one year ; discharged June 17, 1865, expiration of service.

SAMUELS, SOLOMON D. Private 8th Light Battery, mustered May 30, 1862, for six months; discharged Nov. 29, 1862, expiration of service. Re-enlisted private Co. K, 4th Regiment Heavy Artillery, Aug. 18, 1864, for one year ; discharged June 17, 1865, expiration of service.

SANBORN, ALMON. Corporal Co. H, 50th Regiment Infantry, mustered Sept. 29, 1862, for nine months ; discharged Aug. 24, 1863, expiration of service.

SANBORN, CHARLES W. H. Private 14th Light Battery, mustered March 29, 1864, for three years; discharged June 15, 1865, expiration of service.

SANBORN, FRANK. Private 4th Co. Unattached Infantry, mustered May 3, 1864, for ninety days ; discharged Aug. 6, 1864, expiration of service.

SANBORN, FREDERICK G. Private Co. D, 1st Battalion Frontier Cavalry, mustered Jan. 2, 1865, for one year; discharged March 21, 1865, to re-enlist Hospital Steward U. S. A.

SANDS, GEORGE H. Private Co. H, 1st Regiment Infantry, mustered Oct. 3, 1861, for three years ; discharged Nov. 5, 1862, for disability, Mustered Dec. 5, 1863, private Co. I, 1st Regiment Cavalry for three years ; discharged Nov. 18, 1864 ; promoted 1st Lieut. 1st Regiment U. S. C. T. ; date of commission Oct. 12, 1864.

SARGENT, CHRISTOPHER. Private Co. G, 40th Regiment Infantry mustered Sept. 5, 1862, for three years ; appointed Corporal, Jan. 1, 1865 ; discharged June 16, 1865, expiration of service.

SARINGER, CHARLES E. Private V. R. C., mustered June 20, 1864.

SAUNDERS, ALONZO. Wagoner, Co. C, 35th Regiment Infantry, mustered Aug, 19, 1862, for three years ; discharged Nov. 17, 1862, disability.

SAUNDERS, JOHN. Private 6th Light Battery, mustered Dec. 24, 1864, for three years ; discharged Aug. 7. 1865, expiration of service.

SAUNDERS, JOHN H. Private Co. C, 1st Battalion Heavy Artillery, mustered April 22. 1863, for three years ; discharged Oct. 20, 1865, expiration of service.

SAUNDERS, ROBERT A. 2d Lieutenant Co. H, 1st Regiment Infantry, mustered May 25, 1861, for three years ; Sept. 16, 1861, resigned. Mustered Sept. 29, 1862, for nine months, 1st Sergeant Co. H, 50th Regiment Infantry ; discharged Aug. 24, 1863, expiration of service. Mustered Nov. 27, 1863, Veterinary Surgeon 3d Regiment Cavalry ; discharged July 25, 1865. expiration of service.

158

SAWTELLE, ZACHARIAH. Private Co. H, 50th Regiment,
Infantry, mustered Sept. 29, 1862, for nine months ; discharged Aug. 24, 1863, expiration of service.

SAWYER, WILLIAM. Private Co. F, 4th Regiment Cavalry,
mustered Jan. 27, 1864, for three years ; wounded. Died,
June 27, 1864, at Washington, D. C.

SCHATTONULLER, IGNATZ. Private Co. D, 2d Regiment
Infantry, mustered July 6, 1864, for three years ; discharged July 26, 1865, expiration of service.

SCHILLING, WILLIAM. Private Co. E, 43d Regiment Infantry, mustered Oct. 1, 1862, for nine months ; discharged
July 30, 1863, expiration of service.

SCHMIDT, PETER. Private 4th Light Battery, mustered
Feb. 6, 1864, for three years. Deserted, Feb. 5, 1865, at
Kennorville, La. .

SCHOLES, HENRY. Private Co. A, 28th Regiment Infantry,
mustered April 16, 1864, for three years; discharged June
27, 1865, expiration of service.

SCHWENDY, FRITZ. Unassigned recruit 31st Regiment Infantry, mustered April 15, 1864, for three years ; discharged Sept. 9, 1865.

SCOTT, BENJAMIN F. Private Co. H, 2d Regiment Cavalry, mustered May 12, 1864, for three years ; discharged
July 20, 1865, expiration of service.

SCOTT, FRANK J. Private Co. H, 43d Regiment Infantry,
mustered Sept. 20, 1862, for nine months ; discharged
July 30, 1863, expiration of service. Re-entered Medical
Department, Sept. 1864.

SCOTT, SAMUEL. Unassigned recruit 20th Regiment, mustered March 18, 1864, for three years ; transferred to
Navy, April 23, 1864.

SCOTT, WALTER. Unassigned recruit 2d Regiment Infantry, mustered May 13, 1864, for three years.

SEELEY, SAMUEL W. Private Co. I, 1st Regiment Cavalry, mustered Dec. 5, 1863, for three years; discharged June 29, 1865, expiration of service.

SEELEY, WILLIAM D. Corporal 4th Co. Unattached Infantry, mustered May 3, 1864 for ninety days; discharged Aug. 6, 1864, expiration of service.

SEIBERT, GOTTLIEB. Private Co. G, 2d Regiment Cavalry, mustered May 10, 1864, for three years; discharged July 20, 1865, expiration of service; absent, sick.

SEIP, JACOB. Unassigned recruit 20th Regiment Infantry, mustered April 12, 1864, for three years.

SELDON, THOMAS. Private Co. F, 55th Regiment Infantry, mustered June 26, 1863, for three years; discharged Aug. 29, 1865, expiration of service.

SHAEFFER, FREDERICK. Private Co. K, 2d Regiment Infantry, mustered May 25, 1861, for three years. Wounded, Aug. 9, 1862, at Cedar Mountain, Va.; discharged Oct. 2, 1862, disability from wound.

SHANLEY, PATRICK. Private Co. G, 61st Regiment Infantry, mustered Nov. 11, 1864, for one year; discharged July 16, 1865, expiration of service.

SHARKEY, THOMAS. Private Co. F, 16th Regiment Infantry, mustered July 12, 1861, for three years. Deserted, Aug. 17, 1861. Re-enlisted private Co. D, 1st Regiment D. C., Sept. 28, 1861; discharged Sept. 28, 1864. Re-enlisted private Co. F, 61st Regiment Infantry, Oct. 18, 1864, on quota of Stoughton; discharged July 16, 1865, expiration of service.

SHATTUCK, LAFAYETTE. U. S. Artillery, mustered March 17, 1864; discharged April 4, 1865.

SHAW, GEORGE T. Private 4th Co. Unattached Infantry, mustered May 3, 1864, for ninety days ; discharged Aug. 6, 1864, expiration of service.

SHAW, J. W. W. General service U. S. A., mustered March 17, 1864.

SHAW, ROBERT. Private Co. K, 5th Regiment Cavalry, mustered April 12, 1864, for three years ; discharged June 21, 1865, expiration of service.

SHEA, CORNEILLE. Private Co. I, 2d Regiment Cavalry, mustered April 8, 1864, for three years. Died, Jan. 1865, at Danville, Va.

SHEEHAN, PATRICK. Private Co. C, 28th Regiment Infantry, mustered March 15, 1864, for three years; discharged June 19, 1865, expiration of service.

SHEEHAN, WILLIAM. Corporal Co. H, 48th Regiment Infantry, mustered Sept. 25, 1862, for nine months; discharged Sept. 3, 1863, expiration of service.

SHEEK, FRANCIS. Private Co. K, 30th Regiment Infantry, mustered April 13, 1864, for three years. Died, Aug. 12, 1864, at Washington, D. C.

SHELDON, AURELUS B. C. Private Co. E, 2d Regiment Cavalry, mustered March 17, 1863, for three years ; transferred March 4, 1864, to Navy.

SHELDON, JOSEPH W. Private Co. E, 2nd Regiment Cavalry, mustered March 17, 1863, for three years ; discharged July 20, 1865, expiration of service.

SHELHAMMER, JOHN. Private Co. C, 33d Regiment, Infantry, mustered Aug. 6, 1862, for three years. Wounded July 2, 1863, at Gettysburg, Pa. ; transferred Aug. 10, 1864, to V. R. C. ; discharged July 12, 1865.

SHEPPARD, EUGENE. Private Co. E, 2d Regiment Infantry, mustered May 7, 1864, for three years. Died Jan. 1865, at Nashville, Tenn.

SHERMAN, CHARLES F. Private Co. K, 50th Regiment Infantry, mustered Sept. 19, 1862, for nine months ; discharged Aug. 24, 1863, expiration of service.

SHIELDS, WILL. J. General Service U. S. A., March 17, 1864.

SHIPMAN, WILLIAM N. Private Co. H, 50th Regiment Infantry, mustered Sept. 29, 1862, for nine months, discharged Aug. 24, 1863, expiration of service.

SIBLEY, NELSON H. Private Co. G, 40th Regiment Infantry, mustered Sept. 5, 1862, for three years; appointed Corporal Sept. 1, 1863; appointed Sergeant April 9, 1864 ; wounded June 3, 1864, at Cold Harbor, Va.; discharged Dec. 31, 1864, disability from wound.

SILVER, NATHAN B. Private Co. E, 43d Regiment Infantry, mustered Oct. 1, 1862, for nine months; discharged June 2, 1863, expiration of service.

SIMMONS, ENOCH F. Corporal Co. A, 43d Regiment Infantry, mustered Oct. 11, 1862, for nine months; discharged July 30, 1863, expiration of service.

SIMMONS, WILLIAM A. Corporal Co. F, 44th Regiment Infantry, mustered Sept. 12, 1862, for nine months ; discharged June 18, 1863, expiration of service.

SIMONDS, EABUD. Private Co. D, 17th Regiment Infantry, mustered Feb. 10, 1862, for three years; taken prisoner, Feb. 1, 1864, near Newbern, N. C. Died, July 10, 1864, at Andersonville, Ga.

SIMPSON, ALPHONSO. Private Co. F, 44th Regiment Infantry, mustered Sept. 12, 1862, for nine months; discharged June 18, 1863, expiration of service.

SINCLAIR, JOHN G. Private Co. H, 43d Regiment Infantry, mustered Sept. 20, 1862, for nine months; discharged July 30, 1863, expiration of service.

SMALL, WILLIAM H. Private Co. G, 40th Regiment Infantry, mustered Sept. 5, 1862, for three years; discharged June 16, 1865, expiration of service.

SMIDT, JOHN. Unassigned recruit 2d Regiment Cavalry, mustered May 12, 1864, for three years.

SMIDT, PETER. Private Co. K, 2d Regiment Infantry, mustered July 23, 1864, for three years; discharged July 14, 1865, expiration of service, in Hospital since Aug. 10, 1864.

SMILIE, JOHN H. Private V. R. C., mustered Dec. 14, 1864.

SMITH, CHANDLER P. Unassigned recruit 1st Regiment Infantry; no further record in 1st Regiment. Mustered private Co. G, 40th Regiment Infantry, Sept, 5, 1862, for three years; appointed Corporal, June 4, 1863; appointed Sergeant, Nov. 1, 1864; discharged June 16, 1865, expiration of service.

SMITH, CHARLES O. C. Private Co. G, 40th Regiment Infantry, mustered Sept. 5, 1862, for three years; appointed Corporal, Sept. 16, 1862. Died, April 19, 1863, at Washington, D. C.

SMITH, ELIJAH R. Private Co. H, 50th Regiment Infantry, mustered Sept. 29, 1862, for nine months; discharged Aug. 24, 1863, expiration of service.

SMITH, GEORGE H. Corporal Co. H, 42d Regiment Infantry, mustered Sept. 24, 1862, for nine months; discharged Aug. 20, 1863, expiration of service.

SMITH, JAMES. Private Co. B, 2d Regiment Infantry, mustered May 10, 1864, for three years; discharged July 14, 1865, expiration of service.

SMITH, JAMES. Private Co. A, 2d Regiment Infantry, mustered June 11, 1864, for three years.

SMITH, JOHN. Private Co. G, 4th Regiment Cavalry, mustered Jan. 27, 1864, for three years. Deserted, Aug. 20, 1865.

SMITH, JOHN L. General service U. S. A., mustered March 28, 1864.

SMITH, PATRICK. Unassigned recruit 2d Regiment Infantry, mustered Aug. 18, 1864, for three years.

SMITH, THOMAS. Private Co. F, 2d Regiment Cavalry, mustered Aug. 17, 1864, for three years; discharged July 20, 1865, expiration of service.

SMITH, THOMAS. Unassigned recruit 2d Regiment Cavalry, mustered May 25, 1864, for three years; transferred June 26, 1864, to Navy.

SMITH, WILLIAM A. Private Co. H, 1st Regiment Infantry, mustered May 23, 1861, for three years on quota of Boston; appointed Corporal, Oct. 1, 1861; discharged Aug. 18, 1862, for promotion. Commissioned Aug. 18, 1862, 2d Lieutenant Co. G, 40th Regiment Infantry; promoted 1st Lieut., Nov. 1362; promoted Capt. Feb. 26, 1863. Wounded May 16, 1864, at Drury's Bluff, Va.; discharged Sept. 6, 1864, disability from wound.

SMITH, WILLIAM D. Private Co. H, 1st Regiment Infantry, mustered May 23, 1861, for three years. Killed April 26, 1862, at Yorktown, Va.

SMITH, WILLIAM L. Private Co. G, 61st Regiment Infantry, mustered Nov. 19, 1864, for one year ; discharged July 16, 1865, expiration of service.

SNOW, GEORGE W. Assistant Surgeon 28th Regiment Infantry, mustered Sept. 20, 1861 ; discharged March 13, 1863, for promotion. Mustered, March 13, 1863, Surgeon 35th Regiment Infantry; discharged June 9, 1863, expiration of service.

SNOW, ROBERT F. Private Co. E, 16th Regiment Infantry, mustered July 12, 1861, for three years. Killed, Aug. 29, 1862, near Manassas, Va.

SNOW, WILLIAM A. 1st Sergeant Co. L, 3d Regiment Cavalry, mustered Nov. 25, 1861, for three years; discharged March 4, 1863, for promotion. Commissioned 2d Lieut. 1st Regiment La. Cavalry, March 1, 1863 ; commissioned 1st Lieutenant, Aug. 1863.

SOULE, THOMAS H. Private 4th Co. Unattached Infantry, mustered May 3, 1864, for ninety days ; discharged Aug. 6, 1864, expiration of service.

SOUTHER, EDWARD E. Corporal 11th Light Battery, mustered Jan. 2, 1864, for three years ; appointed Sergt., July 9, 1864. Wounded, July 17, 1864, near Petersburg, Va. ; appointed 1st Sergt., Oct. 15, 1864; discharged and commissioned 2d Lieut., Jan. 15, 1865 ; discharged June 16, 1865, expiration of service.

SOUTHER, WILLIAM R. Private Co. H, 1st Regiment Infantry, mustered Sept. 12, 1861, for three years ; discharged July 24, 1862, for disability.

SPELLMAN, JOHN. Private 6th Light Battery, mustered Dec. 20, 1864, for three years; discharged Aug. 7, 1865, expiration of service.

SPOONER, JOHN F. Private Co. H, 43d Regiment Infantry, mustered Sept. 20, 1862, for nine months; discharged July 30, 1863, expiration of service. Died, July 22, 1867, in Texas.

SPOONER, JOSEPH W. Private Co. H, 1st Regiment Infantry, mustered May 23, 1861, for three years. Wounded April 26, 1862, at Yorktown, Va.; discharged May 25, 1864, expiration of service. Died, Aug. 9, 1876, at Everett, Mass.

SPRIGGS, ISAIAH. Private Co. A, 54th Regiment Infantry, mustered March 30, 1863, for three years; discharged Aug. 20, 1865, expiration of service.

STAFFORD, FRANK. Private Co. F, 56th Regiment Infantry, mustered Jan. 12, 1864, for three years; taken prisoner. Died, Nov. 16, 1864, at Salisbury, N. C.

STANDISH, BEN. Unassigned recruit 19th Regiment Infantry, mustered April 9, 1864, for three years.

STANWOOD, WILLIAM E. Private Co. H, 43d Regiment Infantry, mustered Sept. 20, 1862, for nine months; discharged July 30, 1863, expiration of service.

STEARNS, ISAAC R. Private Co. C, 44th Regiment Infantry, mustered Sept. 12, 1862, for nine months; discharged June 18, 1863, expiration of service.

STEARNS, THEODORE R. General service U. S. A., mustered March 1, 1864.

STEELE, ROBERT. Private Co. C, 35th Regiment Infantry, mustered Aug. 19, 1862, for three years; taken prisoner May 24, 1864, at North Anna River, Va.; exchanged, and discharged June 9, 1865, expiration of service.

STEERE, ALPHONSO D. Private Co. B, 2d Regiment Heavy Artillery, mustered Aug. 18 1864, for three years; discharged June 12, 1865, expiration of service.

STETSON, ALBUS R. Private Co. C, 35th Regiment Infantry, mustered Aug. 19, 1862, for three years; discharged June 9, 1865, expiration of service.

STEVENS, GEORGE H. Private Co. G, 18th Regiment Infantry, mustered Aug. 24, 1861, for three years; appointed Corporal, Sept. 21, 1862. Wounded Dec. 13, 1862, at Fredericksburg, Va.; transferred Sept. 1, 1863, to 2d Battalion V. R. C.; discharged Aug. 24, 1864, expiration of service.

STEVENS, GEORGE W. Private Co. E, 47th Regiment Infantry, mustered Oct. 8, 1862, for nine months; discharged Sept. 1, 1863, expiration of service.

STEVENS, NICHOLAS. Private Co. B, 15th Regiment Infantry, mustered April 8, 1864, for three years; transferred July 27, 1864, to 20th Regiment Infantry Co. E; discharged July 16, 1865, expiration of service.

STEVENS, JOHN A. Private Co. H, 2d Regiment Heavy Artillery, mustered Aug. 20, 1864, for three years; discharged Sept. 3, 1865, expiration of service.

STEWART, CHARLES. Private Co. H, 42d Regiment Infantry, mustered Sept. 24, 1862, for nine months. Deserted, Oct. 1, 1864, at Readville, Mass.

STEWART, GEORGE. Unassigned recruit 28th Regiment Infantry, mustered May 7, 1864, for three years.

STODDARD, GEORGE L. Private Co. H, 1st Regiment Infantry, mustered May 23, 1861, for three years; wounded at Yorktown, Va., April 26, 1862. Deserted, Sept. 1862. Served in the Navy from Dec. 1862, to March 1864.

STONE, BENJAMIN. Private Co. H, 42d Regiment Infantry, mustered Sept. 24, 1862, for nine months; discharged Aug. 20, 1863, expiration of service.

STONE, BENJAMIN F. Corporal Co. K, 43d Regiment Infantry, mustered Sept. 16, 1862, for nine months; discharged July 30, 1863, expiration of service.

STONE, CHARLES O. Private Co. F, 29th Regiment Infantry, mustered Dec. 14, 1861, for three years; discharged Jan. 1, 1864, to re-enlist; mustered Jan. 2, 1864 for three years; taken prisoner near Petersburg, Va., March 25, 1865; discharged May 26, 1865, expiration of service.

STONE, GEORGE F. Private Co. D, 22d Regiment Infantry, mustered Sept. 6, 1861, for three years; taken prisoner June 28, 1862, near Richmond, Va.; exchanged Aug. 6, 1862; discharged Oct. 17, 1864, expiration of service.

STONE, GEORGE H. Private Co. H, 1st Regiment Infantry, mustered May 23, 1861, for three years. Wounded, April 26, 1862, at Yorktown, Va.; discharged Oct. 12, 1862, disability from wound. Died, Feb. 16, 1870, at Chelsea.

STONE, SAMUEL P. Private Co. H, 50th Regiment Infantry, mustered Sept. 29, 1862, for nine months; discharged Aug. 24, 1863, expiration of service.

STONE, WILLIAM P. Private Co. C, 35th Regiment Infantry, mustered Aug. 19, 1862, for three years. Wounded and taken prisoner Aug. 19, 1864, near Petersburg, Va.; exchanged, and discharged June 30, 1865, expiration of service. .

STRATTON, JOSEPH JR. Private Co. K, 17th Regiment
Infantry, mustered July 22, 1861, for three years, discharged June 23, 1863, for disability.

STRAW, JEFFERSON H. Private 4th Co. Unattached Infantry, mustered May 3, 1864, for ninety days ; discharged
Aug. 6, 1864, expiration of service.

STREET, FREDERICK. Private 6th Light Battery, mustered
Dec. 2, 1864, for three years ; discharged July 14, 1865,
expiration of service.

STURKES, CHARLES. Private Co. C, 35th Regiment Infantry, mustered Aug. 19, 1862, for three years ; discharged
Jan. 15, 1863, for disability.

SULLIVAN, DANIEL. Private 18th Co. Unattached Infantry, mustered Aug. 6, 1864, for 100 days ; discharged
Nov. 14, 1864, expiration of service.

SULLIVAN, PATRICK. Private Co. I, 33d Regiment, mustered, Aug. 12, 1864, for three years.

SUMMERS, JAMES. Corporal Co. L, 3d Regiment Cavalry,
mustered March 17, 1864, for three years. Died, Feb.
14, 1865.

SUMMERS, JOSEPH B. General service U. S. A., mustered
March 17, 1864.

SWAIN, ROBERT. Private Co. B, 28th Regiment Infantry,
mustered Dec, 13, 1861, for three years. Wounded Aug.
24, 1862, near Manassas, Va. ; discharged Nov. 28, 1862,
disability from wound. Re-enlisted on quota of Gloucester, in 15th Regiment Infantry, Aug. 4, 1863 ; transferred July 27, 1864, to 20th Regiment Infantry. Deserted, May 23, 1865.

SWAIN, WILLIAM. Private Co. C, 2d Regiment Heavy Artillery, mustered Aug. 4, 1863, for three years. Deserted, Aug. 22, 1863.

SWAIN, WILLIAM. Private Co. B, 48th Regiment Infantry, mustered Oct. 10, 1862, for nine months; discharged Dec. 13, 1862, disability.

SWAIN, WILLIAM. Corporal Co. C, 28th Regiment Infantry, mustered Jan. 29, 1864, for three years; appointed Sergeant in 1865; discharged June 17, 1865, expiration of service.

SWAN, WILLIAM R. Captain Co. C, 5th Regiment Infantry, mustered May 1, 1861, for three months; discharged July 31, 1861, expiration of service. Mustered Dec. 13, 1861, Capt. Co. K, 13th Regiment Maine Infantry; discharged March 9, 1864, disability from fever.

SWAN, LOUIS W. Sergeant 2d Light Battery, mustered July 1, 1861, for three years; discharged Feb. 15, 1864, for re-enlistment. Mustered Feb. 15, 1864, 1st Sergeant for three years; discharged Dec. 1, 1864 for promotion. Mustered Dec. 1, 1864, 2d Lieutenant; discharged Aug. 11, 1865, expiration of service.

SWEENEY, FRANK. Private Co. C, 35th Regiment Infantry, mustered Aug. 19, 1862, for three years; taken prisoner May 24, 1864, at North Anna River; paroled Nov. 25, 1864; discharged June 9, 1865, expiration of service.

SWEENEY, JAMES. Private Co. C, 35th Regiment Infantry, mustered Feb, 22, 1863, for three years. Wounded, July 30, 1864, near Petersburg, Va.; wounded Aug. 19, 1864, near Weldon, R. R., Va.; transferred June 9, 1865, to Co. C, 29th Regiment Infantry; discharged June 27, 1865, expiration of service.

SWEENEY, JAMES. Unassigned recruit 2d Regiment Infantry, mustered May 13, 1864, for three years.

SWEENEY, NATHANIEL I. Private Co. C, 25th Regiment Infantry, mustered Aug. 19, 1862, for three years. Killed, Sept. 17, 1862, at Antietam, Md.

SWEETSER, JOHN E. Unassigned recruit 2d Regiment Cavalry, mustered Aug. 12, 1864, for three years.

SWEET, CYRUS E. Private Co. H, 43d Regiment Infantry, mustered Sept. 20, 1862, for nine months; discharged · March 3, 1863, disability. Mustered private 4th Co. Unattached Infantry, May 3, 1864, for ninety days; discharged Aug. 6, 1864, expiration of service.

SWEET, WILLIAM. Private 12th Light Battery, mustered Nov. 20, 1862, for three years; discharged July 25, 1865, expiration of service.

SWEETSER, THOMAS A. Private Co. I, 19th Regiment Infantry, mustered July 26, 1861, for three years. Wounded Sept. 17, 1862, at Antietam, Md.; discharged, March 19, 1863, disability from wound.

SWIFT, EDWARD, General service U. S. A., mustered March 28, 1864.

SWORDS, EDWARD K. Private Co. H, 43d Regiment Infantry, mustered Sept. 20, 1862, for nine months; discharged July 30, 1863, expiration of service.

SYMONDS, FREDERICK W. Private 4th Co. Unattached Infantry, mustered May 3, 1864, for ninety days; discharged Aug. 6, 1864, expiration of service. Died, Sept. 27, 1876, at Chelsea.

T

TABER, BARTHOLOMEW. Private Co. C. 35th Regiment Infantry, mustered Jan. 3, 1864, for three years ; taken prisoner, May 23, 1864. Died, Aug. 1864, at Andersonville, Ga.

TAYLOR, THOMAS. Private Co. G, 2d Regiment Cavalry, mustered June 10, 1864, for three years. Died, June 26, 1864, at Andersonville, Ga.

TEAGUE, FRANCIS. Private Co. G, 2d Regiment Cavalry, mustered March, 1864, for three years ; discharged July 20, 1865, expiration of service.

TENNEY, LYMAN B. Private 4th Co. Unattached Infantry, mustered May 3, 1864, for ninety days ; discharged Aug. 6, 1864, expiration of service.

TEVLIN, MICHAEL. Private Co. D, 2d Regiment Cavalry, mustered Aug. 13, 1864, for three years ; discharged June 20, 1865, expiration of service.

TEWKSBURY, MARTIN G. Private Co. H, 1st Regiment Infantry, mustered Oct. 3, 1861, for three years. Wounded May 5, 1862, at Williamsburg, Va. ; musket stock shattered June 25, 1862, at Fair Oaks, Va. ; wounded Aug. 29, 1862, near Manassas, Va. ; discharged May 27, 1863, disability from wounds.

THAYER, EDWIN L. Private Co. G, 1st Regiment Infantry, mustered May 23, 1861, for three years ; appointed Corporal, Dec. 1, 1862 : taken prisoner May 3, 1863, at Chancellorsville, Va. ; exchanged Sept. 1, 1863 ; appointed Sergeant, Jan. 1, 1864 ; discharged May 25, 1864, expiration of service.

THAYER, JOSEPH W. Private Co. H, 12th Regiment Infantry, mustered June 26, 1861. for three years. Wounded Dec. 13, 1862, at Fredericksburg, Va. ; wounded July 1, 1863, at Gettysburg, Pa. ; transferred Jan. 16, 1864, to 117th Co. 2d Battalion V. R. C. ; discharged June 27, 1864, expiration of service.

THAYER, WALTER B. Private 8th Light Battery, mustered May 30, 1862, for six months ; discharged Nov. 29, 1862, expiration of service.

THEIS, ERNST. Private Co. E, 2d Regiment Infantry, mustered Dec. 7, 1864, for three years. Deserted.

THOMAS, HENRY A. Private Co. G, 40th Regiment Infantry, mustered Sept. 5, 1862, for three years ; appointed Corporal, Jan. 1, 1865 ; discharged June 16. 1865, expiration of service.

THOMAS, JOHN. Unassigned recruit 2d Regiment Infantry, mustered July 17, 1864, for three years.

THOMAS, WILLIAM. Private Co. G, 3d Regiment Cavalry, mustered Nov. 1, 1862, for three years. Deserted, Nov. 1, 1862.

THOMBS, THOMAS. Private Co. H, 1st Regiment Infantry, mustered May 23, 1861, for three years. Wounded, June 30, 1862. at White Oak Swamp, Va. ; discharged May 25, 1864, expiration of service. Died, March 18, 1866, at Chelsea.

THOMPSON, CHARLES. Private V. R. C.

THOMPSON, HENRY. Private Co. K, 2d Regiment Cavalry, mustered June 9, 1864, for three years. Deserted. Oct. 19, 1864.

THOMPSON, HENRY F. Private Co. H, 43d Regiment Infantry, mustered Sept. 20, 1862, for nine months; discharged July 30, 1863, expiration of service.

THOMPSON, JOHN. Unassigned recruit 2d Regiment Cavalry, mustered Aug. 27, 1864, for three years.

THOMPSON, WILLIAM. Private Co. A, 2d Regiment Infantry, mustered June 13; 1864, for three years. Deserted, Aug. 8, 1864, at Atlanta, Ga.

THOMSON, THOMAS J. Private Co. L, 4th Regiment Cavalry, mustered July 7, 1864, for three years; discharged Nov. 14, 1865, expiration of service.

TILDEN, COLMAN Jr. Private Co. H, 43d Regiment Infantry, mustered Sept. 20, 1862, for nine months; discharged July 30, 1863, expiration of service.

TILTON DANIEL P. Private 2d Light Battery, mustered Jan. 4, 1864, for three years; discharged Aug. 11, 1865, expiration of service.

TOBEY, JOHN S. Sergeant Co. C, 35th Regiment Infantry, mustered Aug. 19, 1862, for three years; appointed 1st Sergeant, Oct. 31, 1862; discharged Jan. 24, 1863, for promotion. Mustered 2d Lieut., Jan. 24, 1863, Co. C; promoted 1st Lieut., June 17, 1863; promoted Capt., Dec. 8, 1863; transferred June 9, 1865, to 29th Regiment Infantry; Brevet Major; discharged Aug. 10, 1865, expiration of service. Died, Nov. 14, 1879.

TODD, JAMES. Corporal 12th Light Battery, mustered Nov. 28, 1862, for three years. Died, Oct. 30, 1864, at Port Hudson, La.

TOWER, STEPHEN T. Private Co. H, 1st Regiment Infantry, mustered May 23, 1861, for three years; discharged May 25, 1864, expiration of service. Died, May 18, 1879, in Boston.

TOWLE, AUGUSTUS. Private Co. I, 1st Regiment Infantry, . mustered Oct. 22, 1861, for three years ; discharged May 24, 1864, expiration of service.

TRAFTON, CHARLES H. Private Co. A, 6th Regiment Infantry, mustered July 15, 1864, for 100 days ; discharged Oct. 27, 1864, expiration of service.

TRASK, EDWARD. Private Co. D, 3d Regiment Heavy Artillery, mustered Jan. 4, 1864, for three years ; discharged Sept. 18, 1865, expiration of service.

TRIMPOP, CHARLES. Private Co. G, 2d Regiment Infantry, mustered Dec. 6, 1864, for three years ; discharged July 14, 1865, expiration of service.

TUCKER, BEAVIS. Private Co. C, 35th Regiment Infantry, mustered Aug. 19, 1862, for three years ; transferred July 25, 1864, to Co. H, 19th Regiment V. R. C. ; discharged July 13, 1865, expiration of service.

TUFTS, FRANCIS W. Private Co. B, 44th Regiment Infantry, mustered Sept. 12, 1862, for nine months ; discharged June 18, 1863, expiration of service.

TUFTS, JOHN. Private Co. H, 43d Regiment Infantry ; mustered Sept. 20, 1862, for nine months ; discharged July 30, 1863, expiration of service.

TUFTS, THOMAS JR Private Co. B, 3d Regiment Cavalry, mustered Dec 2, 1863, for three years, discharged Sept. 28, 1865, expiration of service.

TUPPER, GEORGE F. Private Co. E, 5th Regiment Infantry, mustered May 1, 1861 for three months ; discharged July 31, 1861, expiration of service.

TURK, EBEN. Private 11th Light Battery, mustered Aug. 25, 1862, for nine months ; discharged May 23, 1863, expiration of service.

TURNER, EDWARD. 11th Regiment Infantry, U. S. A., mustered Feb. 29, 1864.

TURNER, JOHN. Private 4th Co. Unattached Infantry, mustered May 3, 1864, for ninety days; discharged Aug. 6, 1864, expiration of service.

TURNER, WILLIAM. Sergeant Co. I, 56th Regiment Infantry, mustered Feb. 4, 1864, for three years ; discharged July 12, 1865, expiration of service.

TUTEIN, EDWARD G. Private Co. H, 1st Regiment Infantry, mustered May 23, 1861, for three years ; appointed Sergeant May 25, 1861 ; appointed 1st Sergeant Sept. 8, 1862 ; discharged March 1, 1863, for promotion, mustered same day 2d Lieutenant ; discharged May 25, 1864, expiration of service. Mustered Dec. 9, 1864, for one year, Captain Co. G, 61st Regiment Infantry ; discharged July 16, 1865, expiration of service.

TUTTLE, JOHN S. Private Co. H, 50th Regiment Infantry, mustered Sept. 29, 1862, for nine months ; discharged Aug. 24, 1863, expiration of service.

TUTTLE, JOSEPH P. S. Private Co. B, 12th Regiment Infantry, mustered June 26, 1861. Wounded Sept. 17, 1862, at Antietam, Md. ; appointed Corporal, Oct. 1862 ; wounded July 2, 1863, at Gettysburg, Pa. ; discharged Jan. 18, 1864, disability from wounds. Died, Oct. 8, 1868, at Cambridgeport, Mass.

TWICHELL, JOHN W. Musician, Co. D, 17th Regiment Infantry, mustered Feb. 2, 1862, for three years ; discharged Jan. 1, 1864, to re-enlist. Mustered Jan. 2, 1864, for three years ; taken prisoner Feb. 1, 1864, near Newbern, N. C. Died, Aug. 17, 1864, at Andersonville, Ga.

TWOHILL, EDWARD. Private V. R. C.

TWOMBLEY, CHARLES W. Private Co. H, 43d Regiment Infantry, mustered Sept. 20, 1862, for nine months; discharged July 30, 1863, expiration of service.

TYLER, JOSEPH A. Private V. R. C., mustered June 20, 1864; discharged Sept. 5, 1865, for disability.

▽

VARRILL, JOHN P. Private 1st Co. Sharpshooters, mustered Oct. 25, 1862, for three years; wounded at Gettysburg, Pa., July 3, 1863. Deserted Feb. 11, 1864.

VEAZIE, WILLIAM W. Private Co. E, 4th Regiment Cavalry, mustered Feb. 18, 1864, for three years. Died Sept. 5, 1864, at Davids' Island, N. Y.

VEAZIE, ELI. Private Co. H, 1st Regiment Infantry, mustered May 23, 1861, for three years. Wounded at Locust Grove, Va., Nov. 27, 1863 ;.discharged March 25, 1864, disability from wound.

VICKORY, JOHN. Private Co. H, 2d Regiment Cavalry ; mustered May 10, 1864, for three years ; discharged July 30, 1865, expiration of service.

VINCENT, JAMES N. Private Co. B, 24th Regiment Infantry, mustered Sept. 26, 1861, for three years. Killed, March 14, 1862, at Newbern, N. C.

VOLK, ALGERNON. General service U. S. A., mustered March 17, 1864.

VOSE, FREDERICK A. Private Co. I, 1st Regiment Cavalry, mustered Dec. 5, 1863, for three years. Deserted, Jan. 1865.

VOSE, ORRIN B. Private Co. H, 50th Regiment Infantry, mustered Sept. 29, 1862, for nine months ; discharged Aug. 24, 1863, expiration of service.

WADE, EDWIN L. Private 4th Co. Unattached Infantry, mustered May 3, 1864, for ninety days; discharged Aug. 6, 1864, expiration of service.

WADE. JAMES P. Private Co. C, 5th Regiment Infantry. mustered May 1, 1861, for three months ; discharged July 31, 1861, expiration of service. Mustered Sergeant Co. C, Nov. 2, 1861. for three years ; appointed Sergeant Major July 1. 1862 ; discharged Oct. 21. 1862, for promotion. mustered same day 2d Lieutenant ; promoted May 7, 1863. 1st Lieutenant ; discharged June 29, 1865, expiration of service.

WADE, SETH. Private Co. I. 23d Regiment Infantry, mustered Sept. 28, 1861, for three years ; appointed Corporal Aug. 19, 1862 ; appointed Sergeant Nov. 3. 1862 ; appointed 1st Sergeant March 19, 1864 ; discharged Oct. 14, 1864. for promotion, commissioned same date 1st Lieutenant ; commissioned Captain Oct. 14, 1864 ; discharged June 25, 1865, expiration of service.

WAGNER, FRANK. Private Co. E, 59th Regiment Infantry. mustered Feb 4, 1864, for three years.

WAGNER, HENRY. Private Co. H, 58th Regiment, mustered April 18, 1864, for three years. Deserted Oct. 4, 1864.

WAGNER, JOHAN. Unassigned recruit 2d Regiment Infantry. mustered May 10, 1864, for three years.

WAGNER, JOHN. Private Co. K, 2d Regiment Infantry. mustered July 23, 1864, for three years. Deserted Aug. 9, 1864.

WALKER, CHARLES W. Private Co. E, 4th Regiment Cavalry, mustered Feb. 18, 1864, for three years ; discharged May 19, 1865, expiration of service.

WALKER, EDWARD. Sergeant Co. H, 42d Regiment Infantry, mustered Sept. 24, 1862, for nine months ; discharged Aug. 30, 1863, expiration of service.

WALKER, EDWARD P. Bugler Co. G, 2d Regiment Cavalry, mustered April 9, 1863, for three years ; discharged June 6, 1865, expiration of service.

WALKER, GILMAN S. Private Co. E, 24th Regiment Infantry, mustered Dec. 5, 1861, for three years ; discharged Jan. 3, 1864, to re-enlist. Mustered Jan. 4, 1864, for three years ; discharged Jan. 20, 1866, expiration of service.

WALKER, HENRY. Private Co. H, 1st Regiment Infantry, mustered Sept. 24, 1861, for three years ; discharged April 14, 1863, for disability. Served three months private Co. G, 8th Regiment M. V. M., on quota of Gloucester ; discharged Aug. 1, 1861, expiration of service.

WALKER, SAMUEL JR. Private Co. B, 43 Regiment Infantry, mustered Oct. 11, 1862, for nine months. Deserted, Oct. 11, 1862, at Readville, Mass.

WALKER, WILLIAM G. Musician Co. H, 19th Regiment Infantry, mustered Aug. 28, 1861, for three years ; transferred Dec. 1861, to Co. D ; taken prisoner Aug. 3, 1862, near Richmond, Va. ; exchanged Sept. 13, 1862 : discharged Feb. 7, 1863, disability.

WALLWORK, JOHN B. Private Co. G, 59th Regiment Infantry, mustered July 29, 1864, for three years ; transferred June 1, 1865, to 57th Regiment Infantry ; discharged July 30, 1865, expiration of service.

WALSH, DAVID. Private V. R. C., mustered April 29, 1864.

WALSH, PATRICK. Private 6th Light Battery, mustered Dec. 21, 1861, for three years; discharged Jan. 5, 1864, to re-enlist. Mustered Jan. 6, 1864, for three years; discharged Feb. 6, 1865, expiration of service.

WALSH, WILLIAM. Private Co. F, 28th Regiment Infantry, mustered Dec. 13, 1861, for three years; wounded Sept. 17, 1862, at Antietam, Md.; discharged Jan. 1, 1864, to re-enlist. Mustered Jan. 2, 1864, for three years; wounded March 25, 1865, at Smith's Farm, Va.; discharged July 27, 1865, expiration of service.

WALTER, CHARLES. Unassigned recruit 2d Regiment Infantry, mustered June 11, 1864, for three years.

WALTERS, WILLIAM. Private Co. L, 3d Regiment Heavy Artillery, mustered May 30, 1864, for three years; discharged Sept. 18, 1865, expiration of service.

WARREN, THEODORE B. Private Co. H, 43d Regiment Infantry, mustered Sept. 20, 1862, for nine months; discharged July 30, 1863, expiration of service.

WATERS, JOHN. Private Co. C, 43d Regiment Infantry, mustered Sept. 20, 1862, for nine months. Deserted, Sept. 25, 1862, at Readville, Mass.

WATSON, ISAAC A. Private Co. G, 5th Regiment Infantry, mustered March 4, 1864, for three years; discharged Oct. 31, 1865, expiration of service.

WATSON, JOHN A. Private Co. H, 43d Regiment Infantry, mustered Sept. 20, 1862, for nine months; discharged July 30, 1863, expiration of service. Mustered private 4th Co. Unattached Infantry, May 3, 1864, for ninety days; discharged Aug. 6, 1864, expiration of service. Mustered Oct. 2, 1864, Co. F, 61st Regiment Infantry, for one year on quota of Roxbury; discharged July 16, 1865, expiration of service.

WATSON, NELSON S. Unassigned recruit 3d Regiment Cavalry, mustered Aug. 5, 1864, for three years ; discharged June 3, 1865, expiration of service.

WATSON, ROBERT. Private Co. C, 28th Regiment Infantry, mustered Dec. 13, 1861, for three years ; discharged Jan. 1, 1864, to re-enlist. Mustered Jan. 2, 1864, for three years. Killed May 10, 1864, at Po River, Va.

WATTS, HENRY. Private Co. D, 3d Regiment Cavalry, mustered Jan. 2, 1864, for three years ; transferred July 9, 1864, to Navy.

WAY, GEORGE. Private Co. B, 56th Regiment Infantry, mustered March 19, 1864, for three years. Died at Salisbury, N. C., while prisoner of war.

WEBSTER, GEORGE W. Unassigned recruit 2d Regiment Cavalry, mustered May 13, 1864, for three years.

WELCH, JOHN. Private Co. L, 2d Regiment Cavalry, mustered May 5, 1864, for three years. Deserted May 27, 1864.

WELCH, RICHARD. Private Co. F, 2d Regiment Cavalry, mustered June 9, 1864, for three years. Deserted July 12, 1864.

WELLER, GODFREY. Private 12th Light Battery, mustered Nov. 12, 1862, for three years : discharged July 25, 1865, expiration of service.

WEIR, JOSEPH. Private Co. F, 28th Regiment Infantry, mustered Dec. 13, 1861, for three years ; transferred Sept. 17, 1863, to V. R. C.

WEIR, JOSEPH. Private Co. G, 28th Regiment Infantry, mustered Dec. 13, 1861, for three years ; missing near Fredericksburg, Va., Aug. 12, 1862.

WELLS, CHARLES T. Private Co. G, 32d Regiment Infantry, mustered May 30, 1862, for three years; discharged January 20, 1863, for disability; re-enlisted on quota of Marlboro', private Co. C, 2d Regiment Heavy Artillery, discharged Sept. 3, 1865.

WELLS, IVORY. Private Co. C, 35th Regiment Infantry, mustered Aug. 19, 1862, for three years, discharged June 9, 1865, expiration of service.

WELSH, EDWARD. Unassigned recruit 28th Regiment Infantry, mustered May 11, 1864, for three years.

WELSH, JAMES. Unassigned recruit 26th Regiment Infantry, mustered May 24, 1864, for three years.

WELSH, JOHN. Private Co. B, 28th Regiment Infantry, mustered Jan. 10, 1862, for three years; discharged Jan. 1, 1864, to re-enlist. Mustered Jan. 2, 1864, for three years. Deserted April 1, 1864.

WELSH, JOHN. Unassigned recruit 28th Regiment Infantry, mustered March 22, 1864, for three years. Deserted June 25, 1863; returned Oct. 10, 1863; re-enlisted Jan. 1, 1864, for three years. Deserted April 1, 1864, at Boston.

WELSH, JOHN J. Ordinance Corps, U. S. A., mustered April 13, 1864.

WENTWORTH, ALBERT F. Private Co. H, 1st Regiment Infantry, mustered May 23, 1861, for three years. Killed July 18, 1861, at Blackburn's Ford, Va.

WESCOTT, HENRY A. Private Co. H, 11th Regiment Infantry, mustered June 13, 1861, for three years; appointed Corporal Nov. 1861; wounded May 5, 1862, at Williamsburg, Va.; left regiment; enlisted in Navy Sept. 1862; discharged Nov. 1865.

WEST, JAMES B. 1st Sergeant Co. E, 28th Regiment Infantry, mustered Dec. 13, 1861, for three years ; discharged July 26, 1862, for promotion, mustered same day 2d Lieutenant; promoted 1st Lieutenant Jan. 16, 1863 ; wounded June 3, 1864, at Gaines' Hill, Va., died June 4, of wounds.

WETZLER, HERMAN. Private Co. A, 19th Regiment Infantry, mustered May 6, 1864, for three years : discharged June 30, 1865, expiration of service.

WHEELER, ALVIN L. Private Co. B, 3d Regiment Infantry, mustered March 17, 1864, for three years ; discharged Sept. 28, 1864, expiration of service.

WHEELER, JAMES E. Private Co. H, 50th Regiment Infantry, mustered Sept. 29, 1862, for nine months ; discharged Aug. 24, 1863, expiration of service.

WHEELOCK, MERRILL G. Private C. F, 44th Regiment Infantry, mustered Sept. 12, 1862, for nine months ; discharged June 18, 1863, expiration of service.

WHITFORD, REUBEN. Private Co. H, 43d Regiment, mustered Sept. 20, 1862, for nine months : discharged July 30, 1863, expiration of service.

WHITE, AUSTIN J. Private Co. C, 35th Regiment Infantry, mustered Aug. 19, 1862, for three years : appointed Sergeant, Sept. 18, 1862 : appointed Sergeant-Major, Sept. 13, 1863; discharged Jan. 14, 1864, for promotion. Mustered same day, 1st Lieutenant ; wounded Aug. 19, 1864, near Petersburg, Va. ; commissioned Capt. Sept. 6, 1864 : not mustered. Died, Sept. 15, 1864, from wound, at Chelsea.

WHITE, GEORGE W. Private 4th Co. Unattached Infantry, mustered May 3, 1864, for ninety days ; discharged Aug. 6, 1864, expiration of service.

WHITE, JAMES. Unassigned recruit 2d Regiment Infantry, mustered, July 8, 1864, for three years.

WHITE, SAMUEL. Private Co. K, 5th Regiment Infantry, mustered April 12, 1864, for three years ; discharged July 7, 1865, for disability.

WHITE, WILLIAM. Private Co. K, 33d Regiment Infantry, mustered Aug. 12, 1862, for three years. Killed, May 15, 1864, at Resaca, Ga.

WHITE, WILLIAM R. Private Co. H. 43d Regiment Infantry, mustered, Sept. 20, 1862, for nine months ; discharged July 30, 1863 ; expiration of service. Died, April 29, 1864. at Chelsea.

WHITING, EDWARD. Private Co. H, 43d Regiment Infantry, mustered Sept. 20, 1862, for nine months ; discharged July 30, 1863, expiration of service.

WHITMAN, JOHN. Corporal 4th Co. Unattached Infantry, mustered May 3, 1864, for ninety days ; discharged Aug. 6, 1864, expiration of service.

WHITMARSH, JONATHAN. Private Co. H, 50th Regiment Infantry, mustered Sept. 29, 1862, for nine months ; discharged Aug. 24. 1863, expiration of service. Died at Providence, R. I.

WHITNEY, BENJAMIN F. Private Co. C, 28th Regiment Infantry, mustered April 14. 1864, for three years. Died Dec. 2. 1864, at Annapolis, Md.

WHITTAKER, ABNER G.   Private Go. H, 1st Regiment Infantry, mustered Sept. 10, 1861, for three years; discharged July 28, 1862, for disability.

WHITTEMORE, THOMAS.   Private Co. E. 1st Regiment Cavalry, mustered Oct. 23. 1861, for three years; discharged Mar. 6, 1863, for disability; mustered V. R. C. May 24. 1864, on quota of New Marlboro'; discharged July 12. 1865.   Died Feb. 24, 1871, at Chelsea.

WHITTEMORE, THOMAS, Jr.   Private Co. H. 43d Regiment Infantry, mustered Sept. 20, 1862, for nine months : discharged July 30. 1863, expiration of service.

WHITTEN, GEORGE.   Private Co. G, 2d Regiment Infantry, mustered May 25, 1861, for three years ; discharged May 28, 1864, expiration of service.

WIGGIN, JOHN R.   Private 2d Light Battery, mustered Jan. 5, 1864, for three years ; discharged Aug. 11, 1865, expiration of service.

WILDER, CHARLES M.   Private Co. G, 40th Regiment Infantry, mustered Sept. 5, 1862, for three years ; appointed Corporal Feb., 1864 ; wounded May 16, 1864, at Drury's Bluff, Va.; appointed Sergeant Nov. 1, 1864; discharged June 16, 1865. expiration of service.

WILHELMI, EUGENE.   Private Co. K, 2d Regiment Infantry, mustered May 16, 1864, for three years ; discharged July 14. 1865. expiration of service.

WILKINSON. CHARLES N.   Private Co. I, 44th Regiment Infantry, mustered Sept. 12, 1862, for nine months ; discharged June 18, 1863. expiration of service.

WILKINSON. SAMUEL F.   Wagoner Co. H, 43d Regiment Infantry, mustered Sept. 20, 1862, for nine months ; discharged July 30, 1863, expiration of service.

WILLIAMS, BENJAMIN D. Private Co. C, 35th Regiment Infantry, mustered Aug. 19, 1862, for three years; transferred to V. R. C.. Jan. 15, 1864, discharged June 28, 1865, expiration of service.

WILLIAMS, CHARLES. Private 2d Light Battery, mustered Jan. 5, 1864, for three years; discharged Aug. 11, 1865, expiration of service.

WILLIAMS, CHARLES. Unassigned recruit 28th Regiment Infantry, mustered April 14, 1864, for three years.

WILLIAMS, DANN. Unassigned recruit 28th Regiment Infantry, mustered April 15, 1864, for three years; transferred to Navy, May 17, 1864.

WILLIAMS, GEORGE. Private Co. C, 9th Regiment Infantry, mustered Nov. 9, 1861, for three years; wounded May 31, 1862, at Hanover Court House. Va.; discharged Oct. 22, 1862, disability from wounds.

WILLIAMS HARRY. Private Co. E, 26th Regiment Infantry, mustered Dec. 20, 1864, for three years; discharged Aug. 25, 1865, expiration of service.

WILLIAMS, HORATIO N. Musician, Co. H, 1st Regiment Infantry, mustered May 23, 1861, for three years; discharged Sept. 6, 1862, disability. Re-enlisted private Co. A, 3d Regiment Heavy Artillery, June 10, 1863, for three years; transferred March 11, 1864, to 1st U. S. Light Battery. Wounded near Petersburg, Va., July 30, 1864; wounded, Aug. 30, 1864.

WILLIAMS, JAMES. Private Co. G, 2d Regiment Infantry, mustered June 9, 1864, for three years; discharged June 24, 1865, expiration of service.

WILLIAMS, JOHN. Unassigned recruit 2d Regiment Infantry, mustered May 13, 1864, for three years; transferred May 28, 1864, to Navy.

WILLIAMS, JOHN. Private Co. G, 5th Regiment Cavalry, mustered May 11, 1864, for three years; discharged Oct. 31, 1865, expiration of service.

WILLIAMS, MARTIN. Unassigned recruit 2d Regiment Infantry, mustered May 13, 1864, for three years.

WILLIAMS, ROBERT. Unassigned recruit 28th Regiment Infantry, mustered May 10, 1864, for three years.

WILLIAMS, SAMUEL M. Private 5th Light Battery, mustered Dec. 28, 1863, for three years; discharged June 12, 1865, expiration of service.

WILLIAMS, WINFRED R. Private Co. C, 2d Regiment Cavalry, mustered Dec. 17, 1863, for three years. Deserted Nov. 9, 1864.

WILLIAMSON, DAVID. Private 13th Light Battery, mustered April 15, 1864, for three years; transferred May 17, 1864, to Navy.

WILLIS, CHARLES H. Private Co. G, 40th Regiment Infantry, mustered Sept. 5, 1862, for three years. Died Jan. 22, 1864, chronic diarrhœa, Boston, Mass.

WILSON, CHARLES. Private Co. E, 43d Regiment Infantry, mustered Oct. 1, 1862, for nine months; discharged June 2, 1863, expiration of service.

WILSON, GEORGE. Corporal Co. K, 3d Regiment Heavy Artillery, mustered May 12, 1864, for three years; discharged Sept. 18, 1865, expiration of service.

WILSON, GEORGE. Corporal Co. I, 2d Regiment Infantry, mustered May 10, 1864, for three years. Died, March 12, 1865, at Wilmington, N. C.

WILSON, HENRY. Private Co. H, 43d Regiment Infantry, mustered Sept. 20, 1862, for nine months; discharged July 30, 1863, expiration of service.

WILSON, HENRY JR. Private Co. H, 1st Regiment Infantry, mustered May 23, 1861, for three years; appointed Corporal, Jan. 1, 1864; discharged May 25, 1864, expiration of service.

WILSON, JOHN. Private Co. F, 28th Regiment Infantry, mustered April 14, 1864, for three years. Deserted, June 14, 1864.

WILSON, JOHN. Unassigned recruit 2d Regiment Infantry, mustered May 13, 1864, for three years.

WILSON, NORMAN. Musician Co. H, 43d Regiment Infantry, mustered Sept. 20, 1862, for nine months; discharged July 30, 1863, expiration of service. Mustered Jan. 14, 1864, private Co. I, 1st Regiment Cavalry, for three years; re-enlisted private Co. I, 1st Regiment Cavalry, N. B., Jan. 14, 1864, for three years; wounded May, 1864; appointed Corporal Sept. 18, 1864. Killed Oct. 1, 1864, near Petersburg, Va.

WILSON, WILLIAM. Private Co. G, 1st Regiment Infantry, mustered Aug. 13, 1862, for three years. Prisoner of War, May 3, 1863, no further record.

WINCHESTER, DANIEL. Unassigned recruit 2d Regiment Infantry, mustered May 17, 1864, for three years.

WINSLOW, GEORGE M. Private Co. D, 3d Regiment Heavy Artillery, mustered Aug. 14, 1863, for three years; discharged Sept. 18, 1865, expiration of service.

WISE, WILLIAM C. Private 8th Light Battery, mustered May 30, 1862, for six months; discharged Nov. 29, 1862, expiration of service.

WOLF, LOUIS B. Private Co. F, 2d Regiment Cavalry, mustered June 11, 1864, for three years; discharged June 29, 1865, expiration of service.

WOLFFRAIN, WILLIAM. Private Co. C, 2d Regiment Cavalry, mustered May 5, 1864, for three years. Deserted from Hospital.

WOOD, DAVID. Private 13th Light Battery, mustered April 16, 1864, for three years. Deserted, en route to Battery.

WOOD, EPHRAIM A. 1st Lieutenant 55th Regiment Infantry, mustered July 20, 1863, for three years; Nov. 20 1863, resigned.

WOOD, JOSEPH A. Private Co. H, 43d Regiment Infantry, mustered Sept. 20, 1862, for nine months; discharged July 30, 1863, expiration of service.

WOODS, CHARLES. Private Co. L, 3d Regiment Heavy Artillery, mustered May 30, 1864, for three years; discharged Sept. 18, 1865, expiration of service.

WOODWARD, FREDERICK H. Private Co. H, 50th Regiment Infantry, mustered Sept. 29, 1862, for nine months; discharged Aug. 24, 1863, expiration of service.

WREN, JAMES. Private Co. I, 2d Regiment Cavalry, mustered Aug. 15. 1864, for three years; discharged May 8, 1865, for disability.

WRENN, JOSEPH C. Private Co. K, 35th Regiment Infantry, mustered March 16, 1864, for three years; discharged May 22, 1865, expiration of service.

WRIGHT, EDWARD J. Private Co. B, 1st Regiment Infantry, mustered May 23, 1861, for three years, Deserted, Nov. 7, 1863.

WRIGHT, HENRY E. Private 4th Co. Unattached Infantry, mustered May 3, 1864, for ninety days ; discharged Aug. 6, 1864, expiration of service.

WRIGHT, THOMAS S. Private Co. C, 35th Regiment Infantry, mustered Aug. 19, 1862, for three years ; appointed Sergeant, Oct. 25, 1862 ; appointed 1st Sergt., April 21, 1863; discharged Sept. 6, 1863, for promotion. Mustered same date 1st Lieutenant ; wounded May 18, 1864, at Spottsylvania, Va. ; commissioned Capt., Nov. 14, 1864, mustered March 1, 1865 ; discharged June 9, 1865, expiration of service.

WRIGHT, WILLIAM T. Private Co. H, 1st Regiment Infantry, mustered May 23, 1861, for three years ; wounded April 26, 1862, at Yorktown, Va ; appointed Corporal March 1, 1863 ; discharged May 25, 1864, expiration of service. Died Oct. 19, 1867, at Chelsea.

WYLIE, CHARLES. Private Co. A, 43d Regiment Infantry, mustered Oct. 11, 1862, for nine months; discharged July 30, 1863, expiration of service.

WYLIE, ISAAC. Private Co. H, 43d Regiment Infantry, mustered Sept. 20, 1862, for nine months ; discharged July 30, 1863, expiration of service.

YEATON, RICHARD B. Private 16th Light Battery, mustered March 11, 1864, for three years ; discharged June 21, 1865, for disability.

YOUNG, GEORGE W. Private Co. H, 43d Regiment Infantry, mustered September 20, 1862, for nine months ; discharged July 30, 1863.

YOUNG, ROBERT M. Private Co. H, 50th Regiment Infantry, mustered Oct. 13, 1862, for nine months ; discharged Aug. 24, 1863, expiration of service.

ZALLER, WILLIAM. Private Co. K, 2d Regiment Cavalry, mustered May 10, 1864, for three years; discharged June 27, 1865, for disability.

APPENDIX.

ALLEN, E. C. First Sergeant Co. A, 12th Regiment U. S. Infantry; commissioned 2d Lieut., May 25, 1862; 1st Lieut., Jan. 19, 1863; Capt., Nov. 1863. Died, Dec. 19, 1863, at Baltimore, Md.

AMES, AZEL JR. Hospital Steward U. S. A; commissioned 1st Lieut. 2d La. (colored) Engineers, Aug. 13, 1863.

AMES, GEORGE L. Private Co. B, U. S. Engineer Corps; appointed artificer, Jan. 1, 1862; Corporal, 1864; discharged Dec. 1864.

BIGELOW, BENJAMIN F. Hospital Steward 11th Regiment U. S. Infantry, Aug. 25, 1862; commissioned Acting Assistant Surgeon of Navy, Dec. 1863.

BOYER, WILLIAM. Private 1st R. I. Light Artillery, Battery H, Dec. 31, 1862.

BROWN, GEORGE F. Private 7th Regiment Illinois Cavalry, May 11, 1863.

BURKE, L. O. F. Private Co. F, 3d Regiment N. H. Infantry, March 17, 1862.

CAHILL, PATRICK. Private Co. E, 36th Regiment N. Y, Infantry, June 1861; discharged July 15, 1863.

CLELAND, WILLIAM W. Private 1st Regiment Mo. Infantry, April 25, 1861; discharged July 25, 1861. Re-enlisted same day private 11th Regt. Mo. Infantry; appointed Sergt. Aug. 6, 1861; Sergt.-Major, Aug. 21, 1861; commissioned 2d Lieut., Feb. 21, 1862; 1st Lieut., July 4, 1862; Capt., Sept. 19, 1862; Chief Gen. John E. Smith's Staff, Dec. 1862.

CONNELLY, CORNELIUS. Private Co. G, 6th Regiment California Vols., March 14, 1863; discharged close of war.

CROSS, HENRY C. Private 1st R. I. Light Artillery, Battery D, Dec. 11, 1862; transferred to V. R. C.; commissioned Capt., Colored Regiment.

CUMMINGS, EDWARD H. Sergeant Co. H, 35th Regiment N. Y. Infantry, May 31, 1861 ; appointed 1st Sergt., July 5. 1862 ; discharged June 11, 1863.

CURRIER, AMOS S. Quartermaster of 78th Regiment N. Y. Infantry.

CURRIER, BENJAMIN F. 1st Lieutenant Co. C, 78th Regiment N. Y. Infantry.

CURRY, AMOS P. Private 13th Regiment Ills. Infantry; commissioned 2d Lieut. 10th Regiment Mo. Cavalry, Aug. 1, 1861 : commissioned Captain ; commisioned Col. 1st Regiment Enrolled Militia, Memphis, Tenn, 1865.

DOWNING, HENRY. Private 1st R. I. Light Artillery, Battery C ; wounded July 1, 1862, at Gaines' Mills, Va. ; taken prisoner and discharged Aug. 29, 1862.

DUNN, PATRICK. Private U. S. Marine Corps, Feb. 4, 1865.

EATON, HENRY M. Co. C, 83d Regiment Pa. Infantry; wounded June 26. 1862, near Richmond, Va. ; discharged Nov. 16, 1862.

EDWARDS, SAMUEL J. Private 1st N. H. Battery.

ELDRIDGE, ELLERY W. Hospital Steward U. S. A.

EMERY, CHARLES, 1st Lieutenant Co. G, 12th Regiment Indiana Infantry, May 1861 ; commissioned Capt. Co. E, 55th Regiment Ind. Infantry, June 3, 1861. Wounded and taken prisoner Aug. 30. 1862, at Richmond, Ky.; paroled and exchanged Jan. 15. 1863 ; commissioned Capt. 1st Regiment U. S. (colored) Vols., June 1863.

FANNING, THOMAS. Private 18th Regiment N. H. Infantry.

FLYNN, JOHN. Private 3d Regiment N. H. Infantry.

GERRISH, GEORGE A. Captain 1st N. H. Battery, Sept. 10, 1861 ; taken prisoner at Bull Run, Va., Aug. 1862 ; released Sept. 1862 ; appointed Chief of Artillery 1st Division 1st Army Corps, Nov. 9, 1862. Wounded at Fredericksburg, Va., Dec. 13. 1862 ; resigned March 7, 1863.

GILMAN, ALBERT H. Quartermaster 3d U. S. Artillery.

GRANTMAN, WILLIAM. Capt. 13th Regiment N. H. Infantry, Aug. 18, 1862 ; commissioned Major, June 1, 1863 ; commissioned Lieut. Col. 1864, resigned.

GRAY, MARCELLUS. Private Co. I, 26th Regiment Mo. Infantry ; Oct. 10, 1861 : appointed Corporal, June 1, 1863 ; Sergeant, Oct. 1, 1863.

HALWORTH, THOMAS L. Band, 3d Brigade 3d Division, 24th Army Corps.

HANLON, JOHN. Private 6th N. Y. Battery; transferred from 11th Regt. Mass. Infantry; discharged 1864.

HILL, GEORGE W. 1st Lieut. Co. C, 13th Regiment U. S. Infantry; commissioned Capt., May 20, 1863.

HOLLIS, EBEN H. Corporal 104th Regiment Illinois Infantry, Aug. 1862, transferred to V. R. C., Feb. 1864.

KENNISTON, GEORGE A. Private Co. E, 38th Regiment N. Y. Infantry; discharged Sept. 1862.

LUDWIG, ROSCOE F. Co. A, 23d Regiment, Me., nine months.

LOOMIS, CHARLES E. Sergeant Co. G, 57th Regiment N. Y. Infantry. Wounded near Richmond, Va., June 13, 1862 ; discharged Oct. 9, 1862.

LOVETT, THOMAS. 11th U. S. Infantry.

MANCHESTER, WILLIAM. Hospital Steward 9th Regiment Illinois Infantry; discharged Aug., 1862.

McCANN, BERNARD. Private U. S. Marine Corps, 1865.

McDONALD, JOHN S. Private Co. K, 2d Regiment N. H. Infantry; June 8, 1861, discharged ; 1st Lieutenant, June 30, 1864.

MERRIAM, SAMUEL N. Private Co. E, 104th Regiment Illinois Infantry. Wounded Dec. 7, 1862, at Hartsville, Tenn. ; died, Dec. 21, 1862.

NORRIS, PHINEAS B. Sergeant Co. H, 42d Regiment N. Y. Infantry.

NOYES, HENRY E. 2d Lieutenant 2d U. S. Cavalry, June 24, 1861 ; commissioned 1st Lieutenant Co. G, Feb. 15, 1862.

PATRICK, FRANCIS. Private Co. C, 10th Regiment Wis. Infantry, 1861. Wounded at Chickamauga in 1863 ; wounded and taken prisoner, Sept. 20, 1863, at Lookout Mountain.

PRATT, FRANK H. Private Maine (Fessenden's) Sharpshooters.

PROUTY, GEORGE. Bugler, U. S. Cavalry.

PROCTOR, JOSEPH L. 1st Lieutenant 18th Regiment U. S. Infantry, May 14, 1861 ; commissioned Capt., Jan. 15, 1863.

RAY, ALFRED C. Private Co. D, 64th Regiment N. Y. Infantry, June 20, 1861.

RESTIEAUX, E. B. W. Capt. Assistant Quarter-master's U. S. Volunteers.

ROLLINS, HIRAM. Capt. Co. K, 2d Regiment N. H. Infan-
try. Wounded July 21, 1861, at Bull Run, Va.; resigned
Nov. 1862 ; commissioned Capt. V. R. C., 1863.
SPARKS, RUFUS T. Private Co. A, 64th Regiment Ill. In-
fantry, Sept. 25, 1861 ; appointed Corporal, July 1862.
SUTHERLAND, GEORGE F. Sergeant Co. H, 2d Regiment
N. H. Infantry, June 1861.
THAYER, JOHN D. Sergeant-Major 2d Regiment Ohio Cav-
alry ; discharged Sept. 30, 1862.
TOWER, CHARLES W. Private Co. G, 1st Regiment N. Y.
Infantry, April 1862. Died, March 13, 1864, at New Or-
leans, La.
WILDER. CHARLES B. Capt. Assistant Quarter-master U.
S. Volunteers, Feb. 1863.
WILLIAMS, ARTHUR S. Private Co. C, U. S. Corps Engi-
neers ; discharged Aug. 22, 1862.
WILLIS, GEORGE H. 2d Lieutenant 3d N. C (37th) U. S.
Infantry, Nov. 1863.
WINSLOW, GEORGE C. Capt. Assistant Quarter-master,
U. S. Volunteers, Aug. 1863.
WRIGHT, EDWARD J. Smith's New York Battery. Desert-
ed from Co. B, 1st Regiment Mass. Infantry.

CHELSEA RESIDENTS ON OTHER QUOTAS.

BENT, JOHN S. Private Co. E, 50th Regiment Infantry,
quota of Boston, mustered Sept. 19, 1864, for nine months ;
discharged Aug. 24, 1863. Died in New Orleans, La.
BRANON, OWEN. Private Co. A, 28th Regiment Infantry,
quota of Dracut. mustered Aug. 22, 1864, for three years.
Killed at Hatchers Run, Va., March 25, 1865.
BRYANT, CALEB. Private Co. C, 1st Regiment Infantry,
quota of Boston. mustered May 27, 1861, for three years ;
discharged July 20, 1861, disability.
BUTLER, HENRY P. Private Co. B, 1st Regiment Infantry,
quota of Boston, mustered May 23, 1861, for three years ;
discharged Nov. 26, 1862, disability.
BUTLER, JACOB W. Sergeant Co. G, 61st Regiment Infantry, quota of Medway, mustered Dec. 9, 1864, for one year ;
discharged July 16, 1865.
CARNAN, JOHN. Private Co. I, 61st Regiment Infantry,
quota of Lynn, mustered Jan. 25, 1865, for one year ; discharged July 16, 1865.

CALLAHAN, CHARLES H. Private Co. H, 20th Reg. Inf., quota of Andover, mustered Aug. 24, 1861, for three years; discharged April 14, 1862, for disability. Died, May 29, 1862.

CLIFFORD, LOREN C. Private Co. M, 3d Regiment Cavalry, quota of Marlboro', mustered Dec. 31, 1864 for one year; discharged Sept. 28, 1865.

CONROY, JOHN. Private Co. I, 61st Regiment Infantry, quota of Needham, mustered Jan. 17, 1865, for one year; discharged July 16, 1865.

CULLY, ELI. Private Co. K, 43d Regiment Infantry, quota of Weymouth, mustered Oct. 1, 1862, for nine months ; discharged July 30, 1863.

DILLINGHAM, CHARLES. Private Co. G, 2d Regiment Infantry, quota of Brewster, mustered Feb. 15, 1862, for three years. Wounded, Aug. 9, 1862, at Cedar Mountain, Va. ; died of wounds Sept. 10, 1862, at Alexandria, Va.

DOHERTY, WILLIAM. Private Co. F, 1st Regiment Cavalry, quota of Boston. mustered Dec. 26, 1863, for three years ; discharged Dec. 18, 1864, for disability.

DRURY, MARTIN V. B. Corporal Co. G, 61st Regiment Infantry, mustered Nov. 23, 1864, for one year, quota of Boston; discharged July 16, 1865.

EATON, SIDNEY P. Private Co. H, 30th Regiment Infantry, mustered Dec. 12, 1861, for three years on quota of North Bridgewater. Died, March 1, 1862, at New Orleans, La.

ECCLES, JOHN. Private Co. C, 61st Regiment Infantry. mustered Sept. 14, 1864, for one year on quota of Quincy ; discharged June 4, 1865, expiration of service. Died, Feb. 22, 1878, in Chelsea.

EMERSON, NATHANIEL B. Private Co. H, 1st Reg. Inf., mustered Sept. 22, 1862, for three years on quota of Boston. Wounded at Fredericksburg, Va., Dec. 13, 1862; wounded at Chancellorsville, Va., May 3, 1863; discharged May 25, 1864.

FALT, HENRY. Private Co. G, 4th Regiment Cavalry, mustered Jan. 27, 1864, for three years on quota of Easthampton; discharged July 18, 1865.

FROST, JOHN H. Private Co. C, 35th Regiment Infantry, mustered Aug. 19, 1862, for three years on quota of Roxbury. Died, Aug. 6, 1864, at Camp Dennison, Ohio.

GOOKIN, GEORGE E. Private Co. H, 24th Regiment Infantry, mustered July 29, 1862, for three years on quota of Boston; discharged Dec. 3, 1864.

GRAVES, WILLIAM R. Private Co. H, 61st Regiment Infantry, mustered Dec. 12, 1864, for one year on quota of Charlestown ; discharged July 16, 1865.

HENDERSON, GEORGE F. Sergeant Co. H, 61st Regiment Infantry, mustered Jan. 5, 1865, for one year on quota of Charlemont; discharged July 16, 1865.

HILL, CHARLES B. Private 1st Light Battery; mustered Aug. 28, 1861 for three years on quota of Boston; discharged Nov. 17, 1862, for disability.

HODGE, CHARLES H. Private Co. G, 61st Regiment Infantry, mustered Nov. 16, 1864, for one year on quota of Sherburne; discharged July 16, 1865.

HUNT, SAMUEL. Quarter-master's Sergeant 5th Regiment Infantry, mustered May 1, 1861, for three months on quota of Charlestown; discharged July 31, 1861.

HURTER, ALVAH K. Private Co. L, 3d Regiment Cavalry, mustered Dec. 12, 1861, for three years on quota of Boston; discharged Dec. 27, 1864.

JONES, CHARLES H. Private Co. I, 1st Regiment Cavalry, mustered Dec. 5, 1863, for three years on quota of Boston; discharged June 29, 1865.

JONES, ISAAC H. 1st Sergeant Co. C, 1st Regiment Infantry, mustered May 27, 1861, for three years, Boston; discharged July 20, 1861, for disability.

KELLEY, WILLIAM B. Private Co. H, 19th Regiment Infantry, mustered July 21, 1863, for three years on quota of Lynn; transferred to 20th Regiment, Jan. 14, 1864; taken prisoner June 22, 1864; discharged July 16, 1865.

KENNEDY, JAMES. Private Co. G, 28th Regiment Infantry, mustered Jan. 4, 1862, for three years. Killed, Dec. 13, 1862, at Fredericksburg, Va.

LEWIS, WENDELL. Private Co. A, 55th Regiment Infantry, mustered Dec. 8, 1863, for three years on quota of Boston. Died, July, 1865.

LLOYD, THOMAS W. Private Co. K, 1st Regiment Cavalry, mustered Jan. 4, 1862, for three years; credited to New York; transferred to Co. K, 4th Cavalry; discharged, Oct. 18, 1864.

LOW, LYMAN H. Private Co. B, 13th Regiment Infantry. mustered July 16, 1861, for three years, on quota of Boston; discharged Aug. 1, 1864.

LYNCH, MICHAEL. Private Co. G, 61st Regiment Infantry, mustered Nov. 30, 1864, for one year, quota of Chelmsford; discharged July 16, 1865.

McGILLICK, JOHN. Private Co. C, 28th Regiment Infantry, mustered Aug. 18, 1862, for three years, quota of Boston; discharged Jan. 2, 1863, for disability. Died at Chelsea January 27, 1863.

McLEOD, EDWARD. Private Co. C, 35th Regiment Infantry, mustered Aug. 19, 1862, for three years, quota of Salisbury Mills; appointed Corporal Jan. 21, 1863; transferred to V. R. C. March 16, 1864; discharged April 22, 1864.

MERRIAM, WARREN L. Private Co. M, 4th Regiment Cavalry, mustered Jan. 3, 1864, for three years, quota of Rockport; discharged Nov. 14, 1865.

MITCHELL, JOHN. Private Co. I, 1st Regiment Infantry, mustered Aug. 13, 1862, for three years, quota of Boston; discharged Dec. 27, 1862, for disability.

MURPHY, JOHN. Private Co. H, 50th Regiment Infantry, mustered Sept. 29, 1862, for nine months, quota of Malden; discharged Aug. 24, 1863.

NOBLE, THOMAS B. Private Co. D, 1st Battalion Frontier Cavalry, mustered Jan. 2, 1865, for one year, quota of Cambridge; discharged June 30, 1865.

O'RILEY, WILLIAM E. Private Co. G, 61st Regiment Infantry, mustered Nov. 16, 1864, for one year, quota of Sherborn; discharged July 16, 1865.

OTIS, LEMUEL T. Corporal Co. I, 1st Regiment Cavalry, mustered Dec. 5, 1863, quota of Boston; discharged June 29, 1865.

PARK, THOMAS E. Private Co. G, 3rd Regiment Heavy Artillery, mustered Oct. 20, 1863, for three years, quota of North Chelsea; discharged Sept. 18, 1865.

PEARCE, EDWARD T. 1st Lieut. 12th Regiment Infantry; mustered June 26, 1861, quota of Gloucester; discharged July 8, 1864. Died at New Orleans, La.

PETTINGILL, WILLIAM E. Private Co. G, 61st Regiment Infantry, mustered Dec. 3, 1864, for one year, quota of Medway; discharged July 16, 1865.

PHELPS, FRANK. Private Co. H, 61st Regiment Infantry, mustered Jan. 7, 1865, for one year, quota of Hanover; discharged July 16, 1865.

PROCTOR, ALPHEUS. Private Co. G, 61st Regiment Infantry, mustered Dec. 6, 1864, for one year on quata of Medway; discharged July 16, 1865.

QUINN, WILLIAM T. Corporal Co. H, 61st Regiment Infantry, mustered Jan. 5, 1865, for one year on quota of Charlemont; discharged July 16, 1865.

REGAN, JAMES. Private Co. B, 28th Regiment Infantry; mustered Dec. 13, 1861, for three years on quota of Boston; discharged Dec. 4, 1862, for disability.

RICH, GEORGE L. Private Co. H, 61st Regiment Infantry, mustered Jan. 5, 1865, for one year on quota of Hingham; discharged May 15, 1865.

RICH, HARRIS R. Private Co. K, 61st Regiment Infantry; mustered Jan. 12, 1865, for one year on quota of Charlestown; discharged July 16, 1865.

ROOKE, WILLIAM. Private Co. H, 50th Regiment Infantry, mustered Sept. 29, 1862, for nine months, quota of Malden; discharged Aug. 24, 1863.

SMITH, ALBERT E. Sergeant 8th Light Battery, mustered May 30, 1862, for six months on quota of Sharon; discharged Nov. 29, 1862. Commissioned 1st Lieutenant 2d Regiment Heavy Artillery, Aug. 14, 1863, on quota of Boston; discharged Sept. 3, 1865.

SMITH, WILLIAM F. 2nd Lieutenant 1st Regiment Cavalry, mustered Jan. 16, 1864, on quota of Boston; discharged for promotion Nov. 13, 1864. Commissioned same day 1st Lieutenant; discharged June 26, 1865.

STRATTON, HOMER R. Private Co. K, 17th Regiment Infantry, mustered July 22, 1861, for three years on quota of Malden; discharged April 17, 1863, for disability; re-enlisted Sergeant 2d Regiment Maine Cavalry, 1863.

SUTHERLAND, CHARLES H. Private Co. A, 22d Regiment Infantry, mustered Sept. 2, 1861, for three years on quota of Boston; discharged Nov. 5, 1862, for disability.

WATSON, JOHN A. Private Co. F, 61st Regiment Infantry, mustered Oct. 2, 1864, for one year on quota of Roxbury; discharged July 16, 1865.

WEBBER, LINCOLN E. Private Co. B, 11th Regiment Infantry, mustered Sept. 5, 1864, for three years on quota of Dartsmouth; discharged June 4, 1865.

WELD, THEODORE C. Private Co. H, 61st Regiment Infantry, mustered March 8, 1865, for one year on quota of Rockport. Died, May 25, 1865, at Alexandria, Va.

WHITE, GEORGE W. Private Co. M, 4th Regiment Cavalry, mustered Nov. 14, 1864, for three years on quota of Dorchester; discharged Nov. 14, 1865.

WILLARD, JAMES H. Private Co. H, 21st Regiment Infantry, mustered Aug. 5, 1861, for three years on quota of Ashburnham. Sent by General Court Martial, Oct. 1863, to hard labor; discharged Aug. 15, 1864.

WORSLEY, BARDON E. Corporal Co. L, 1st Regiment Heavy Artillery, mustered Nov. 26, 1861, for three years on quota of Ipswich; discharged Dec. 15, 1864.

The following are complete Rosters of organizations that entered into the Army as Chelsea companies, and were there known and recognized as such.

ROSTER OF COMPANY H,

First Mass. Infantry Volunteers,

COL. ROBERT COWDIN.

MUSTERED INTO U. S. SERVICE, MAY 22D, 1861 ; 3 YEARS.

[The letter R, opposite a name stands for Recruit, and N. R., for Non Resident.]

Sumner Carruth, Captain.
Albert S Austin, 1st Lieutenant.
Robert A. Saunders, 1st Lieutenant.
Horatio Roberts, 1st Lieutenant.
John M. Mandeville, 1st Lieutenant.
William P. Drury, 1st Lieutenant.
Edward G. Tutein, 2d Lieutenant.
Lionel D. Phillips, 1st Sergeant, N R.
Charles H. Carruth, Sergeant, N. R.
Edward L. Jones, Sergeant.
Thomas Harding, Sergeant.
James R. Gerrish, Sergeant.
John Harvey, Sergeant.
Samuel S. Pratt, Sergeant, N. R.
Thomas H. Bigelow, Sergeant.
Isaac Alston, Sergeant.
Samuel B. Bassett, Sergeant.
Patrick J. Donovan, Sergeant, N. R.
Orville Bisbee, Corporal.
George E. Miller, Corporal, N R.
George H. Green, Corporal, R. & N. R.
Charles A. Lord, Corporal, R.
Henry Wilson, Jr., Corporal.
David McClure, Corporal, N. R.
William D. Grover, Corporal, N. R.
John P. Jones, Corporal.
Jonathan J. Frost, Corporal.
William A. Smith, Corporal.
John H. Newling, Corporal.
Henry Pierce, Corporal, N. R.
William T. Wright, Corporal
George O. Jewett, Corporal.
Horace A. Sawyer, Musician, N. R.
Horace N. Williams, Musician.

PRIVATES.

Allen, Nathaniel.
Allen, Hiram W.
Andrews, Robert, N. R.
Alger, Charles H.
Appleby, Mark H., N. R.
Appleton, Charles A. J
Andrews, Walter B., R. & N. R.

Bacon, George.
Batchelder, Ezra A.
Bigelow, J. H.
Bridges, William E., N. R.
Blaisdell, Sargent, R. & N. R.
Baker, Alexander B., R.
Batcheler, William C., R. & N. R.
Bailey, Henry S., R. & N. R.
Blanchard, Benjamin, R. & N. R.
Campbell, William H.
Clement, William B.
Childs, Samuel, N. R.
Chittick, Thomas, N. R.
Cooper, Oliver C., N. R.
Crowell, Philander.
Cudworth, John R.
Campbell, George W.
Chessman, John W., R. & N. R.
Clark, Leonard, R. & N. R.
Cornell, Enoch C., R. & N. R.
Cushing, William, R. & N. R.
Chaffee, Charles M., N. R.
Davis, Nathaniel T.
Day, John W., N. R.
Dinsmore, William J.
Drawbridge, Thomas N.
Drown, John C., R. & N. R.
Donegan, Thomas, R. & N. R.
Everdean, Charles S.
Everdean, Wilbur F.
Emerson, Nathaniel H., R. & N. R.
Emerson, Stephen G., R. & N. R.
Fellows, Charles O.
Fletcher, Calvin T., N. R.
Flagg, Darius C., R. & N. R.
Flanders, George I., N. R.
Florence, Thomas, R. & N. R.
Fox, William A., R. & N. R.
Gerrish, William.
Gilbert, Charles, N. R.
Grantman, William, N. R.
Grover, Fitz Roy, R. & N. R.
Grover, Christopher C., R. & N. R.
Grover, Amaziah, R. & N. R.

Gray, George W., N. R.
Gafferney, James, R. & N. R.
Gross, Edward, R. & N. R.
Hadley, Edward F., N. R.
Haskell, Theodore F.
Huse, Nelson S.
Holden, Leverett D.
Hassett, Edward F., R. & N. R.
Heald, Timothy F., R. & N. R
Horton, Augustus E., N. R.
Hallgreen, William C., R. & N. R.
Hallgreen, Robert B., R. & N. R.
Heald, Samuel C., R. & N. R.
Ilsley, Johnathan C.
Jackson, Charles A.
Jennings, Stephen E.
Jewett, William M.
Johnson, Henry.
James, John M.
Jacobs, Edward C., R. & N. R.
Kingsbury, Allen A., N. R.
Kelley, John, R. & N. R.
Kelley, Lawrence H.
Lamos, Horace A., N. R.
Lane, William H., N. R.
Loud, Nathan N.
Learned, Samuel F. H.
Learned, George G.
Luke, William
Luke, John A.
Lynch, William, R. & N. R.
Mason, Henry,
Mason, Nathaniel E.
Moody, Francis O.
Moore, John G., N. R.
Murphy, James H.
Montague, William H., R.
Morrison, Richard L.
McConnell, William, R.
Needham, Thomas.
Noyes, George A.
Osborn, David W., N. R.
Parsons, Joshua, N. R.
Perley, Elbridge G.

Perkins, Calvin, N. R.
Peabody, Edward M, R. & N. R.
Rogers, F. H., R.
Smith, William D.
Spavin, Robert, N. R.
Spooner, Joseph W.
Stoddard, George L.
Stone, George H.
Smith, William H., R. & N. R.
Spofford, Daniel H., R. & N R.
Sullivan, Thomas O., R. & N. R.
Sullivan, George S., R. & N. R.
Savelle, James H., R. & N R.
Seavey, William M., R. & N. R.
Sands, George H., R.
Souther, William R, R.
Sawyer, Thorndyke H, R. & N. R.
Smith, Chauncey C., R. & N. R.
Tower, Stephen T.
Thombs, Thomas.
Toppan, John Q. A., N. R.
Thurston, Joseph W., R. & N. R.
Totten, William A. P., R. & N. R.
Tewksbury, Martin G., R.
Taylor, John, R. & N. R.
Veazie, Eli.
Wentworth, Albert F.
Welch, William, R. & N. R.
Wyman, Frederick, R. & N. R.
Woods, Lemuel F., R. & N. R.
Ward, George, R. & N. R.
Whittaker, Abner G., R. & N. R.
Walker, Henry, R. & N. R.
York, John, R. & N. R.
Everdean, Joseph B., Captain's Page.
Prescott, William A., 1st Lieut's Page.

OFFICERS OF CO. H, 1ST MASS. INFANTRY
VOLUNTEERS, 1864.

Carruth, Frank W., Captain, N. R.
Wiley, John S., 1st Lieutenant, N. R.
Maguire, Rufus M., 2d Lieutenant, N. R.

ROSTER OF COMPANY C,

35th Mass. Infantry Volunteers,

COL. EDWARD A. WILDE.

MUSTERED INTO U. S. SERVICE, AUG. 18TH, 1862; 3 YEARS.

ORIGINAL ORGANIZATION.

Cheever, Tracy P., Captain.
Blanchard, Clifton A., 1st Lieutenant.
Minck, Franklin B., 2d Lieutenant.
Fowler, Stephen D., 1st Sergeant.
Ricker, Horace S., Sergeant.
Tobey, John S., Sergeant.
Bowen, Henry, Sergeant.
Matthews, William H., Sergeant.
Davidson, Robert C., Corporal.
McCulloch, Robert, Corporal.
Remick, Clark H., Corporal.
Blanchard, Alfred Jr., Corporal.
Couillard, Elijah, Corporal.
Harvey, Henry E., Corporal.
Hutchinson, Allen, Corporal.
White, Austin J., Corporal.
Pierce, Charles A., Musician.
Reynolds, David B., Musician.
Saunders. Alonzo, Wagoner.

PRIVATES.

Alden, George W.
Austin, Henry.
Ayers, Charles.
Batchelder, Josiah H.
Bates, Charles G.
Bowen, William.
Blakeley, Frederick F.
Butler, Alfred C.
Brewster, Alpheus.
Brown, Alfred M.
Birdsall, H.
Briggs, Elijah E.
Cummings, William R. S.
Crooker, Alfred L.
Capen, Edmund A.
Conant, Walter S.
Clark, Henry
Cushing, Hosea G. Jr.
Chute Richard H.
Cossitt, George F.
Colby, Eugene D
Channell, John T.
Copeland, Henry.
Cummings, Henry.
Cushing, Elisha A.
Clough, Henry A.
Denham, Robert H.
Dam, Charles E.
Dempsey, Jeremiah.
Dearborn, George A.
Everdean, George W.
Farley, Henry B.
Frost, John H.
Fuller, Alonzo W.
Gilman, Charles W.
Goodrich, J. Henry.

Green, William.
Gipson, Montgomery.
Gillings, George E.
Goulding, Joseph M.
Gardner, Andrew B.
Holmes, Elmer W.
Holbrook, Preston.
Hicks, William H.
Holmes, Sidney.
Hodges, John W.
Howard, Noah P.
Haskell, Marcus M.
Ide, James A.
Ilsley, Hosea Jr.
Jellison, Greenleaf S.
Leveratt, John.
Lane, John A.
Lincoln, Jesse P.
Lord, James A.
Mason, Wm. J.
McLeod, Edward.
Morrill, Benjamin.
Oakman, William C.
Peterson, John.
Paine, Edwin R.
Pratt, Joseph T.
Reed, George H.
Ross, Charles H.
Richards, Francis D.
Robinson, George L.
Ransom, Robert C.
Ridlon, Joseph H.
Sweeney, Frank.
Steele, Robert.
Stranger, Heman F.
Smith, John G.
Stone, Wm. P.
Sweeney, Nathaniel I.
Stetson, Albus R.
Sturkes, Charles.
Tucker, Beavis.
Willis, Ivory.
Williams, Benjamin D.
Welch, Michael.
Wright, Thos. S.
Wellington, Theodore F.
Anderson, John; Capt's Page.
Mitchell, George L.; Lieut's Page.
Gill, John F.; 2d Lieut's Page.

RECRUITS.

Rawson, Charles M.
Taber, Bartholomew.
Peterson, John.
Putnot, James,
Sweeney, James.

ROSTER OF COMPANY G,

40th Mass. Infantry Volunteers,

COL. BURR PORTER.

MUSTERED INTO U. S. SERVICE, SEPT. 8TH, 1862 ; 3 YEARS.

Marshall, George E., Captain.
Jenkins, Horatio Jr., 1st Lieutenant.
Smith, William A., 2d Lieutenant.
Currier, Charles A., 1st Sergeant.
Campbell, Charles A., Sergeant.
Willis, George H., Sergeant.
Clapp, George W., Sergeant.
Bowen, Daniel E., Sergeant.
Green, John, Sergeant.
Gerrish, Israel H., Corporal.
Cheever, Joseph C. F., Corporal.
Hutchins, Levi, Corporal.
Dodge, Benjamin F., Corporal.
Bacon, Andrew J., Corporal.
Smith, Charles O. C., Corporal.

PRIVATES.

Adams, George Q.
Bacon, Lewis.
Breed, Henry W.
Bender, Daniel.
Bailey, Joshua M.
Bailey, Henry S. P.
Buck, Theodore H.
Buck, George H.
Baker, Joseph.
Barrington, John F.
Brown, Frank A.
Batchelder, Samuel, Jr.
Brackett, Samuel P.
Bayley, George F. H.
Bayley, Granville B.
Buzzell, Hiram H.
Butler, Benjamin H.
Coyne, Michael.
Cole, Herbert S.
Crocker, Henry M.
Clark, George L.
Colby, Oscar F.
Corcum, Levi F.
Cox, Charles G.
Cutting, Frederick L.
Donaghy, James.
Dearborn, Charles H
Dearborn, Charles L.
Daniels, William B.
Dunn, John V.

Everdean, Joseph B.
Ellery, Alphonso.
Earle, George W.
Edwards, Edward E.
Easterbrook, Kimball, Jr.
Field, Warren S.
Galusha, Florilla B.
Gibson, Frederick M.
Gibby, William H.
Glover, Benjamin F.
Hutchins, Isaiah M.
Heenan, John.
Hammond, Frank.
Howard Charles A.
Hurley, Daniel E.
Hodgkins, William H
Hubbard, Charles H.
Howe, Frank T.
Hatch, Isaac J., Jr.
Holden, John B.
Jackson, George F. C.
Johnson, George H.
Knowles, Benjamin F.
Linscott, Benjamin H.
Lawton, William H.
Lewis, George A.
Merrill, Israel H.
McLaughlin, James.
Mayo, Benjamin H.
McKenney, Alfred H.
Moses, James (recruit).
Niland, Thomas.
Pearson, Samuel F.
Parker, Nathan W.
Parkhurst, Eugene D. C.
Plummer, Joseph.
Rigby, William H.
Ribero, Joseph W.
Ring, Charles T.
Sibley, Nelson H.
Sargent, Christopher.
Small, William H.
Smith, Chandler P.
Sweeney, Dennis (recruit).
Thomas, Henry A.
Toppan, Edwin.
Wilkinson, Richard.
Wilder, Charles M.
Willis, Charles H.

ROSTER OF COMPANY H,

42d Mass. Infantry Volunteers,

COL. ISAAC S. BURRILL.

MUSTERED INTO U. S. SERVICE SEPT. 24TH, 1862 ; 9 MONTHS.

Bailey, D. W., Captain.
Gould, Augustus L., 2d Lieutenant.
Jewett, Wm. M., 1st Sergeant.
Jones, Edward L., Sergeant.
O'Brien, Dennis A., Sergeant.
Davis, John, Sergeant.
Marden, Charles M., Corporal.
Smith, George H., Corporal.
Walker, Edward, Corporal.
Hinds, Wm. A., Corporal.

PRIVATES.

Bird, James H.
Barrett, John.
McLaughlin, Charles.
Mahoney, Edward.
Haley, James.
McGowan, James.
McGowan, Thomas.
Stone, Benjamin.

ROSTER OF COMPANY H,

43d Mass. Infantry Volunteers.

COL. CHARLES L. HOLBROOK.

MUSTERED INTO U. S. SERVICE SEPT. 20TH, 1862; 9 MONTHS.

[The letters N. R. opposite a name, stands for Non Resident.]

Hanover, George B., Captain.
Bradbury, William, 1st Lieutenant.
Colesworthy, Daniel C., 2d Lieutenant.
Edmunds, John, Jr., 1st Sergeant.
Butts, Charles G., 2d Sergeant.
Perry, John H., 3d Sergeant.
Eldridge, Horace P., 4th Sergeant.
Ilsley, Daniel P., 5th Sergeant
Adams, Charles T., Corporal.
King, Thomas, Corporal.
Bryant, Southworth, Corporal.
Coburn, Charles M., Corporal.
Pitman, John T., Corporal.
Barnes, Franklin O., Corporal.
Butler, Alfred M. S., Corporal.
Colesworthy, George E., Corporal.
Humphrey, Charles L., musician.
Wilson, Norman, musician.
Wilkinson, Samuel F., wagoner.

PRIVATES.

Adams, Sylvester R.
Adams, Jonathan S.
Bunten, Gilbert.
Bryant, William B.
Blanchard, Edward B.
Beatley, Charles S.
Bassett, Charles Z.
Burtt, Joseph A. N. R.
Butts, Edwin H.
Ballsdon, George.
Benner, Edwin.
Bettis, Jonas A.
Carruth, Isaac S. N. R.
Colesworthy, Charles J.
Dade, David B.
Emerson, George H.
Evans, Thomas H
Evans, Frank S.
Folsom, William J.
Farley, James A. N. R.
Fracker, John.
Fisher, Charles R.
Gooding, George
Goodwin, Clement F.
Gilling William F.
Geary, George W.
Garrighty, John F.
Hayden, John.
Harlow, Dexter.
Hopkins, John P. N R.

Hall, Charles W. N. R.
Harrison, John L.
Hemmenway, George S. H.
Judkins, Hiram.
Jones, John T.
Johnson, Samuel W. N. R.
Kimball, James H.
Knowles, Henry F
Lombard, George E.
LeBlanc, Remi.
Lovejoy, Joseph F.
Loach, James W.
Lord, George F.
McIntire, James.
McKenzie, William.
Maynard, Cornelius D. N. R.
Morrill, George E.
Mason, Walter.
Menrs, George.
Merritt, Martin
Patrick, Albert E.
Perry, Almon.
Pierce, George F. N. R.
Parker, Merritt. N. R.
Perkins, Charles W.
Pratt, George W.
Pickford, Henry.
Richardson, Zanoni A. N. R.
Rackliff, Benjamin.
Rogers, Edward H.
Stanwood, William E.
Spaulding, William A. N. R.
Sinclair, John G.
Spooner, John F.
Swords, Edward K.
Swett, Cyrus E.
Scott, Frank J.
Thompson, Henry F.
Twombly, Charles W.
Tilden, Colman, Jr.
Tutts, John.
Teel, Abner G. N. R.
Whittemore, Thomas, Jr.
Whitford, Reuben.
Whiting, Edward.
Warren, Theodore B.
Watson, John A.
Wilson, Henry.
Wylie, Isaac.
White, William R.
Wood, Joseph A.
Young, Geo. W.

ROSTER OF COMPANY H,

50th Mass. Infantry Volunteers,

COL. CARLOS P. MESSER.

MUSTERED INTO U. S. SERVICE SEPT. 29TH, 1862 ; 9 MONTHS.

[The letters N. R. opposite a name, stands for Non Resident.]

Hobbs, Cyrus, Captain.
Holmes, Henry T., 1st Lieutenant.
Daniels, William P., 2d Lieutenant.
Saunders, Robert A., 1st Sergeant.
Carlton, Willard F., Sergeant.
Lord, George F., Sergeant.
Grant, James S., Sergeant.
Hurley, John W., Sergeant.
Proctor, James Henry, Corporal.
Sanborn, Almon, Corporal.
Forsaith, James L., Corporal.
Grant, Joseph H , Corporal
Brackett, Edwin F. A., Corporal.
Dunning, John N., Corporal.
Lucas, Charles H., Corporal.
Hall, Samuel R., Corporal.
Snow, William F., Musician, N. R.
Pike, Joseph A., Musician, N. R.
Collier, George G., Wagoner.

PRIVATES.

Averill, Charles S.
Aylward, John.
Briggs, Edward P.
Bickers, Joseph P.
Bickford, Henry P.
Bickford, George F.
Bailey, John D.
Burnham, Edward W.
Butler, Charles H., N R.
Butler, Orville W.
Butters, Silas, N. R.
Burkett, Henry A.
Brown, George F.
Bohan, Daniel.
Cole, Solomon A.
Calef, Isaac W.
Calef, Horatio S.
Clark, Lewis.
Carter, Horace.
Cross, Henry.
Cobb, George H., N. R.
Durgin, Augustus.
Dempsey, Patrick.
Dixon, Horatio.
Dickson, Thomas, N. R.
Dickson, John P., N. R.
Dean, Charles, N. R.
Edgecombe, Joseph W.
Ely, Samuel B., N. R.
Edgar, George B., N. R.
Gifford, Albert D.

Grover, Thomas.
Gillen, John, N. R.
Green, Henry.
Giles, John Henry.
Gnelpa, John B.
Griffin, Jacob E.
Hight, Henry W.
Holmes, John W.
Henry, William S.
Holbrook, John W.
Hodgkins, Francis P.
Hammond, James R.
Hatch, Charles H.
Hawkes, Harrison.
Hawes, Augustus W.
Hooper, James L., N. R.
Holden, Horace G.
Hunnewell, Richard.
Hinckley, Charles E.
Holland, Adelbert.
Jennings, Philip M.
Jones, Thomas.
Jones, Henry.
Kennefick, John.
Murphy, John, N. R.
McLaughlin, James R., N. R.
Nyman, Edgar A.
Niland, Patrick J.
Nichols, Jos. A.
Pearson, Reuben.
Pearson, W. Everett.
Proctor, George.
Proctor, Frederick, N. R.
Patten, Thaddeus, N. R.
Quigley, Edward, N. R.
Quinn, Charles.
Ripley, Robert.
Reed, Luther A.
Roberts, Myron C.
Raymond, Alfred.
Rooke, William, N. R.
Sale, John.
Sawtelle, Zachariah.
Smith, Elijah R.
Sampson, Eden.
Stone, Samuel P.
Shipman, William N.
Tuttle, John S.
Vose, Orin B.
Woodward, Fred. H.
Whitmarsh, Jonathan.
Wheeler, James E.
Young, Robert M.

OFFICERS, SAILORS, ETC.

The following is a partial list of Chelsea men who served, during the war, in the Navy and on other Government vessels.

This list is incomplete, but as full and accurate as is possible to make it with present resources.

AUSTIN, CHARLES. Seaman, Gunboat South Carolina, May 17, 1861. Re-enlisted Sept. 1862, on steamer Rhode Island. Discharged May, 1863.

ALLEN, GEORGE. 1st class fireman, Canandaigua, Aug. 4, 1862. Discharged Sept. 5, 1864.

BEARD, ROBERT. Landsman.

BRAGG, I. W. Assistant Surgeon, Receiving Ship Ohio. Frigate Roanoke, Dec. 1861. Hospital Ship, Fortress Monroe, April, 1862. Wachusett, May 1862. San Jacinto, June 1862.

BURKE, WILLIAM. Musician, Mississippi. N. R. Discharged, 1862.

BOYNTON, JOHN T.

BAKER, PATRICK. Marine.

BOYER, WILLIAM. Carpenter, Young Rover, Aug. 1861, to Aug. 1862.

BOYER, CHRISTIAN. Carpenter, Young Rover, Aug. 1861, to Aug. 1862. Re-entered as seaman, Aug., 1864.

BURGESS, HENRY C. Acting Paymaster, Ohio.

BUTLER, WILLIAM F. Seaman, Saxon.

BURNS, JAMES. Seaman, Vermont.

BURNS, JAMES H. Fireman, Kensington.

BESSEY, JOHN. Seaman, Portsmouth.

BIGELOW, BENJ. F. Acting Assistant Surgeon, Dec. 1863.

BOLTON, WM. H. Master's Mate, Malvern, Dec. 23, 1863. Transferred to Commodore Jones.

BRANNAN, MICHAEL, Jr. Seaman, Ceres, April, 1863.

CUNNINGHAM, ENOS T. Musician, Mississippi. Discharged, 1862.

CASS, FREDERICK. Seaman, Massachusetts.

CUMMINGS, WILLIAM R. S. Landsman, South Carolina. Discharged. Enlisted, 35th Mass., Aug. 1862.

COTTER, EDWARD T. Landsman, Sabine.

COYNE, MICHAEL. Landsman, Cumberland. Discharged April, 1862. Enlisted, 40th Mass., Aug. 1862.

CUSHING, WM. B. Passed Midshipman, Cambridge. Lieutenant Commander, 1865.

CULLEN, PATRICK. Seaman, Katahdin. Died, Feb. 23, 1863.

COBURN, GEORGE H. Paymaster's Clerk, Vermont.

CUTTING, GEORGE H. Coalheaver.

CLARK, CHARLES E. Acting Ensign, Iron-clad Nahant. Resigned, 1863.

CURRY, DAVIS H. Carpenter, Gunboat Louisiana, Feb. 1862.

DILLINGHAM, JOHN. Acting Master, Preble. Morning Light. Oct. 1862. Taken prisoner Jan. 1863. Paroled and exchanged, —, 1864. Resigned ——, 1865.

DILLINGHAM, JAMES S., Jr. Acting Master, Rhode Island. Resigned Oct. 9, 1861.

DURAN, ANDREW. Seamen, Bainbridge.

DRURY, MICHAEL B. Seaman, Kearsarge. Jan. 12, 1862. Discharged Nov. 29, 1864. Re-entered, seaman, Jan. 5, 1865.

DEMOITT, LEWIS. Seaman, Saxon.

DAWSON, F. B. Acting Assistant Surgeon, Steamer Patron.

DIGNAN, STEPHEN. Coalheaver, Nantasket.

DAVIS, NATHANIEL T. Paymaster's Clerk, Alabama, May, 1864.

DIGNAN, JAMES. Landsman, July 30, 1864.

DYKE, JAMES H. Seaman, July 18, 1864.

ENGLES, S. ALLEN. Surgeon, Vincennes, till June, 1862.
On retired list, Aug. 1863. Died at Chelsea, Feb. 27, 1865.

EDGERLY, HIRAM O. Seaman, Housatonic, July, 1862,
to Aug. 1863.

ERICKSON, C. J. Seaman, March 3, 1864.

FRENCH, CHARLES A. Acting Master, Minnesota. Transferred to Whitehead. Appointed Commander, ——. 1862.

FARLEY, THOMAS S. Master's Mate, Mississippi. Resigned
Jan. 1862.

FITZPATRICK, JOHN. Marine, Westfield. Transferred to
Clifton, Dec. 1862. On board Flag Ship, Jan. 1863.

FROST, LOUIS W. Midshipman, Constitution, Aug. 1862.

FRENCH, OLIVER H. Paymaster's Clerk, Whitehead.

HOLLIS, GEORGE F. Master's Mate, Louisiana. Appointed
Ensign, Octorora, Aug. 10, 1862. Acting Master, June 11,
1864.

HORNE, DAVID B. Acting Master, Nightingale. Resigned
June 29, 1863.

HARRIS, THOMAS W. Musician, Mississippi. Discharged,
1862.

HALLIHAN, THOMAS. Carondolet. Died. at Vicksburg,
July 22, 1862.

HOYT, EBEN, JR. 1st Assistant Engineer, Richmond. Spe-
cial duty, Iron-clad steamers, Boston, July, 1863.

HIGGINS, JOSIAH P. Yeoman, Kennebec.

HAWES, WM. H. Master's Mate, Jamestown.

HILLS, FREDERICK C. Acting Assistant Paymaster, Gunboat Isaac Smith. Taken prisoner, Stono River, Jan. 1863.
Paroled May 4, 1863. Exchanged May 6, 1863. Ordered
to De Soto, ——, 1863.

HUTCHINS, SAMUEL. Seamen, Minnesota.

HOLT, JAMES E. Landsman, Iron-clad Galena, April 16,
1862, to June 17, 1863.

HANNAH, WM. AUGUSTUS. Master's Mate. Sept. 15,
1863.

HOWARD, JOHN. Seaman.

HURSCH, CHAS. F. Acting 2d Assistant Engineer, Trefoil.

ILSLEY, JONATHAN C. Seaman, Brooklyn. Transferred to Richmond, Sept. 1863.

JANVRIN, EDWIN. Master's Mate, Vincennes. Appointed Acting Ensign, June, 1862. On board Rachael, Seaman.

KENNEDY, JOHN. Seaman, Massachusetts.

KYLE, THOMAS. Coalheaver.

KERSE. PATRICK. Coalheaver, Saco. Jan. 1864.

KELEY, WILLIAM. Seaman, March 8, 1864.

LENNAN, BENJ. C. Musician, Mississippi. N. R. May, 1861, to Jan. 1862.

LACY, JAMES. Landsman, Cambridge. Discharged ——. Re-enlisted ——, 1865.

LEONARD, EZRA. Acting Master, Varuna. Transferred to Tennessee. Transferred to Monongahela, June, 1863.

LEWIS, THOMAS D. Seaman, Colorado.

LEWIS, JOEL W., JR. Steward, San. Jacinto.

LOW, PHILIP B. Acting Ensign, Com. Morris, Oct. 1862. Resigned Sept. 9, 1863.

LANGLEY, WILLIAM A. Coalheaver, Genesee.

LORING, STAUNTON D. 3d Assistant Engineer, Ladona.

LORING, W. F. Seaman, Genesee.

LOWELL, WM. C. Yeoman, Monticello, Dec. 1863.

MOORE, WILLIAM N. Seaman, Fearnought.

MAIES, WILLIAM H. Master's Mate, Cambridge. Appointed Acting Master, March 26, 1862. Taken prisoner in North Carolina, Nov. 17, 1862. Paroled. Exchanged Jan. 13, 1863. Ordered to Iron-clad Nantucket, Jan. 15, 1863.

MAILLEY, OWEN. Landsman.

MERRILL, JOHN M. Acting Master, Kingfisher.

McGIVERN. Lawrence, Landsman.

McKIERNON, JOHN. Marine.

MURPHY, JOHN. Landsman. Aug. 1, 1861. Transferred to Mississippi Squadron, Nov. 1862. Discharged Aug. 1864.

MITCHELL, CHARLES F. Acting Master, Norwich, from Dec. 1861, to Sep. 1863. In command Gunboat E. B. Hale, Sept. 8, 1863.

MERRYMAN, J. Walter. Master's Mate.

MALLARD, W. H. Acting Master, Sebago.

MAHON, JOSEPH. Coalheaver.

MURPHY, DANIEL S. Acting Master, Hartford.

MASON, N. EMMONS. Surgeon's Steward, Gunboat New National, April, 1863. Steward, Naval Hospital, Memphis, Tenn., ——, 1863.

McNAMARA, TIMOTHY. Gunboat Kanawha.

McQUADE, CHAS. From 1st Cavalry, May 3, 1864.

MAYO, HENRY A. Master's Mate, Buckthorn.

NYMAN, FRANCIS W. 3d Engineer.

ORCUTT, JOHN A. Master's Mate, Tacony.

OLIVER, GEO. F. Seaman, Ethan Allen.

PEPPER, DANIEL. Coast Pilot, Colorado, till June, 1862.

PEPPER, GEORGE. Seaman, Saxon.

PHILLIPS, JOHN F. Engineer's Steward, Colorado.

PRESCOTT, ALEX. H. Surgeon's Mate, South Carolina.

PRESCOTT, W. A. Master's Mate, Gunboat Port Royal.

PILSBUBY, J. ELLIOT. Midshipman, Constitution, Aug. 1862.

PALMER, W. H. Acting Assistant Paymaster, Nahant, Oct. 25, 1864.

PLUNKETT, JOHN. (O. Q.) ——, 1864.

RICE, GEORGE H. Master's Mate, Preble. Morning Light, Oct. 1862. Wounded Dec. 1862. Taken prisoner Jan. 21, 1863. Released Feb. 26, 1865.

RAY, RICHARD L. Gunner, Potomac.

ROWE, EDWARD F. Acting Master's Mate, April 15, 1862. Acting Ensign, Nahant, ——, 1863.

RINGOT, CHARLES. Ensign, Sagamore. Killed near James River, Va., Nov. 25, 1862.

RYAN, MICHAEL. Landsman, Alabama, March, 1864. Discharged April 10, 1865.

ROGERS, HENRY A. Master's Mate, Buckthorn, March, 1864.

STONE, EDWIN C. Minnesota.

SIMMS, PATRICK. Coalheaver, Whitehead.

SIBLEY, ARTHUR. Acting Assistant Paymaster, Gunboat Linden, Dec. 1862.

STEVENS, A. L. Sailmaker's Mate, Albatross, Aug., 1862, to Aug., 1863. Re-entered as Master's Mate, Owasco, March 8, 1864.

STODDARD, GEORGE L. Seaman, Dec. 1862.

SAWTELLE, ISAIAH L. 3d Engineer, Gunboat Britannia.

SAUNDERS, CHAS. H. L. Fireman, Gunboat Aries, Sept. 19, 1863. Discharged, ——, 1864. Re-entered 3d Assistant Engineer, Paul Jones, ——, 1865.

SEMON, E. N. Acting Ensign, Storeship Release, Dec. 19, 1862. Attached to steamer Nyphon, Oct. 22, 1862.

SMITH, LEONARD M. Tonawanda. Discharged Aug. 26, 1863.

SAWYER, GEO. K. Seaman, Colorado, Aug. 17, 1862. Discharged Sept. 8, 1863. Re-entered, Com. Hull, Oct. 11, 1863. Discharged Oct. 16, 1864.

SCOTT, STEPHEN C. Landsman. (O. Q.) ——, 1864.

TURNER, LEVI W. Master's Mate, Lno. Resigned.

TUTEIN, FRED. J. Bandmaster, Mississippi. May 15, 1861, to June, 1862.

THORNTON, JOHN T. Landsman, Sabine.

TOOTHAKER, SAMUEL G. Seaman, Ethan Allen. Discharged ——, 1862. Appointed Acting Ensign, Macedonian, Jan. 1863.

THORNTON, HENRY H. Landsman, Sabine.

TOPPAN, BENJAMIN F. Seaman.

TURNER, HENRY T. Paymaster's Clerk, South Carolina.

THORNTON, J. S. Lieutenant Commander, Kearsage.

TUCKER, GEORGE. Seaman. (O. Q.) ——, 1865.

VERY, S., JR. Acting Master, Cambridge. 1st Lieutenant, Gemsbok.

VERY, SAMUEL W. Yeoman, Gemsbok.

WHITE, JOSEPH R. Musician, Mississippi. Discharged, 1862.

WINCH, GEORGE HENRY. Landsman, Fearnought.

WELLER, JOHN. Seaman, Aug. 1, 1861. Detailed at Fort Ellsworth, near Washington, August to October, 1861. Transferred to Minnesota and to Gunboat Whitehead. Appointed Quarter-master, Jan. 1, 1862. Wounded, Oct. 3, 1862, at Franklin, Va. Discharged March 28, 1863. Died at Chelsea, March 23, 1864.

WELLS, HENRY M. Surgeon.

WESTCOTT, HENRY A. Sept. 1862.

WHITE, W. L. Hendrick Hudson. Sept. 1863.

WINDE HENRY A. Master's Mate, Buckthorn, March, 1864.

www.ingramcontent.com/pod-product-compliance
Lightning Source LLC
Chambersburg PA
CBHW030821270326
41928CB00007B/840